Complete
Canadian
Curriculum

Grade 3

Revised and Updated!

Math
English
Social Studies
Science

Credits

Photos (Cover "boy" Andres Rodriguez/123RF.com, "buildings" Songquan Deng/123RF.com, "totem pole" Gunther Fraulob/123RF.com, "schoolkids" Dmitriy Shironosov/123RF.com, "Northern Lights" pilens/123RF.com)

Copyright © 2015 Popular Book Company (Canada) Limited

Printed in China

 ISBN: 978-1-77149-031-3

Mathematics

English

ISBN: 978-1-77149-031-3

Social Studies

Science

ISBN: 978-1-77149-031-3

MATHEMATICS

* The Canadian penny is no longer in circulation. It is used in the units to show money amounts to the cent.

ISBN: 978-1-77149-031-3

Numbers to 100

- Compare, order, and write whole numbers in words up to 100.
- Count backward by 2's, 5's, and 10's from 100.
- Round 2-digit numbers to the nearest ten.

10 beads in a group

I have thirty-two beads.

Fill in the missing numbers.

① 35 36 ____ 38 ____ ____ ____ 42 ____

② 69 70 ____ ____ 73 ____ ____ ____ 77

③ 87 88 ____ ____ ____ 92 93 ____ ____

④ 55 56 ____ 58 ____ ____ ____ ____ 63

Circle the greater number.

⑤ 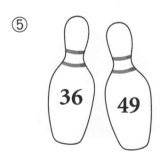 36 49

⑥ 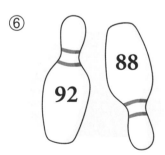 92 88

⑦ 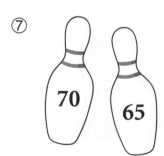 70 65

Put the numbers in order from least to greatest.

⑧ 39 58 63 18 _____

⑨ 44 30 81 53 _____

⑩ 64 16 46 14 _____

ISBN: 978-1-77149-031-3

Count and write the numbers in words.

⑪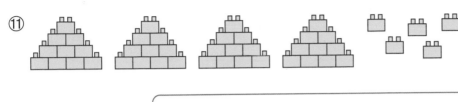

I have _____ blocks.

⑫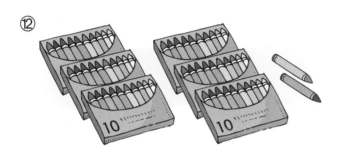

_____ crayons

⑬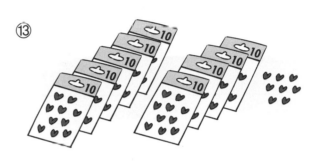

_____ stickers

Write the numbers.

⑭ twenty-six   _____   ⑮ forty-five   _____

⑯ ninety-one   _____   ⑰ eighty   _____

⑱ sixty-four   _____   ⑲ thirty-eight   _____

⑳ seventy-two   _____   ㉑ fifty-three   _____

㉒ a number greater than 65   _____

㉓ a number greater than 28 but smaller than 37   _____

㉔ a 2-digit number with 0 in its ones column   _____

㉕ a 2-digit number with 4 in its tens column   _____

ISBN: 978-1-77149-031-3

Follow the patterns to write numbers and draw arrows on the number lines.

㉖

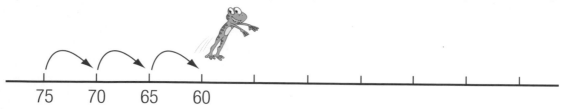

75   70   65   60

㉗

100   90   80   70

㉘

88   86   84   82

Count backward by 2's, 5's, or 10's to find the missing numbers. Write the numbers.

㉙   74 _____ 70   68 _____ _____ 62 _____ _____ 56

㉚   90   85 _____ _____ 70 _____ _____ _____ 50   45

㉛   100 _____ _____ 70   60 _____ _____ 30 _____ 10

Put the numbers in order from greatest to least. Then fill in the blanks.

㉜   32   30   34   28

In order: _____

I can count backward by
_____'s from _____
to get these numbers.

㉝   45   60   50   55

In order: _____

I can count backward by _____'s
from _____ to get these numbers.

Rounding a 2-digit number to the nearest ten:

e.g. 46 ← It is between 40 and 50.

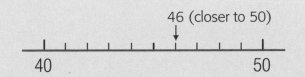

46 (closer to 50)

40   50

46 is rounded to __50__ .

A number halfway between 2 numbers should be rounded up. For example, 35 is rounded up to 40.

Use an arrow to locate each number on the number line. Then round the number to the nearest ten.

㉞
53

50   60

53 is rounded to _____ .

㉟
88

80   90

88 is rounded to _____ .

㊱
69

60   70

69 is rounded to _____ .

㊲
17

10   20

17 is rounded to _____ .

Fill in the blanks.

㊳

The number of candies in the jar is between 75 and _____ .

㊴

The number of beads in the box is between _____ and _____ .

Beads
about 50

ISBN: 978-1-77149-031-3

Addition and Subtraction of 2-Digit Numbers

- Add and subtract 2-digit numbers.
- Estimate and check the answers.
- Solve word problems.

They cost 70¢ only.

35¢ each   35¢ each

Do the addition.

①
$$\begin{array}{r} 37 \\ + 16 \\ \hline \end{array}$$

②
$$\begin{array}{r} 42 \\ + 39 \\ \hline \end{array}$$

③
$$\begin{array}{r} 18 \\ + 63 \\ \hline \end{array}$$

④ 45 + 48 = _____

⑤ 27 + 60 = _____

⑥ 34 + 19 = _____

⑦ 42 + 38 = _____

Round each number to the nearest ten. Do the estimate. Then find the exact answer.

⑧
$$\begin{array}{r} 46 \\ + 33 \\ \hline \end{array}$$
Estimate
+ _____

⑨
$$\begin{array}{r} 24 \\ + 58 \\ \hline \end{array}$$
Estimate

⑩
$$\begin{array}{r} 12 \\ + 56 \\ \hline \end{array}$$
Estimate

⑪
$$\begin{array}{r} 9 \\ + 29 \\ \hline \end{array}$$
Estimate

Complete Canadian Curriculum • Grade 3

ISBN: 978-1-77149-031-3

The answer to each question is the number of cookies in each cookie jar. Do the subtraction. Then answer the questions.

⑫

A

$$\begin{array}{r} 7\ 8 \\ -\ 2\ 6 \\ \hline \end{array}$$

B

$$\begin{array}{r} 4\ 0 \\ -\ 1\ 7 \\ \hline \end{array}$$

C

$$\begin{array}{r} 5\ 2 \\ -\ 3\ 9 \\ \hline \end{array}$$

D

$$\begin{array}{r} 8\ 1 \\ -\ 6\ 3 \\ \hline \end{array}$$

E

$$\begin{array}{r} 4\ 3 \\ -\ \ 8 \\ \hline \end{array}$$

F

$$\begin{array}{r} 3\ 5 \\ -\ \ 7 \\ \hline \end{array}$$

G

$74 - 37 =$ _____

H

$55 - 49 =$ _____

I

$60 - 35 =$ _____

J

$93 - 75 =$ _____

⑬   Which jars have the same number of cookies?   _____

⑭   Which jar has the most cookies?   _____

⑮   Which jar has 10 more cookies than jar C?   _____

Round each number to the nearest ten. Do the estimate. Then find the exact answer.

⑯ —————————— **Estimate** —   ⑰ —————————— **Estimate** —

$$\begin{array}{r} 7\ 4 \\ -\ 3\ 9 \\ \hline \end{array}$$

$$\begin{array}{r} 6\ 8 \\ -\ 4\ 1 \\ \hline \end{array}$$

ISBN: 978-1-77149-031-3   Complete Canadian Curriculum • Grade 3

Use addition to check the answer of subtraction.

e.g. Is 46 – 27 = <u>**29**</u> correct?

1st Add the shaded numbers.

$$\begin{array}{r} 4\ 6 \\ -\ 2\ 7 \\ \hline 2\ 9 \end{array}$$

2nd If the answer is 46, "29" is the correct answer.

$$\begin{array}{r} 2\ 9 \\ +\ 2\ 7 \\ \hline 5\ 6 \end{array} \leftarrow \text{not 46}$$

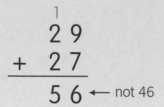

46 – 27 = 29 is not correct.
The correct answer is 19.

Check the answer to each question. Put a check mark ✔ in the space provided if the answer is correct; otherwise, put a cross ✗ and find the correct answer.

⑱ **Check**

$$\begin{array}{r} 7\ 3 \\ -\ 2\ 4 \\ \hline 5\ 9 \end{array} \qquad \begin{array}{r} 2\ 4 \\ +\ 5\ 9 \\ \hline \end{array}$$

⑲ **Check**

$$\begin{array}{r} 6\ 0 \\ -\ 4\ 5 \\ \hline 1\ 5 \end{array}$$

Do the subtraction. Then check the answers.

⑳
$$\begin{array}{r} 9\ 0 \\ -\ 1\ 6 \\ \hline \end{array}$$
Check
$$+ \underline{}$$

㉑
$$\begin{array}{r} 5\ 9 \\ -\ 2\ 4 \\ \hline \end{array}$$
Check

㉒
$$\begin{array}{r} 3\ 3 \\ -\ 1\ 6 \\ \hline \end{array}$$
Check

㉓
$$\begin{array}{r} 8\ 4 \\ -\ 6\ 6 \\ \hline \end{array}$$

Check

ISBN: 978-1-77149-031-3

Solve the problems.

㉔

a. How many candies are there in 2 bags?

_____ = _____

_____ candies

b. How many more candies are there in a jar than in a bag?

_____ = _____

_____ more

㉕

Tim's Cards

36

42

a. How many fewer baseball cards than hockey cards does Tim have?

_____ = _____

_____ fewer

b. How many cards does Tim have in all?

_____ = _____

_____ cards

㉖

62¢

a. A tin soldier costs 5¢ less than a matchbox car. How much does a matchbox car cost?

_____ = _____

_____ ¢

b. *I pay 75¢ for a tin soldier. What is my change?*

_____ = _____

_____ ¢

Numbers to 1000

I've packed 556 dolls already.

- Write, compare, and order whole numbers up to 1000.
- Identify and represent the value of a digit in a 3-digit number.
- Count by 2's, 5's, 10's, 25's, and 100's.

Count and write the numbers.

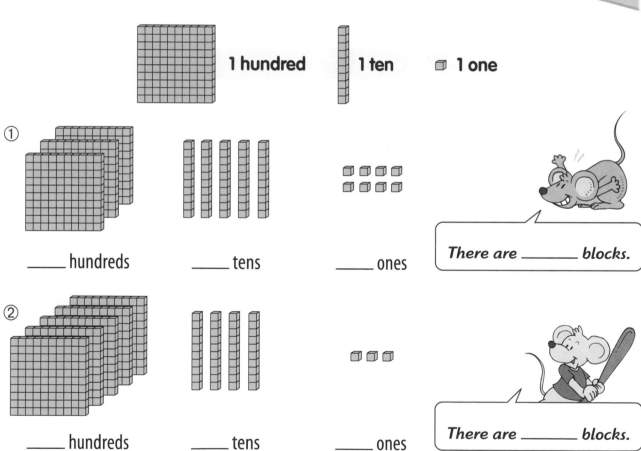

1 hundred   **1 ten**   **1 one**

① _____ hundreds   _____ tens   _____ ones

There are _____ blocks.

② _____ hundreds   _____ tens   _____ ones

There are _____ blocks.

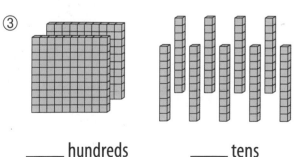

③ _____ hundreds   _____ tens   _____ ones

There are _____ blocks.

ISBN: 978-1-77149-031-3

Write the numbers. Then answer the questions.

④ **A** _____ = 6 hundreds 5 tens 7 ones

B _____ = 5 hundreds 2 tens 4 ones

C _____ = 9 hundreds 7 tens 6 ones

D 375 = ___ hundreds ___ tens ___ ones

E 581 = _____

⑤ Which numbers are between 400 and 600?

_____

⑥ Which numbers have 5 in its hundreds column?

_____

Put the numbers in order from greatest to least.

⑦ 652 256 625   _____

⑧ 788 887 878   _____

⑨ 490 940 904   _____

Write the numbers that the arrows are pointing at.

⑩

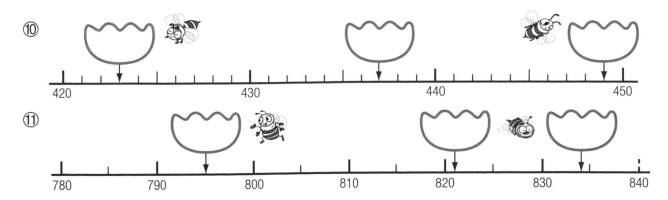

420   430   440   450

⑪

780   790   800   810   820   830   840

See how many apples were sold in the past three days. Write the numbers. Then answer the questions.

⑫

_____ apples   _____ apples   _____ apples

⑬ On which day were the most apples sold?   _____

⑭ If 4 more apples will be sold on Thursday than on Wednesday, how many apples will be sold on Thursday?   _____ apples

⑮ If 3 fewer apples will be sold on Friday than on Tuesday, how many apples will be sold on Friday?   _____ apples

Follow the patterns to draw arrows and write the numbers. Then fill in the blanks to tell how to skip count.

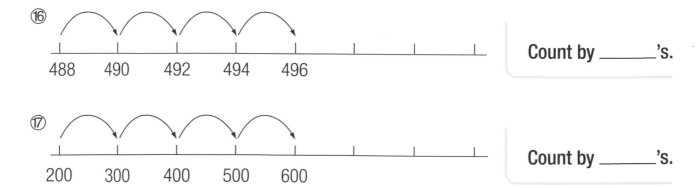

⑯ 488 490 492 494 496   Count by _____'s.

⑰ 200 300 400 500 600   Count by _____'s.

ISBN: 978-1-77149-031-3

Tell how to skip count in each group. Then write the next 5 numbers.

⑱ 425, 450, 475, 500, 525

   Count by _____'s: _____

⑲ 700, 710, 720, 730, 740

   Count by _____'s: _____

⑳ 690, 695, 700, 705, 710

   Count by _____'s: _____

Answer the questions.

㉑

What are the greatest and the least 3-digit numbers?

_____ ; _____

㉒

What are the next five numbers after 398?

_____

㉓

Write 5 numbers that are greater than 388 but smaller than 436.

_____

㉔

How many 3-digit numbers can be formed with these balls? What are they?

_____

_____

ISBN: 978-1-77149-031-3

Addition and Subtraction of 3-Digit Numbers (1)

- Add 3-digit numbers with or without grouping.
- Subtract 3-digit numbers with or without borrowing.

No. of Audience Members:
$$\begin{array}{r} 1\ 1 \\ 8\ 9 \\ +\ 1\ 2\ 5 \\ \hline 2\ 1\ 4 \end{array}$$
Adults
Children
in all

I welcome all 214 of you tonight.

Do the addition.

①
$$\begin{array}{r} 2\ 3\ 4 \\ +\ 1\ 0\ 5 \\ \hline \end{array}$$

②
$$\begin{array}{r} 2\ 1\ 6 \\ +\ 4\ 8\ 3 \\ \hline \end{array}$$

③
$$\begin{array}{r} 4\ 1\ 1 \\ +\ \ \ 8\ 4 \\ \hline \end{array}$$

④
$$\begin{array}{r} 6\ 5\ 3 \\ +\ 1\ 1\ 4 \\ \hline \end{array}$$

⑤
$$\begin{array}{r} 5\ 2\ 1 \\ +\ \ \ 4\ 7 \\ \hline \end{array}$$

⑥
$$\begin{array}{r} 6\ 5 \\ +\ 1\ 0\ 3 \\ \hline \end{array}$$

⑦ 712 + 124 = _____

⑧ 335 + 161 = _____

⑨ 188 + 210 = _____

⑩ 427 + 402 = _____

Find the answers. Then match the socks with the correct drawers. Write the letters.

⑪

A 224 + 224
= _____

B 205 + 183
= _____

C 73 + 315
= _____

D 157 + 340
= _____

Answers greater than 450

Answers smaller than 450

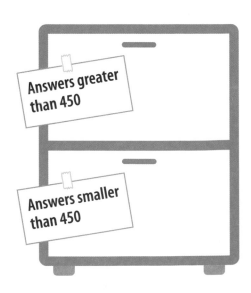

ISBN: 978-1-77149-031-3

Do the addition.

⑫
```
    ○
  3 2 7
+ 4 5 9
```

⑬
```
    ○
  4 3 6
+ 1 2 7
```

⑭
```
   ○○
    8 5
+ 5 1 6
```

⑮
```
   ○○
  6 5 2
+ 1 4 9
```

⑯
```
   ○○
  5 8 4
+ 2 6 6
```

⑰
```
   ○○
  2 9 8
+ 2 9 8
```

⑱ 381 + 65 = _____

⑲ 289 + 350 = _____

⑳ 743 + 79 = _____

㉑ 157 + 644 = _____

㉒ 329 + 165 = _____

㉓ 590 + 286 = _____

Find the answers.   Match the toys with the boxes that have the same answers. Write the letters.

㉔
A 363 + 174 = _____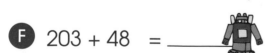

B 92 + 139 = _____

C 402 + 88 = _____

D 246 + 309 = _____

E 465 + 137 = _____

F 203 + 48 = _____

G 159 + 159 = _____

Steps to do subtraction:

1st Subtract the ones. If the ones are too small, borrow from the tens.

2nd Subtract the tens. If the tens are too small, borrow from the hundreds.

3rd Subtract the hundreds.

$$6 \ 10 \ 15$$
$$\begin{array}{r} 7\!\!\!/\ 7\!\!\!/\ 5\!\!\!/ \\ -\ 2\ 4\ 8 \\ \hline 4\ 6\ 7 \end{array}$$

15 − 8 = 7
10 − 4 = 6
6 − 2 = 4

715 − 248 = **467**

Do the subtraction.

㉕
$$\begin{array}{r} 4\ 7\ 5 \\ -\ 2\ 3\ 4 \\ \hline \end{array}$$

㉖
$$\begin{array}{r} 5\ 2\ 9 \\ -\ 1\ 0\ 8 \\ \hline \end{array}$$

㉗
$$\begin{array}{r} 6\ 8\ 3 \\ -\ 4\ 7\ 2 \\ \hline \end{array}$$

㉘
$$3 \ 13$$
$$\begin{array}{r} 5\ 4\!\!\!/\ 3\!\!\!/ \\ -\ 2\ 3\ 4 \\ \hline \end{array}$$

㉙
$$6 \ 12 \ 12$$
$$\begin{array}{r} 7\!\!\!/\ 3\!\!\!/\ 2\!\!\!/ \\ -\ 4\ 5\ 8 \\ \hline \end{array}$$

㉚
$$3 \ 9 \ 15$$
$$\begin{array}{r} 4\!\!\!/\ 0\!\!\!/\ 5\!\!\!/ \\ -\ \ \ \ 6\ 7 \\ \hline \end{array}$$

㉛ 354 − 179 = _____

㉜ 602 − 381 = _____

㉝ 710 − 563 = _____

㉞ 934 − 685 = _____

Find the answers. Then put the necklaces in order from the one with the greatest number to the one with the least.

㉟
A 539 − 142 = _____

B 700 − 464 = _____

C 351 − 209 = _____

D 802 − 381 = _____

In order: _____

ISBN: 978-1-77149-031-3

Solve the problems.

㊱ Tim has 245 marbles and George has 173 marbles.

a. How many marbles do the boys have in all?

b. How many more marbles does Tim have than George?

_____ marbles

_____ more

㊲ Lucy has 318 stickers. Katie has 57 fewer stickers than Lucy.

a. How many stickers does Katie have?

b. How many stickers do the girls have in all?

_____ stickers

_____ stickers

㊳ Look at Mrs. Cowan's gifts.

a. What is the price difference between the gifts?

$ _____

b. What is the total cost of the gifts?

$ _____

$287

$362

ISBN: 978-1-77149-031-3

Addition and Subtraction of 3-Digit Numbers (2)

- Add and subtract 3-digit numbers.
- Check and estimate answers.
- Understand the relationship between addition and subtraction.
- Solve word problems.

No. of Cheese Cubes:

```
  1 1
  3 2 6
+ 2 8 9
-------
  6 1 5
```

I can move 615 cheese cubes.

Add or subtract.

①
```
  3 2 4
+ 1 8 3
```

②
```
  4 6 3
+ 2 8 7
```

③
```
  5 0 6
- 2 7 7
```

④
```
  9 8 4
- 3 9 9
```

⑤
```
  7 2 1
- 4 6 8
```

⑥
```
  3 7 4
+ 5 3 3
```

⑦ 65 + 708 = _____

⑧ 217 − 94 = _____

Do the subtraction. Then check the answers.

⑨
```
  5 2 4
- 1 6 2
```
Check

+ _____

⑩
```
  2 0 0
- 1 5 4
```
Check

+ _____

⑪
```
  4 0 5
- 1 7 3
```
Check

+ _____

⑫
```
  3 7 1
- 3 1 8
```
Check

+ _____

ISBN: 978-1-77149-031-3

Round each number to the nearest hundred.   Estimate.   Then find the exact answer.

⑬

```
   394
 + 219
```

Estimate

```
   400
 + 200
```

⑭

```
   706
 +  92
```

Estimate

_____

⑮

```
   827
 - 183
```

Estimate

_____

⑯

```
   586
 - 328
```

Estimate

_____

Find the sum and difference for each pair of numbers.

⑰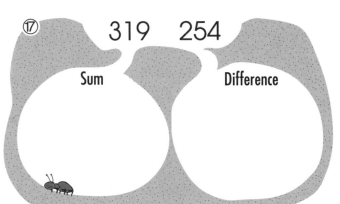

319   254

Sum   Difference

⑱

608   73

Sum   Difference

⑲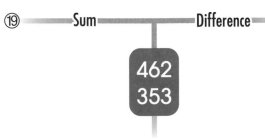

Sum ——— Difference

462
353

⑳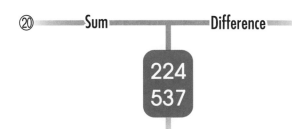

Sum ——— Difference

224
537

㉑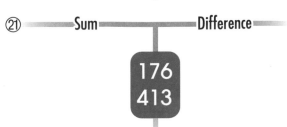

Sum ——— Difference

176
413

㉒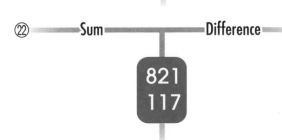

Sum ——— Difference

821
117

ISBN: 978-1-77149-031-3

Relating addition and subtraction:

125 + 239 = 364   364 − 125 = 239

239 + 125 = 364   364 − 239 = 125

125, 239, and 364 are in a family.

Use the given number sentences to find the answers.

㉓ 84 + 237 = 321

a. 237 + 84 = _____

b. 321 − 84 = _____

㉔ 503 − 276 = 227

a. 227 + 276 = _____

b. 503 − 227 = _____

㉕ 413 − 165 = 248

a. 165 + 248 = _____

b. 413 − 248 = _____

㉖ 188 + 547 = 735

a. 547 + 188 = _____

b. 735 − 547 = _____

Help the children complete their tables. Then fill in the blanks.

㉗ **Tina's Score**

	1st Round	2nd Round	Total
A	263 points	points	503 points
B	177 points	413 points	points
C	points	316 points	497 points

㉘ **Matthew's Score**

	1st Round	2nd Round	Total
A	points	164 points	471 points
B	525 points	76 points	points
C	367 points	points	604 points

I got my highest score in _____ .

I got my highest score in _____ .

Solve the problems.

No. of Pizzas Sold		
	Pepperoni	Vegetarian
MON	218	182
TUE	174	203

㉙ How many pepperoni pizzas were sold on Monday and Tuesday?

_____ = _____

_____ pepperoni pizzas

㉚ How many vegetarian pizzas were sold on Monday and Tuesday?

_____ = _____

_____ vegetarian pizzas

We have pizzas in 2 sizes: large and small.

㉛ 79 small vegetarian pizzas were sold on Monday. How many large vegetarian pizzas were sold on that day?

_____ = _____

_____ large vegetarian pizzas

㉜ How many more vegetarian pizzas than pepperoni pizzas were sold on Tuesday?

_____ = _____

_____ more

㉝ I have 154 slices of pizza. If I give 68 slices to my friends, how many slices of pizza will I have left?

_____ = _____

_____ slices of pizza

ISBN: 978-1-77149-031-3

Length and Distance

See, we are both about 1 m tall.

You're not quite 1 m tall.

- Estimate, measure, and record length, height, and distance, using standard units such as centimetre, metre, and kilometre.
- Choose the most appropriate standard unit to measure length, height, and distance.
- Compare and order objects, using attributes measured in centimetres and metres.

**Choose the best units to do the measurement.
Write "km", "m", or "cm" in the circles.**

①

②

③

④

⑤

⑥

ISBN: 978-1-77149-031-3

Fill in the blanks with "km", "m", or "cm" to complete the sentences.

⑦  The length of a ball of yarn is about 36 _____ .

⑧  The thickness of a book is about 3 _____ .

⑨ The distance between Toronto and New York is about 550 _____ .

⑩ Uncle Tim is shorter than 2 _____ .

⑪ Lucy found an earthworm in her backyard. It was about 12 _____ long.

Estimate the length of each line. Then measure and record the actual measurement. Use the given words if needed.

⑫

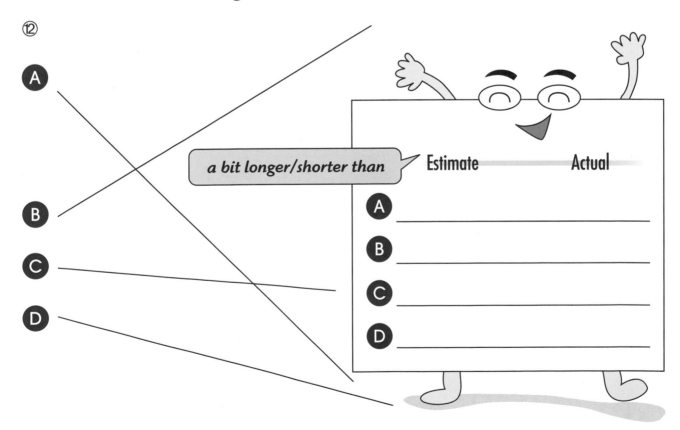

a bit longer/shorter than

	Estimate	Actual
A	_____	_____
B	_____	_____
C	_____	_____
D	_____	_____

ISBN: 978-1-77149-031-3

Measure and record the length or height of each thing. Then draw and record the measurement of each item.

⑬

about _____ long

about _____ long

Draw a pencil that is 2 cm longer than the nail.

⑭

Ⓐ

Ⓑ

about _____ high   about _____ high   about _____ high

Draw a tree that is taller than A but shorter than B.

Measure and record the length of each line in centimetres.

⑮

Ⓐ

Ⓑ

Ⓒ

Length

Ⓐ _____

Ⓑ _____

Ⓒ _____

ISBN: 978-1-77149-031-3

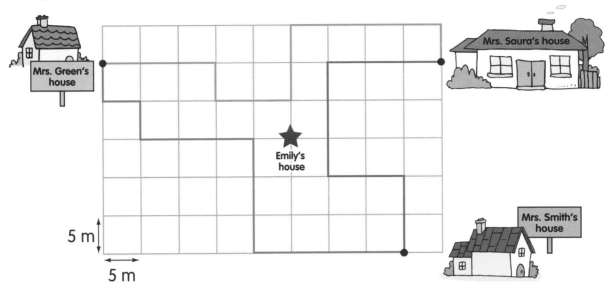

Look at the diagram. Find the lengths of the routes. Then draw lines on the diagram and answer the questions.

⑯   a.   From Mrs. Green's house to Mrs. Saura's house: _____ m

      b.   From Mrs. Green's house to Mrs. Smith's house: _____ m

      c.   From Mrs. Saura's house to Mrs. Smith's house: _____ m

⑰   a.

> *Use a red pen to draw a new route on the diagram to show Mrs. Green the shortest route she can take from her house to Mrs. Saura's house.*

      b.   The length of the route is _____ m.

⑱   a.

> *Use a green pen to draw a new route on the diagram to show Mrs. Smith the shortest route she can take from her house to Mrs. Saura's house.*

      b.   The length of the route is _____ m.

⑲

> *I want to visit the lady that lives closest to me. Who am I going to visit?*

_____

ISBN: 978-1-77149-031-3

Perimeter and Area

- Understand the meaning of perimeter and area.
- Estimate, measure, and record the perimeter of 2-D shapes.
- Estimate, measure, and record the area of shapes.

The perimeter of the mat is about 150 cm.

The area of the mat is about the same as the total of 9 tiles.

Use a red pen to trace the perimeter of each shape.

①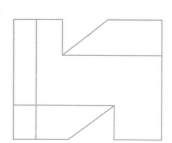

②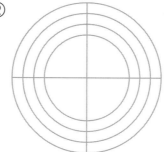

③

Find the perimeter of each shape.

④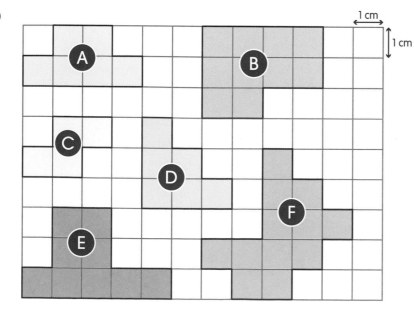

1 cm
1 cm

	Perimeter
A	
B	
C	
D	
E	
F	

ISBN: 978-1-77149-031-3

Estimate the perimeter of each shape. Then measure and record the actual perimeter.

⑤

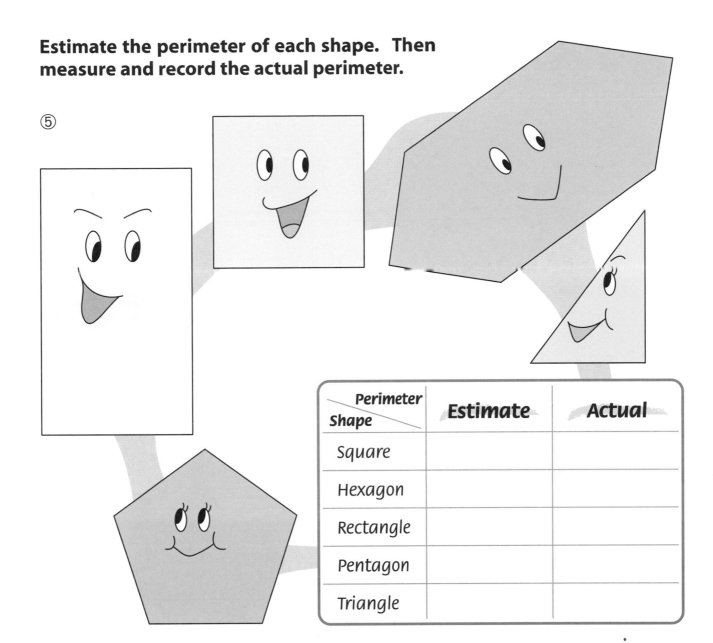

Perimeter / Shape	Estimate	Actual
Square		
Hexagon		
Rectangle		
Pentagon		
Triangle		

Draw the shapes on the grid.

⑥

> Draw a square with a perimeter of 12 cm and a rectangle with a perimeter of 14 cm.

Combine the parts to find areas.

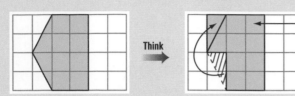

Think ➡️

Take out the part with stripes and put it to a place that can form squares. Then count the number of squares in the combined figure.

The area of this figure is 10 ☐.

Colour each figure. Draw lines to complete the grid. Estimate and find the area of each figure. Then answer the questions.

⑦

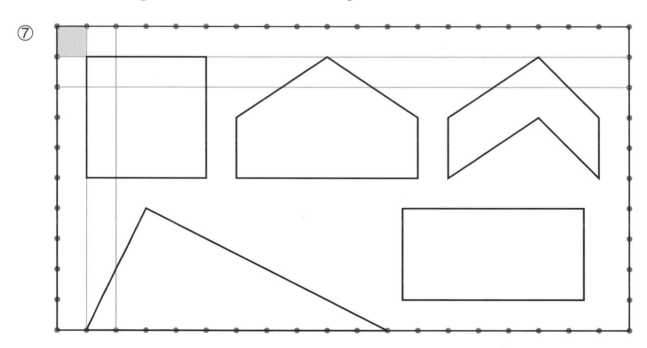

⑧

Figure / Area	Estimate	Actual
Square		
Pentagon		
Hexagon		
Triangle		
Rectangle		

⑨ Which figure has the greatest area?

_____

⑩ If the square is cut into two identical triangles, what is the area of each triangle?

_____

ISBN: 978-1-77149-031-3

Draw the shapes on the grid.

⑪

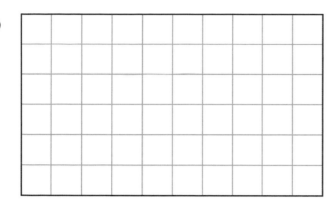

Draw a square with an area of 4 ☐ and a rectangle with an area of 15 ☐.

The children used two different grids to measure the area of a placemat. Help them record the measurements. Then answer the questions.

⑫

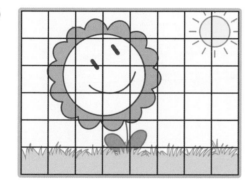

_____ ☐   _____ ☐

⑬ The greater the area of a unit is, the smaller / greater the number of units used to cover a surface.

⑭

How many triangles are needed to cover the placemat?

_____ ◹

ISBN: 978-1-77149-031-3

You finished the plate of French fries in 2 minutes.

Start
05 42

Finish
05 44

Time and Temperature

- Read and write time in 12-hour notation.
- Find time intervals.
- Read water and air temperatures to the nearest degree Celsius.

Fill in the blanks to tell the times in 2 ways.

① 3 : __05__

__5__ min past 3

② __6__ : 40

20 min to __7__

③ 8 : __20__

__20__ min past 8

Tell the times in 2 ways.

④

A __11:25__ ;
__25 min past 11__

B __5:55__ ;
__55 min past 5__

C __2:35__ ; __35 min past 2__

D __12:10__ ; __10 min past 12__

E __11:50__ ; __50 min past 11__

ISBN: 978-1-77149-031-3

Match the clocks with the times in words. Write the letters.

⑤
_B_ thirty-three minutes after two o'clock

_A_ twenty-three minutes after eight o'clock

_F_ twelve minutes after three o'clock

_D_ fifty-eight minutes after two o'clock

_C_ twenty-three minutes after three o'clock

_e_ eight minutes after twelve o'clock

A 8:23

B 2:33 (crossed out)

C 3:23

D 2:58 (crossed out)

E 12:08

F 3:12 (crossed out)

Help Jason write the times to complete his schedule. Then put his activities in order from 1 to 5.

⑥

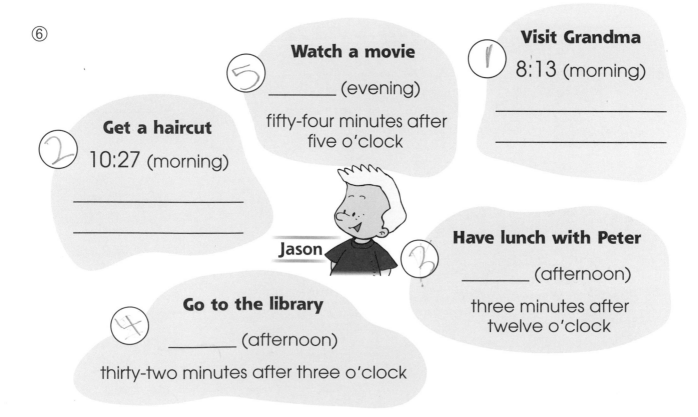

Watch a movie
5
_____ (evening)
fifty-four minutes after five o'clock

Visit Grandma
1
8:13 (morning)
_____
_____

Get a haircut
2
10:27 (morning)
_____
_____

Have lunch with Peter
3
_____ (afternoon)
three minutes after twelve o'clock

Go to the library
4
_____ (afternoon)
thirty-two minutes after three o'clock

Jason

You can use **subtraction** to find time intervals.

e.g.  Think:

$$\begin{array}{r} 4\,1 \\ -\ 2\,6 \\ \hline 1\,5 \end{array}$$

The time interval is 15 minutes.

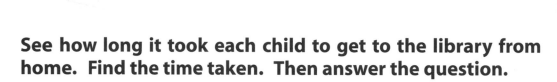

See how long it took each child to get to the library from home. Find the time taken. Then answer the question.

⑦ From `9:14` to `9:53`

 Tom

It took me _____ minutes to walk to the library.

⑧ From `11:08` to `11:21`

 Sally

It took me _____ minutes to walk to the library.

⑨ From `3:27` to `3:39`

 Jacob

It took me _____ minutes to ride my bicycle to the library.

⑩ Who lives closest to the library? _____

ISBN: 978-1-77149-031-3

Water Temperature:

- Water freezes at 0°C.
- Water boils at 100°C.

The air temperature on a warm day is about 20°C, but water at 20°C feels cool. I like to have a hot drink at 45°C.

Colour the thermometers to show the temperatures. Then match the thermometers with the correct pictures. Write the letters.

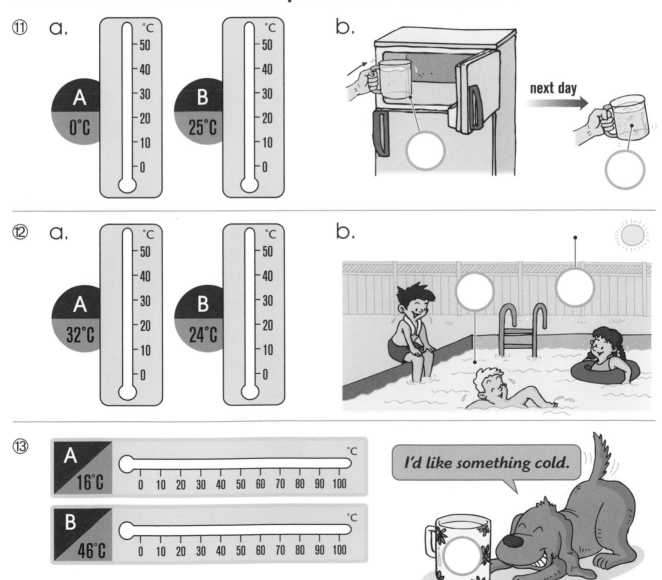

⑪ a.

A 0°C   B 25°C

b. next day

⑫ a.

A 32°C   B 24°C

b.

⑬

A 16°C

B 46°C

I'd like something cold.

9

Money

- Describe the relationships between coins and bills up to $10.

- Estimate and write money amounts up to $10.

- Add money amounts to make purchases up to $10.

I have 10 dollars.

I have 5 toonies.

Don't you know that a 10-dollar bill is the same as 5 toonies?

Check ✔ the correct number of coins or bills to match the highlighted amount.

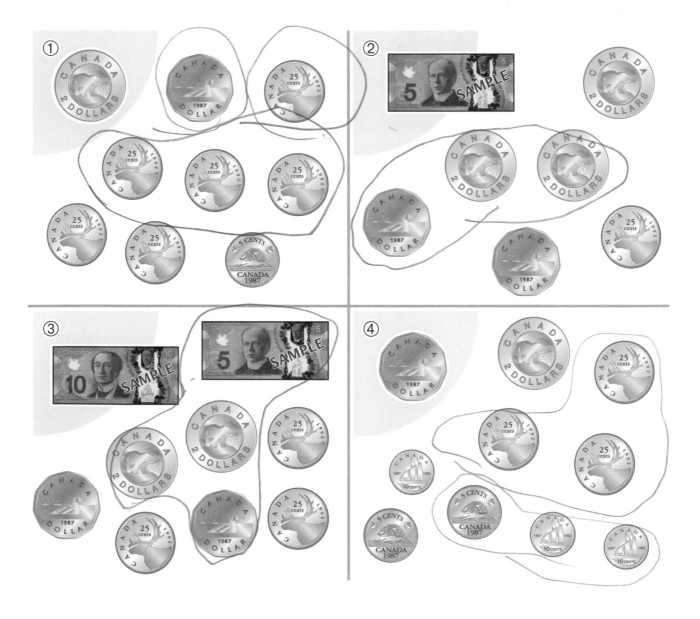

Estimate and find the exact amount of money each child has. Then answer the questions.

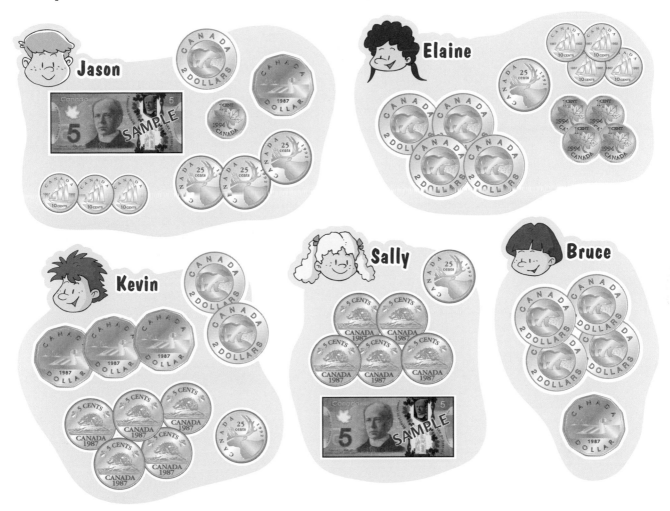

⑤

	Estimate			Actual	
Jason	9	dollars	6 cents	dollars	cents
Elaine	8	dollars	69 cents		
Kevin	7	dollars	50 cents		
Sally	5	dollars	50 cents		
Bruce	9	dollars			

⑥ Who has the most money?

⑦ Who has the least money?

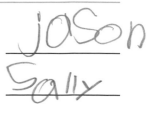

Jason

Sally

ISBN: 978-1-77149-031-3

Ways to write the amount:

Here are 3 dollars 36 cents.

dollars ← → cents

3 dollars 36 cents = **$3.36**

There are 100 cents in 1 dollar.

Write the amount in each piggy bank in 2 ways.

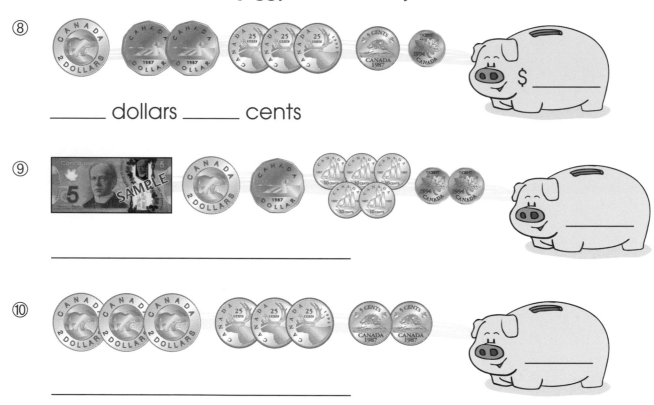

⑧ _____ dollars _____ cents $ _____

⑨ _____

⑩ _____

Fill in the blanks.

⑪ **245 cents**

= 200 cents and ____ cents

= ____ dollars and ____ cents

= $ _____

⑫ **408 cents**

= ____ cents and 8 cents

= ____ dollars and ____ cents

= $ _____

ISBN: 978-1-77149-031-3

Draw the fewest bills and coins to show the cost of each robot.

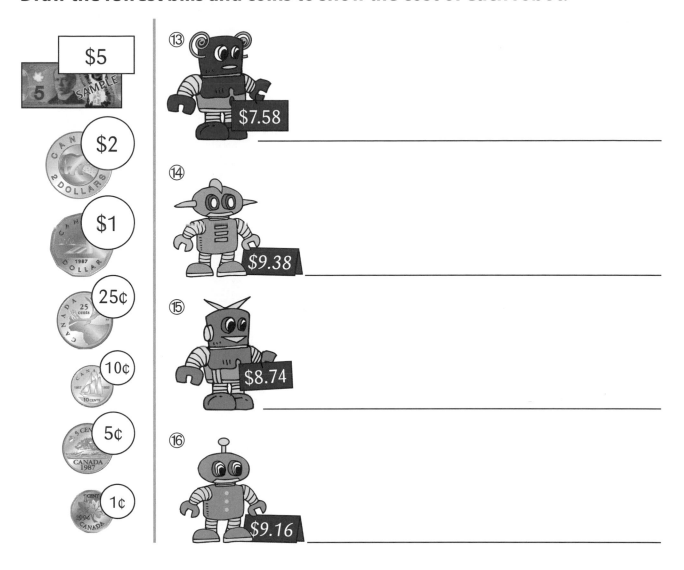

⑬ $7.58

_____

⑭ $9.38

_____

⑮ $8.74

_____

⑯ $9.16

_____

Read what the girl says. Draw the fewest bills and coins to show the money that she has.

⑰

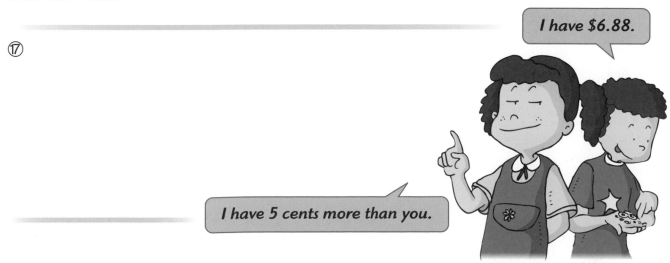

I have $6.88.

I have 5 cents more than you.

ISBN: 978-1-77149-031-3

Addition and Subtraction with Money

$5 = 4 dollars
100 cents

- Add and subtract money amounts to make purchases and change up to $10.
- Solve money problems.

My change is $2.51, isn't it?

Look at the pictures. Find the costs and answer the question.

dollar	cent
4	100
− 2	49
2	51

 **A** $3.21

 **B** $2.38

 **C** $3.27

D $4.49

①
	dollar	cent
A		
B +		

②
	dollar	cent
B		
C +		

③
	dollar	cent
A		
D +		

④
	dollar	cent
C		
D +		

⑤
	dollar	cent
B		
D +		

⑥
	dollar	cent
A		
C +		

⑦ *Which pair of toys costs the most?*

_____

ISBN: 978-1-77149-031-3

Look at the toys on the previous page. Find how much each child pays and which toy he wants. Then find the change.

⑧ John pays $ _____ for **A** .

dollar cent

_____ **Change: $** _____

⑨ Kenny pays $ _____ for **C** .

dollar cent

_____ **Change: $** _____

⑩ Louis pays $ _____ for **B** .

dollar cent

_____ **Change: $** _____

⑪ Frankie pays $ _____ for **D** .

dollar cent

_____ **Change: $** _____

ISBN: 978-1-77149-031-3

Adding money:

dollar	cent
1	
3	8 7
+ 1	4 9
5	3 6

87 + 49 = 136
Carry 100 cents to the dollar column.

$3.87 + $1.49
= **$5.36**

Subtracting money:

dollar	cent
4	129
5̶	2̶9̶
− 1	6 8
3	6 1

Borrow 1 from the dollar column.
100 + 29 = 129

$5.29 − $1.68
= **$3.61**

$1 = 100¢

Fill in the missing information on each receipt.

Detergent
$1.88

Puzzle
$4.89

Crackers
$3.19

$2.16

---

⑫ **R & A Superstore**

Puzzle	$ _____
Crackers	$ _____
Total	$ _____
CASH	$ 10.00
CHANGE	$

⑬ **R & A Superstore**

Detergent	$ _____
Bread	$ _____
Total	$ _____
CASH	$
CHANGE	$ 0.21

⑭ **R & A Superstore**

Crackers	$ _____
Bread	$ _____
Total	$ _____
CASH	$ 6.00
CHANGE	$

⑮ **R & A Superstore**

Detergent	$ _____
Detergent	$ _____
Total	$ _____
CASH	$
CHANGE	$ 1.24

⑯ **R & A Superstore**

Bread	$ _____
_____	$ _____
Total	$ 7.05
CASH	$
CHANGE	$ 0.20

⑰ **R & A Superstore**

Crackers	$ _____
_____	$ _____
Total	$ 5.07
CASH	$
CHANGE	$ 4.93

ISBN: 978-1-77149-031-3

Solve the problems.

⑱   Mrs. Smith pays $5 for a book that costs $3.77. What is her change?

$ _____

⑲   Jordan has $4.25. If he wants to buy a key chain that costs $6.42, how much more does he need?

$ _____

⑳   A box of chocolates costs $3.66. How much do 2 boxes of chocolates cost?

$ _____

㉑   Adam has $5.27 and his brother has $3.64. How much do the boys have in all?

$ _____

㉒

> I have $9.50. Do you think I have enough money to buy 2 sundaes for my parents? If not, how much more do I need?

Special

$4.77

_____

Capacity and Mass

- Estimate, measure, and record the capacity of containers using litres and parts of a litre.
- Estimate, measure, and record the mass of objects using kilograms and parts of a kilogram.

You have 5 kg of sand.

It's getting heavier and heavier.

Sort the containers. Then answer the questions.

① A

 B

 C Juice

 D

 E

 F Milk 1 L

 G

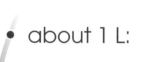 H

 I

- about 1 L:

  _____

- less than 1 L:

  _____

- more than 1 L:

  _____

② Which container holds the most? _____

③ Which container holds the least? _____

Draw the water level in each container.

④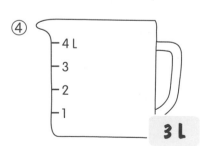
- 4 L
- 3
- 2
- 1

3 L

⑤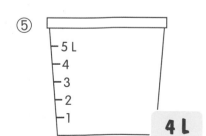
- 5 L
- 4
- 3
- 2
- 1

4 L

⑥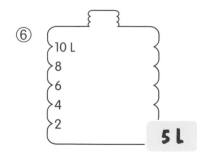
- 10 L
- 8
- 6
- 4
- 2

5 L

ISBN: 978-1-77149-031-3

Which capacity seems reasonable?   Circle the correct answer.

⑦

about 50 L

more than 200 L

⑧

less than 5 L

about 100 L

⑨

less than 1 L

about 10 L

Each container has a capacity of 1 L.   Write how much water is in each container with the given words.

⑩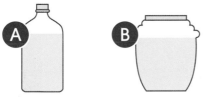

a quarter   half   three quarters

Ⓐ _____ of a litre

Ⓑ _____

Ⓒ _____

Ⓓ _____

Look at the containers.   Fill in the blanks.

⑪ The juice box can hold _____ of a litre of juice.   It takes about _____ juice boxes of water to fill up the ice cream tub.

⑫ The big water bottle can hold _____ of water. It takes about _____ pails of water to fill up the big water bottle.

ISBN: 978-1-77149-031-3

Write the mass of each object. Then answer the questions.

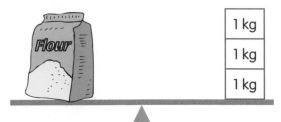

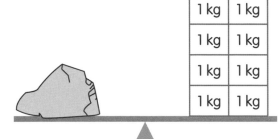

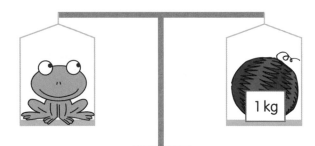 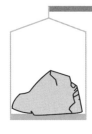

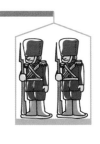

⑬

━━━ **Mass** ━━━

Flour: _____

Pumpkin: _____

Rock: _____

Frog: _____

Watermelon: _____

Tin soldier: _____

⑭ The _____ and the _____ have the same weight.

⑮ _____ bags of flour are needed to balance the frog.

⑯ Draw the correct number of $\boxed{1\,kg}$ to balance the objects.

   ISBN: 978-1-77149-031-3

Each container can hold 1 kg of sugar. Write how much sugar is in each container with the given words.

a quarter   half   three quarters

⑰

Ⓐ   Ⓑ

Ⓒ   Ⓓ

Ⓐ _____ of a kilogram

Ⓑ _____

Ⓒ _____

Ⓓ _____

Look at the pictures. Fill in the blanks.

⑱ a. Half of a watermelon weighs _____ kg.

b. The whole watermelon weighs _____ kg.

c. If Jason cuts the half watermelon in half again, each piece will weigh _____ kg.

⑲ a. 4 boxes of chocolates weigh _____ kg.

b. Each box of chocolates weighs _____ than 1 kg.

c.

> If I can lift 10 kg at a time, how many boxes of chocolates can I lift in one go?

_____ boxes of chocolates

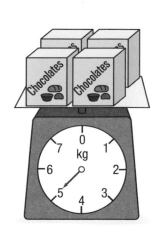

ISBN: 978-1-77149-031-3   Complete Canadian Curriculum • Grade 3   **49**

Multiplication (1)

- Understand multiplication as repeated addition.
- Multiply to 7 x 7.
- Multiply a 1-digit number by 8 or 9 with the help of pictures.

$$\begin{array}{r} 4 \\ \times\ 5 \\ \hline 2\ 0 \end{array}$$

Give me back all 20 rings!

Circle the objects. Then fill in the blanks.

① Circle every 3  .

3 + 3 + 3 + 3 + _____

= ____ groups of 3

= ____ x 3

= _____

② Circle every 4 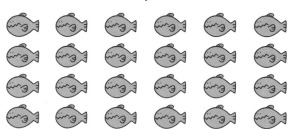 .

4 + _____

= ____ groups of ____

= ____ x ____

= _____

③ Circle every 5  .

5 + _____

= ____ groups of ____

= ____ x ____

= _____

ISBN: 978-1-77149-031-3

Look at the pictures. Fill in the blanks.

④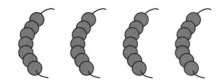

_____ groups of 7

= _____ times 7

= _____ x 7

= _____

⑤

_____ groups of 9

= _____ times 9

= _____ x 9

= _____

⑥

_____ groups of 5

= _____ times 5

= _____ x 5

= _____

⑦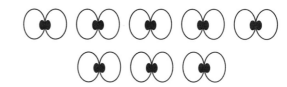

_____ groups of 2

= _____ times 2

= _____ x 2

= _____

Write a multiplication sentence to match each group of items.

⑧

_____ x _____ = _____

⑨

_____ x _____ = _____

⑩

_____ x _____ = _____

⑪

_____ x _____ = _____

ISBN: 978-1-77149-031-3

Draw arrows to continue the patterns. Then count by 3's, 4's, or 7's to write the missing numbers.

⑫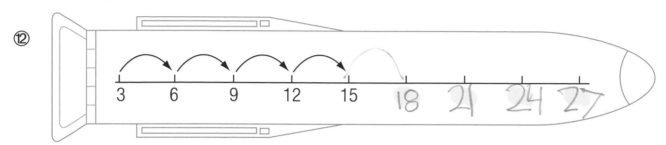

3   6   9   12   15   18 21 24 27

⑬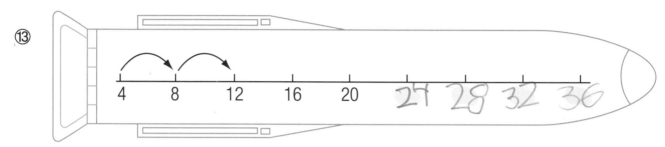

4   8   12   16   20   24 28 32 36

⑭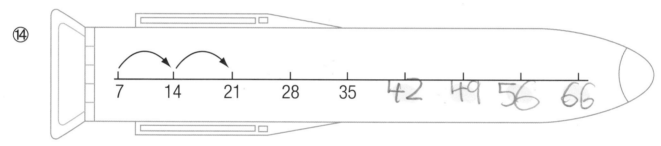

7   14   21   28   35   42 49 56 66

Complete the multiplication tables.

⑮ 1 x 6 = 6
2 x 6 = 12
3 x 6 = 18
4 x 6 = 24
5 x 6 = 30
6 x 6 = 36
7 x 6 = 42
8 x 6 = 48
9 x 6 = 56

⑯ 1 x 2 = 2
2 x 2 = 4
3 x 2 = 6
4 x 2 = 8
5 x 2 = 10
6 x 2 = 12
7 x 2 = 14
8 x 2 = 16
9 x 2 = 18

⑰ 1 x 5 = 5
2 x 5 = 10
3 x 5 = 15
4 x 5 = 20
5 x 5 = 25
6 x 5 = 30
7 x 5 = 35
8 x 5 = 40
9 x 5 = 45

ISBN: 978-1-77149-031-3

Multiplication charts:

multiplication sign →

x	1	2	3	4	5	6	7
1							
2					10 ◄		
3							
4							
5		10 ◄					
6							
7							

A number from

□   □

2 **x** 5

5 **x** 2

Complete the multiplication chart. Then find the answers.

⑱

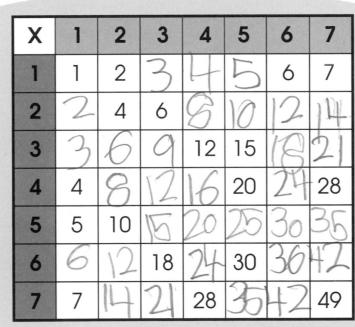

X	1	2	3	4	5	6	7
1	1	2	3	4	5	6	7
2	2	4	6	8	10	12	14
3	3	6	9	12	15	18	21
4	4	8	12	16	20	24	28
5	5	10	15	20	25	30	35
6	6	12	18	24	30	36	42
7	7	14	21	28	35	42	49

⑲ 4 x 6 = __24__

⑳ 5 x 3 = __15__

㉑ 2 x 7 = __14__

㉒ 6 x 6 = __36__

㉓ 4 x 5 = __20__

㉔ 6 x 7 = __42__

㉕

Lily, Louis, Michael, and I each have 6 lollipops. How many lollipops do we have in all?

__24__ lollipops

Multiplication (2)

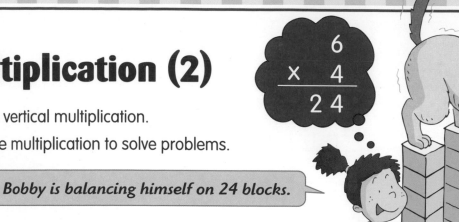

- Do vertical multiplication.
- Use multiplication to solve problems.

Bobby is balancing himself on 24 blocks.

Do the multiplication.

①
$$\begin{array}{r} 3 \\ \times\ 9 \\ \hline 27 \end{array}$$

②
$$\begin{array}{r} 4 \\ \times\ 8 \\ \hline 32 \end{array}$$

③
$$\begin{array}{r} 6 \\ \times\ 5 \\ \hline 30 \end{array}$$

④
$$\begin{array}{r} 7 \\ \times\ 6 \\ \hline 42 \end{array}$$

⑤
$$\begin{array}{r} 2 \\ \times\ 7 \\ \hline 14 \end{array}$$

⑥
$$\begin{array}{r} 5 \\ \times\ 5 \\ \hline 25 \end{array}$$

⑦
$$\begin{array}{r} 4 \\ \times\ 6 \\ \hline 24 \end{array}$$

⑧
$$\begin{array}{r} 5 \\ \times\ 3 \\ \hline 15 \end{array}$$

⑨
$$\begin{array}{r} 3 \\ \times\ 8 \\ \hline 24 \end{array}$$

⑩
$$\begin{array}{r} 7 \\ \times\ 4 \\ \hline 28 \end{array}$$

⑪
$$\begin{array}{r} 5 \\ \times\ 9 \\ \hline 45 \end{array}$$

⑫
$$\begin{array}{r} 4 \\ \times\ 9 \\ \hline 36 \end{array}$$

⑬
$$\begin{array}{r} 6 \\ \times\ 8 \\ \hline 48 \end{array}$$

⑭
$$\begin{array}{r} 7 \\ \times\ 5 \\ \hline 35 \end{array}$$

Fill in the missing numbers.

⑮
$$\begin{array}{r} 3 \\ \times\ \\ \hline 2\,4 \end{array}$$

⑯
$$\begin{array}{r} 7 \\ \times\ \\ \hline 4\,9 \end{array}$$

⑰
$$\begin{array}{r} 6 \\ \times\ \\ \hline 1\,8 \end{array}$$

⑱
$$\begin{array}{r} 4 \\ \times\ \\ \hline 2\,8 \end{array}$$

ISBN: 978-1-77149-031-3

See how many candies the children get if they trade these things with Sally. Help the children solve the problems.

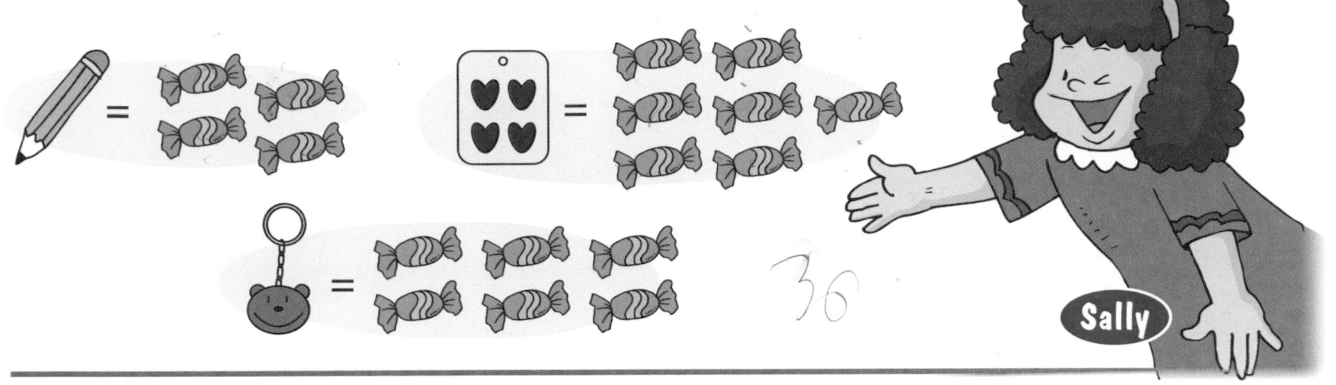

36

Sally

⑲ Mary trades 6 pencils for candies. How many candies does she get?

___24___ candies

6 x 4 = 24

⑳ John trades 3 key chains for candies. How many candies does he get?

___18___ candies

3 x 6 = 18

4 x 7 = 28

㉑ Lily has 4 sheets of stickers. If she wants to trade them for candies, how many candies will she get?

___28___ candies

㉒ Katie wants to trade either 5 sheets of stickers or 6 key chains for candies. Which should she trade for more candies?

___key chains___

Read what the children say. Solve the problems.

㉓ a.
How many apples are there in 4 baskets?

_____ apples

b.
Each apple costs 7¢. How much does a basket of apples cost?

_____ ¢

㉔ a.
How many coins are there on 3 pages?

_____ coins

b.
1 coin weighs the same as 5 paper clips. How heavy are the coins on each page?

_____ paper clips

㉕ a.
There are 6 muffins in a box. How many muffins are there in 5 boxes?

_____ muffins

b.
There are 7 members in my family. If each member eats 2 muffins a day, how many muffins do we eat every day?

_____ muffins

ISBN: 978-1-77149-031-3

Help the girls find how many points each player gets. Complete the table. Then answer the questions.

Each of us can pick 6 cards.

7 points   **5 points**   **4 points**

㉖

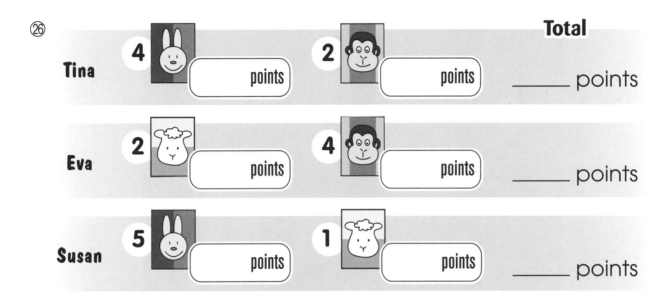

			Total
Tina	4 _____ points	2 _____ points	_____ points
Eva	2 _____ points	4 _____ points	_____ points
Susan	5 _____ points	1 _____ points	_____ points

㉗ Who has the most points? _____

㉘ Who has the fewest points? _____

㉙ If Eva picks 2 🐰 instead of 2 🐑, will she be the winner? _____

㉚

I have taken 2 🐵 from Eva. How many points does Eva have now?

_____ points

14

Division (1)

- Divide a set of objects into groups of a certain number.
- Divide a set of objects into equal shares.
- Solve division problems.

You've used all 28 beads to make 4 bracelets with 7 beads each.

Circle the items. Then fill in the blanks.

① Circle every 3 apples.

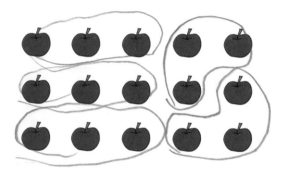

There are ___15___ apples. If I eat 3 apples a day, it will take me ___5___ days to finish all of them.

② Circle every 7 cherries.

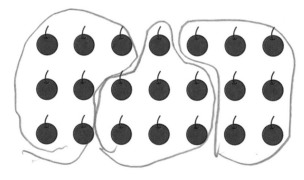

There are ___21___ cherries. If there are 7 cherries in a group, there will be ___3___ groups in all.

③ Circle every 5 peanuts.

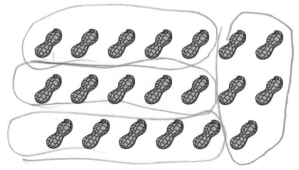

There are ___20___ peanuts. If I put 5 peanuts in a bag, I will need ___4___ bags in all.

Draw the things in the spaces provided. Then fill in the blanks.

④ Put 28 nails equally into 4 boxes.

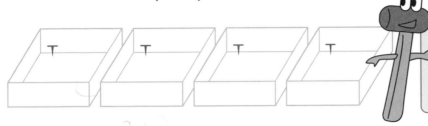

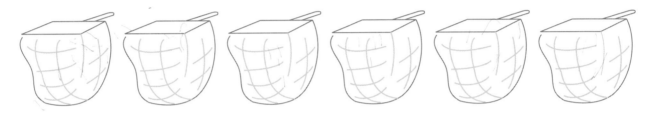

> Put 1 nail into a box at a time and continue until you've put in all 28 nails.

There are _____ nails in each box.

⑤ Put 12 fish equally into 6 nets.

There are _____ fish in each net.

⑥ Put 15 potatoes equally into 5 pots.

There are _____ potatoes in each pot.

⑦ Give 18 flowers equally to 3 bees.

Each bee has _____ flowers.

Draw the missing items. Then fill in the blanks.

⑧ 24 fish in 4 rows

There are ___ fish in each row.

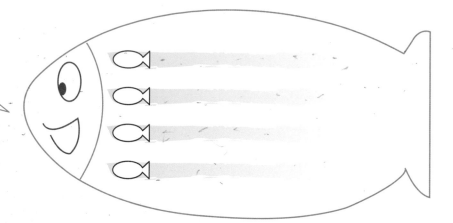

⑨ 21 windows on 3 floors

There are ___ windows on each floor.

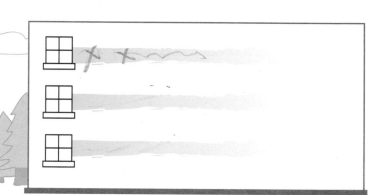

⑩ 35 sun stickers put in rows of 7

There are ___ rows of sun stickers.

⑪ 12 footprints found in rows of 4

There are ___ rows of footprints.

ISBN: 978-1-77149-031-3

Look at the pictures. Fill in the blanks.

⑫ a. Mrs. Smith has __15__ rings.

b. If Mrs. Smith puts 5 rings in a box, she needs __3__ boxes in all.

c. If she puts 3 rings in a box, she needs __5__ boxes in all.

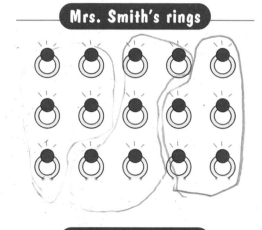

Mrs. Smith's rings

⑬ a. Bobby has _____ bones.

b. If Bobby puts 8 bones in a hole, he needs _____ holes in all.

c. If Bobby eats 4 bones a day, it will take him _____ days to finish all the bones.

Bobby's bones

Read what Linda says. Check ✔ the correct letter.

⑭

> I will share my candies with my 2 friends. Each of us will get 9 candies. Which group of candies is mine?

Ⓐ

Ⓑ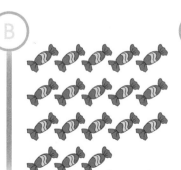

Ⓒ

Division (2)

I've helped you put 13 lollipops equally on 4 stands and there's 1 left. So, I should keep it.

13 ÷ 4 = 3R1

- Use the division sign to write division sentences.
- Do long division and division with remainder.
- Solve division problems.

See how Mrs. Green packs her muffins. Complete the division sentences.

① 20 muffins divided into groups of 4

  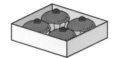 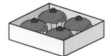 

20 ÷ 4 = __5__   There are __5__ groups of 4.

② 15 muffins divided into groups of 5

15 ÷ 5 = __3__   There are __3__ groups of 5.

③
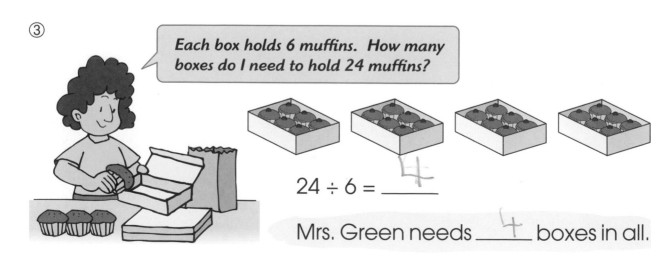

Each box holds 6 muffins. How many boxes do I need to hold 24 muffins?

24 ÷ 6 = __4__

Mrs. Green needs __4__ boxes in all.

If I want to put 10 carrots into 2 groups equally, how many carrots are there in each group?

There are 5 carrots in each group.

Long division

$$2 \overline{)\begin{array}{c} 5 \\ 10 \\ 10 \end{array}}$$

Think:
1 x 2 = 2
2 x 2 = 4
3 x 2 = 6
4 x 2 = 8
5 x 2 = 10

Colour the pictures. Then use long division to find the answers.

④ Jason colours every 3 balls with the same colour. If he has 18 balls, how many different colours does he use?

$$3 \overline{)\begin{array}{c} 6 \\ 18 \end{array}} = 6$$

He uses ___6___ different colours.

⑤ Anita has 20 flowers. How many different colours does she use if she colours every 5 flowers the same colour?

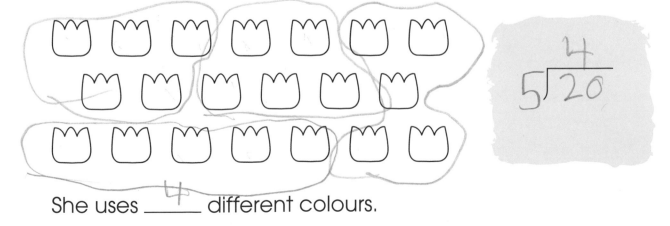

$$5 \overline{)\begin{array}{c} 4 \\ 20 \end{array}}$$

She uses ___4___ different colours.

Do the division.

⑥

$5 \overline{)3\,0}$

⑦

$8 \overline{)2\,4}$

⑧

$2 \overline{)1\,6}$

⑨

$7 \overline{)4\,2}$

⑩　$15 \div 3 = $ _____

⑪　$20 \div 4 = $ _____

⑫　$24 \div 6 = $ _____

⑬　$12 \div 4 = $ _____

⑭　$18 \div 6 = $ _____

⑮　$21 \div 3 = $ _____

⑯　$25 \div 5 = $ _____

⑰　$49 \div 7 = $ _____

⑱　$30 \div 6 = $ _____

Solve the problems.

⑲　May, Sam, and Ted share 27 cookies equally. How many cookies does each child have?

_____ cookies

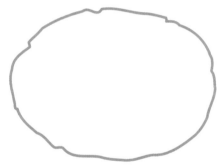

⑳　Each doll costs $2. How many dolls can Linda buy with $16?

_____ dolls

㉑　Mary has 30 stickers. If she puts every 5 stickers in a box, how many boxes does she need to hold all the stickers?

_____ boxes

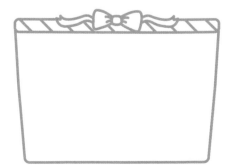

ISBN: 978-1-77149-031-3

I have 13 apples. If I put every 2 apples on a plate, how many plates do I need? How many apples are left?

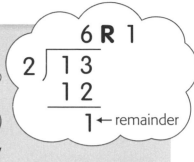

$$\begin{array}{r} 6\ \textbf{R}\ 1 \\ 2\overline{)13} \\ 12 \\ \hline 1 \end{array}$$ ← remainder

$13 \div 2 = \underline{6R1}$

You need 6 plates. 1 apple is left.

Do the division.

㉒ $4\overline{)15}$ _____ R _____

㉓ $3\overline{)20}$ _____ R _____

㉔ $7\overline{)18}$ _____ R _____

㉕ $11 \div 5 =$ _____

㉖ $19 \div 6 =$ _____

㉗ $18 \div 4 =$ _____

㉘ $14 \div 3 =$ _____

Solve the problems.

㉙ Judy has 25 stickers. If she puts every 7 stickers in a bag, how many bags does she need? How many stickers are left?

_____ ÷ _____ = _____

She needs _____ bags. _____ stickers are left.

㉚

I want to share my candies with my two friends equally. How many candies does each of us get? How many candies are left?

_____ ÷ _____ = _____

Each gets _____ candies. _____ candies are left.

ISBN: 978-1-77149-031-3

Multiplication and Division

- Do multiplication and division.
- Understand the relationship between multiplication and division.
- Solve word problems.

Each row has 3 cookies.
4 x 3 = 12

No. of cookies that each of us has:
12 ÷ 2 = 6

I've made 12 cookies.

We can each have 6 cookies.

Find the answers.

①
$$\begin{array}{r} 3 \\ \times\ 6 \\ \hline 18 \end{array}$$

②
$$\begin{array}{r} 4 \\ \times\ 9 \\ \hline 36 \end{array}$$

③
$$\begin{array}{r} 5 \\ \times\ 7 \\ \hline 35 \end{array}$$

④
$$\begin{array}{r} 2 \\ \times\ 8 \\ \hline 16 \end{array}$$

⑤ $8 \overline{)40}$ $\quad 5$

⑥ $5 \overline{)41}$ R ___

⑦ $6 \overline{)24}$

⑧ $4 \overline{)36}$

⑨ $7 \overline{)42}$

⑩ $3 \overline{)20}$ R ___

⑪ $2 \times 4 = $ ____

⑫ $6 \times 6 = $ ____

⑬ $15 \div 4 = $ ____

⑭ $28 \div 7 = $ ____

⑮ $3 \times 5 = $ ____

⑯ $8 \times 6 = $ ____

⑰ $9 \times 3 = $ ____

⑱ $32 \div 4 = $ ____

ISBN: 978-1-77149-031-3

Write a multiplication sentence and a division sentence to match each group of pictures.

⑲

$$\underline{3} \times \underline{6} = \underline{18}$$
$$\underline{18} \div \underline{3} = \underline{6}$$

⑳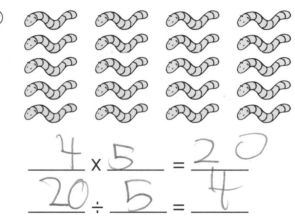

$$\underline{8} \times \underline{2} = \underline{16}$$
$$\underline{16} \div \underline{2} = \underline{8}$$

㉑

$$\underline{7} \times \underline{4} = \underline{28}$$
$$\underline{28} \div \underline{7} = \underline{4}$$

㉒

$$\underline{4} \times \underline{5} = \underline{20}$$
$$\underline{20} \div \underline{5} = \underline{4}$$

Choose the correct numbers to write a multiplication sentence and a division sentence.

㉓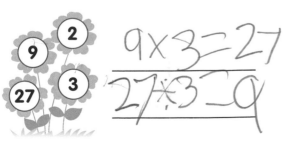
16 15 3 5

$$5 \times 3 = 15$$
$$15 \times 3 = 5$$

㉔
4 5 6 24

$$4 \times 6 = 24$$
$$24 \times 4 = 6$$

㉕
2 9 3 27

$$9 \times 3 = 27$$
$$27 \times 3 = 9$$

㉖
7 28 3 4

$$4 \times 7 = 28$$
$$28 \div 7 = 4$$

Help the boys solve the problems. Check ✔ the correct number sentences and find the answers.

㉗

A big box can hold 6 muffins and a small box can hold 4. If Mrs. Smith has 7 small boxes of muffins, how many muffins does she have in all?

(A) $7 \times 6 =$ _____   (B) $7 \times 4 =$ _____

She has _____ muffins in all.

㉘

How many big boxes are needed to hold 24 muffins?

(A) $24 \div 6 =$ _____   (B) $24 \div 4 =$ _____

_____ big boxes are needed.

㉙

I have 6 green and 42 red marbles. How many marbles do I have in all?

(A) $42 \div 6 =$ _____   (B) $42 - 6 =$ _____

(C) $6 + 42 =$ _____   (D) $42 \times 6 =$ _____

Jason has _____ marbles in all.

㉚

If I put my marbles equally into 6 groups, how many marbles are there in each group?

(A) $42 \div 6 =$ _____   (B) $6 \times 6 =$ _____

(C) $48 \times 6 =$ _____   (D) $48 \div 6 =$ _____

There are _____ marbles in each group.

ISBN: 978-1-77149-031-3

Solve the problems.

㉛ Each pumpkin costs $4. How much do 8 pumpkins cost?

$ _____

㉜ Each basket holds 7 apples. How many baskets are needed to hold 28 apples?

_____ baskets

㉝ If Joey shares a box of 27 cards with 2 friends, how many cards will each child get?

_____ cards

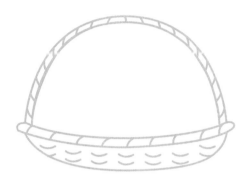

㉞

A bag can hold 5 cookies. How many cookies are there in all in 7 bags?

_____ = _____

_____ cookies

㉟

How many bags are needed to hold 49 cookies?

_____ = _____

_____ bags

ISBN: 978-1-77149-031-3

Fractions

- Divide whole objects and sets of objects into equal parts.
- Identify the parts using fractional names.
- Compare and order fractions.

> You have this and I will have the rest.

> What? I can only have one sixteenth of the pizza?

Draw lines to cut each shape into equal parts. Then do the colouring and fill in the blanks.

①

Cut it into 8 equal parts and colour 2 parts.

Two _____ of the square is coloured.

②

Cut it into 6 equal parts and colour 5 parts.

Five _____ of the hexagon is coloured.

③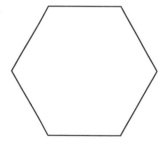

Cut it into 10 equal parts. Then colour 2 parts blue and 5 parts orange.

Two _____ of the rectangle is blue and

five _____ is orange.

Write a fraction to describe the coloured part in each figure.

④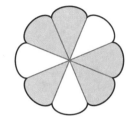

_____ eighths

⑤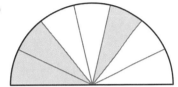

_____

⑥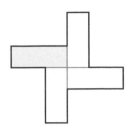

_____

⑦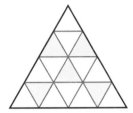

_____

⑧

_____

⑨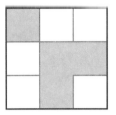

_____

Write a fraction to describe the coloured animals in each group.

⑩

_____

⑪

_____

⑫

_____

⑬

_____

ISBN: 978-1-77149-031-3

Draw lines to divide the items in each group into equal parts. Then colour the parts and fill in the blanks with fractional names.

⑭

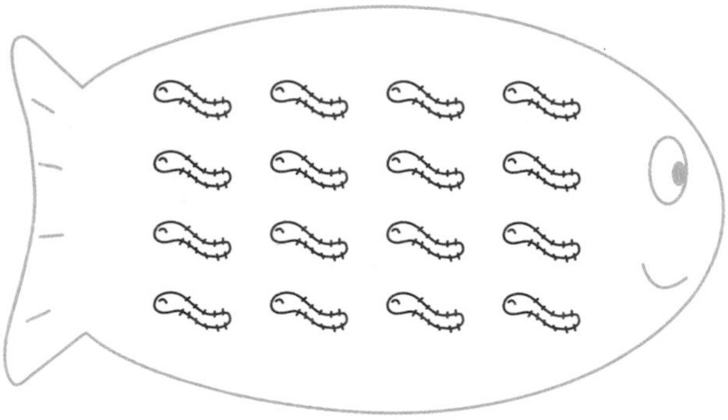

Divide the worms into 8 equal parts and colour 3 parts.

Three _____ of the worms are coloured.

⑮

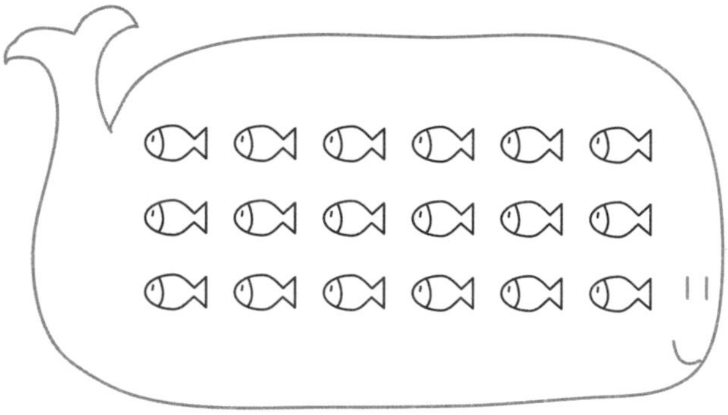

Divide the fish into 6 equal parts and colour 2 parts.

_____ _____ of the fish are coloured.

⑯

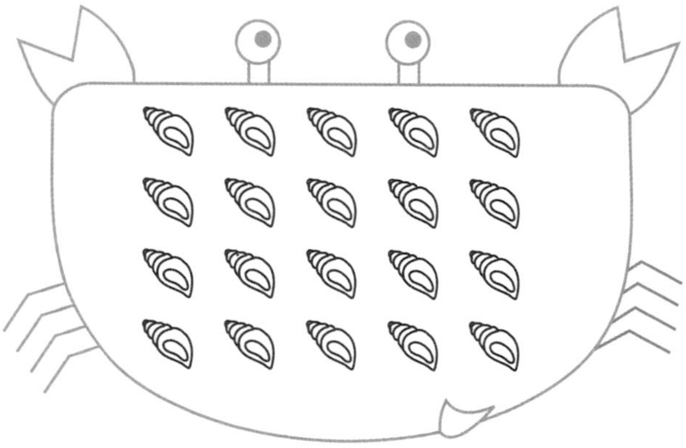

Divide the shells into 5 equal parts and colour 4 parts.

_____ _____ of the shells are coloured.

⑰

Divide the stars into 3 equal parts and colour 2 parts.

_____ _____ of the stars are coloured.

ISBN: 978-1-77149-031-3

Draw lines and colour the correct number of parts of the diagrams to match the fractions. Then circle the greater fraction.

⑱ four tenths three fifths

⑲ three eighths two fourths

⑳ five ninths two thirds

㉑ five sixths three fifths

Colour the correct number of parts to match each fraction. Then put the fractions in order. Write the letters.

㉒ **A** two sixths

B three fifths

C three tenths

From greatest to least:

____ , ____ , ____

㉓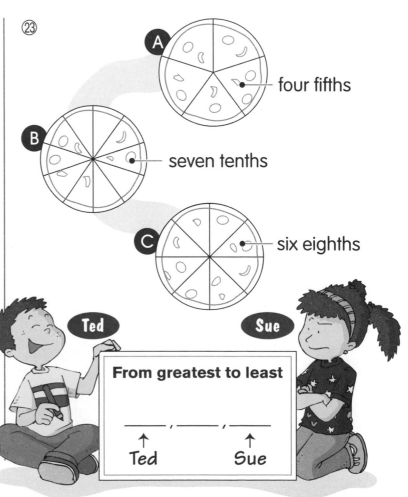

A four fifths

B seven tenths

C six eighths

Ted

Sue

From greatest to least

____ , ____ , ____
↑ ↑
Ted Sue

2-D Shapes (1)

- Identify and compare polygons.
- Sort polygons by geometric properties, such as number of sides and side lengths.
- Identify congruent 2-D shapes.

Each side is 48 cm.

Mr. Square
- 4 sides
- 4 vertices

Colour and name the polygons. Then sort them.

① **A**

B

C

_____

D

E

F

_____

G

H

I

_____

②

Polygon

Irregular   Regular

ISBN: 978-1-77149-031-3

Draw the missing side of each shape. Circle the vertices. Then record the number of sides and the number of vertices.

③

- _____ sides
- _____ vertices

④

- _____ sides
- _____ vertices

⑤

- _____ sides
- _____ vertices

⑥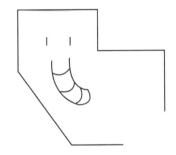

- _____ sides
- _____ vertices

⑦

- _____ sides
- _____ vertices

⑧

- _____ sides
- _____ vertices

Read each sentence. If it is correct, put a check mark ✔ in the circle; otherwise, put a cross ✘ and correct the number or word in bold to make the sentence true.

⑨ A pentagon has 5 sides and **6** vertices. ◯ ; _____

⑩ A **triangle** has 4 vertices and 4 equal sides. ◯ ; _____

⑪ An octagon has **8** sides and 8 vertices. ◯ ; _____

⑫ A hexagon has **1** side more than a pentagon. ◯ ; _____

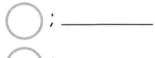

Two shapes are congruent when they have the same size and shape.

e.g. Which shape is congruent to the white square?

Congruent Shapes

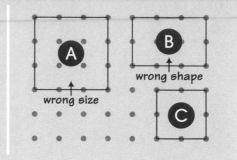

C is congruent to the white square.

Put a check mark ✔ in the circle if the shapes in each pair are congruent.

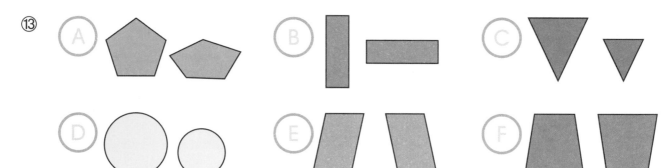

⑬ Ⓐ Ⓑ Ⓒ

Ⓓ Ⓔ Ⓕ

Colour the shape that is congruent to each coloured shape.

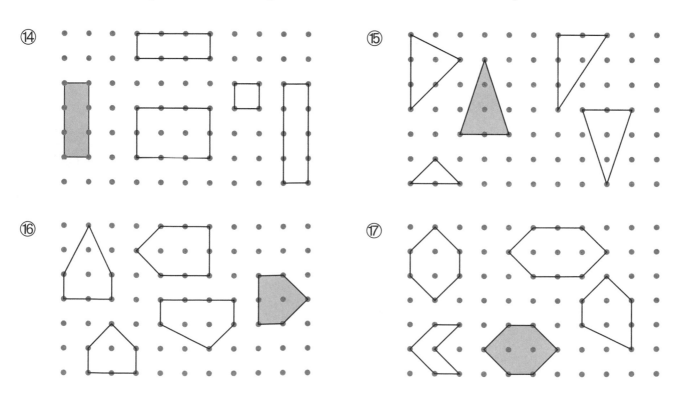

⑭ ⑮

⑯ ⑰

ISBN: 978-1-77149-031-3

Draw a shape that is congruent to each given figure.

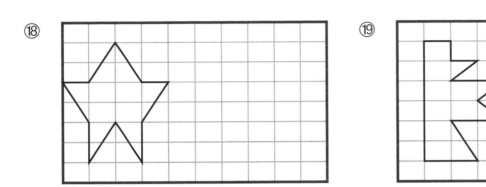

⑱   ⑲

Sort the polygons by their side lengths. Write the letters.

⑳

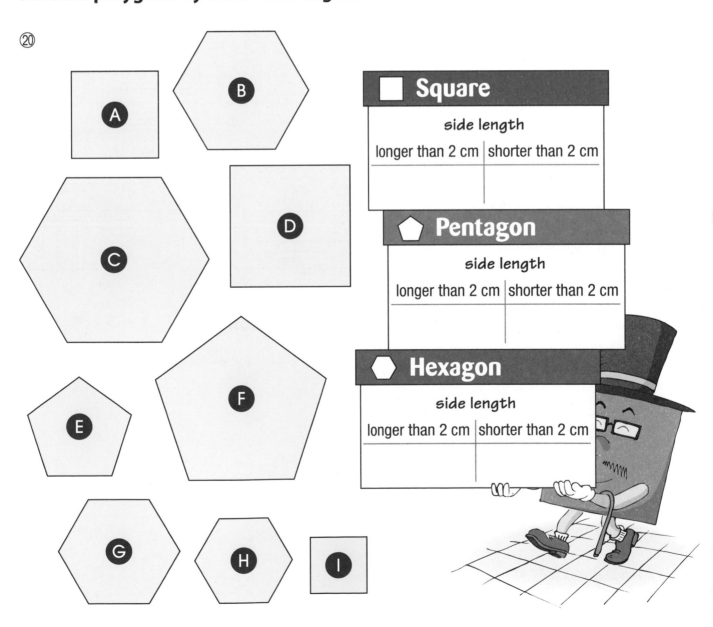

⬜ **Square**	
side length	
longer than 2 cm	shorter than 2 cm

⬠ **Pentagon**	
side length	
longer than 2 cm	shorter than 2 cm

⬡ **Hexagon**	
side length	
longer than 2 cm	shorter than 2 cm

ISBN: 978-1-77149-031-3

2-D Shapes (2)

- Identify right angles and describe angles.
- Sort polygons by their number of interior angles and right angles.
- Understand the relationship among different types of quadrilaterals.
- Draw symmetrical shapes.

Colour the things that have right angles.

①

Trace the dotted lines. Then check ✔ the right angles.

②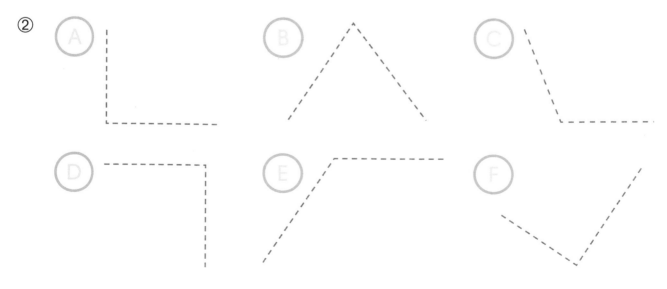

ISBN: 978-1-77149-031-3

Use the words below to describe the given angles. Then draw another angle for each type.

greater than a right angle	a right angle	smaller than a right angle

③

④

⑤

⑥

Mark the interior angles. Then colour them as specified.

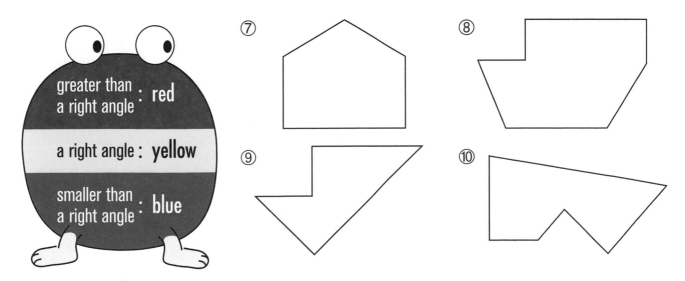

greater than a right angle : **red**

a right angle : **yellow**

smaller than a right angle : **blue**

⑦

⑧

⑨

⑩

ISBN: 978-1-77149-031-3

Quadrilateral:
- a polygon with 4 sides

e.g.

Rectangle: a quadrilateral in which opposite sides are equal, and all interior angles are right angles

Parallelogram: a quadrilateral whose opposite sides are parallel

Look at the interior angles of each quadrilateral. Colour them if they are right angles.

⑪

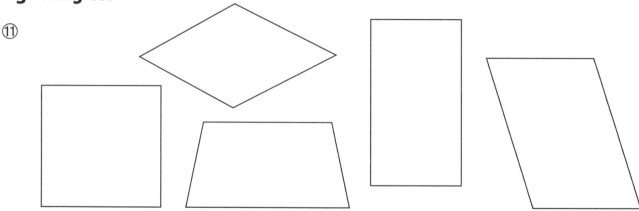

Look at each pair of quadrilaterals. Fill in the blanks and circle the correct answer.

⑫
- 4 sides
- _____ right angles

- 4 equal sides
- _____ right angles

⑬
- opposite sides equal
- _____ pairs of opposite sides

- _____ sides equal
- _____ pairs of opposite sides

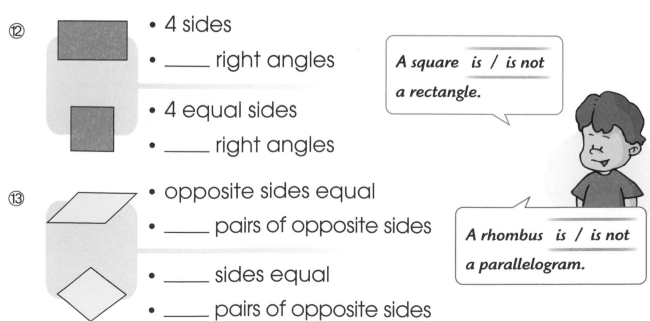

A square   is / is not   a rectangle.

A rhombus   is / is not   a parallelogram.

ISBN: 978-1-77149-031-3

Check ✔ the picture if the dotted line is the line of symmetry of each design.

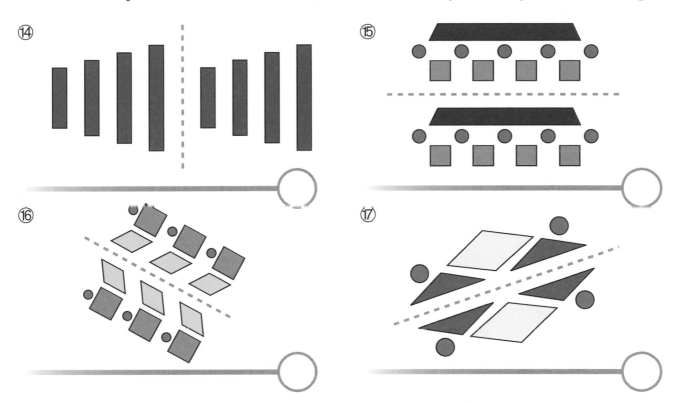

Draw the missing parts of each symmetrical picture.

3-D Figures (1)

- Describe and name prisms and pyramids by the shapes of their bases.

- Sort prisms and pyramids by the number of faces, edges, and vertices.

It is a triangular prism.

Colour the bases of each prism. Then name the shape of the bases and the prism.

①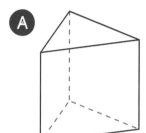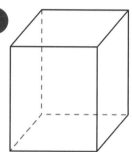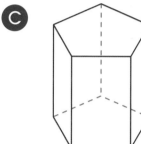

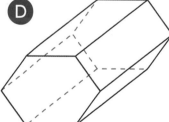 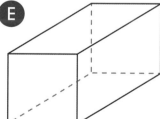 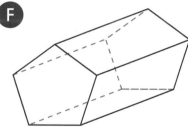

	Shape of Bases	Name of Prism
A		
B		
C		
D		
E		
F		

Colour the base of each pyramid. Then name the shape of the base and the pyramid.

②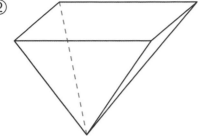

Base: _____

③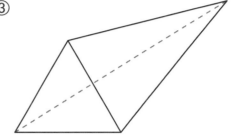

Base: _____

④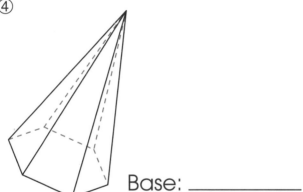

Base: _____

⑤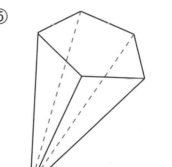

Base: _____

⑥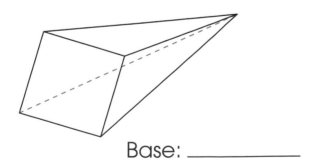

Base: _____

⑦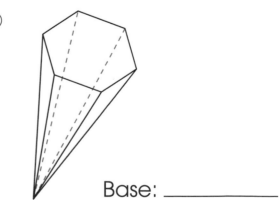

Base: _____

ISBN: 978-1-77149-031-3

Draw the missing edges and circle the vertices of each prism or pyramid. Count and write the numbers. Then sort the solids. Write the letters.

⑧ **A**
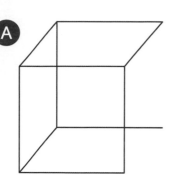

____ faces

____ edges

____ vertices

B

____ faces

____ edges

____ vertices

C

____ faces

____ edges

____ vertices

D
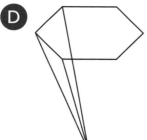

____ faces

____ edges

____ vertices

E

____ faces

____ edges

____ vertices

F
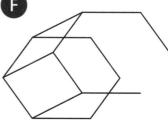

____ faces

____ edges

____ vertices

⑨ **Faces**

fewer than 5: _____

5 or more: _____

⑩ **Edges**

fewer than 12: _____

12 or more: _____

⑪ **Vertices**

fewer than 6: _____

6 or more: _____

ISBN: 978-1-77149-031-3

Name the solid that can be built by the given sticks and marshmallows in each group.

⑫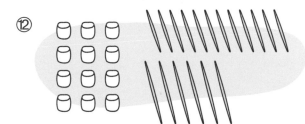

_____

⑬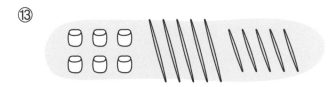

_____

⑭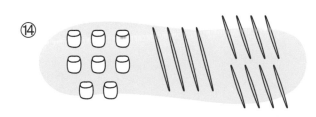

_____

⑮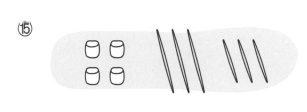

_____

Check ✔ the correct answers.

⑯ Which solid has more than 6 faces?

Ⓐ triangular prism   Ⓑ square-based pyramid

Ⓒ rectangular prism   Ⓓ hexagonal pyramid

⑰ Which solid has more than 14 edges?

Ⓐ hexagonal pyramid   Ⓑ triangular prism

Ⓒ pentagonal prism   Ⓓ rectangular prism

⑱ _Which solids have more than 5 faces but fewer than 9 vertices?_

Ⓐ 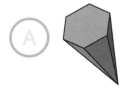   Ⓑ   Ⓒ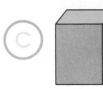

ISBN: 978-1-77149-031-3

3-D Figures (2)

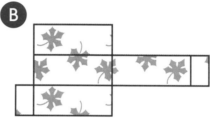

This is Rectangular Prism.

Hi.

- Construct rectangular prisms and describe geometric properties of prisms.

- Identify and describe the 2-D shapes that can be found in a 3-D figure.

Colour the net that can form a rectangular prism.

①

A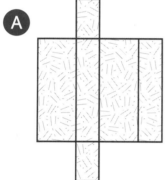

B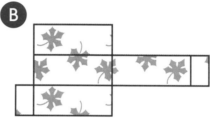

C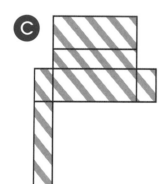

D

E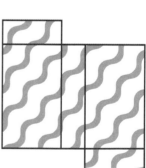

F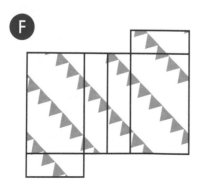

G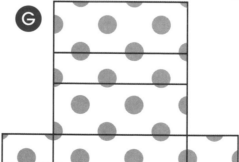

ISBN: 978-1-77149-031-3

Draw the missing parts of each net of a rectangular prism. Then match each net with the rectangular prism. Write the letter.

②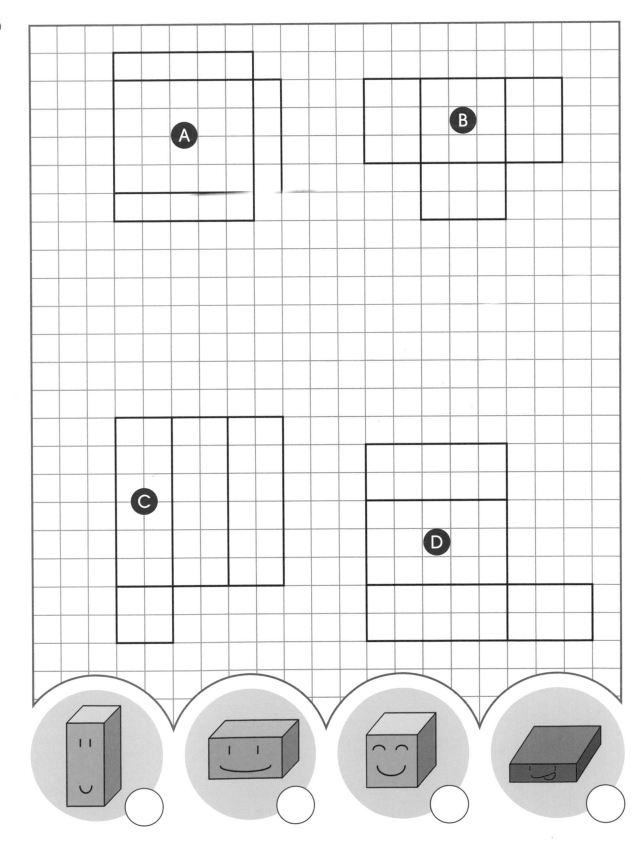

Colour each pair of congruent faces with the same colour in each net. Then answer the questions.

③ **A** 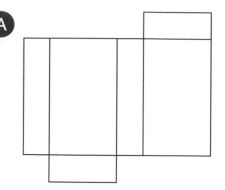   **B**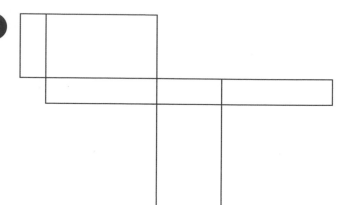

④ How many faces are there in a rectangular prism?

_____ faces

⑤ What shape are the faces?

_____

⑥ *How many pairs of congruent faces are there?*

_____ pairs

Look at the solids. Name the shapes of the coloured faces.

⑦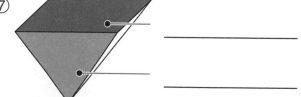

_____

_____

⑧

_____

_____

⑨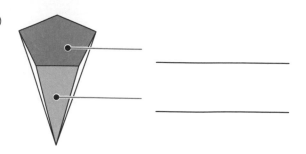

_____

_____

⑩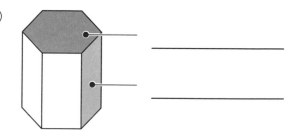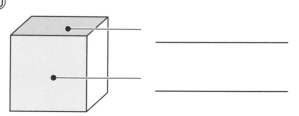

_____

_____

ISBN: 978-1-77149-031-3

Colour all the faces of each solid that you can see. Then write the name of the solid and the numbers.

⑪

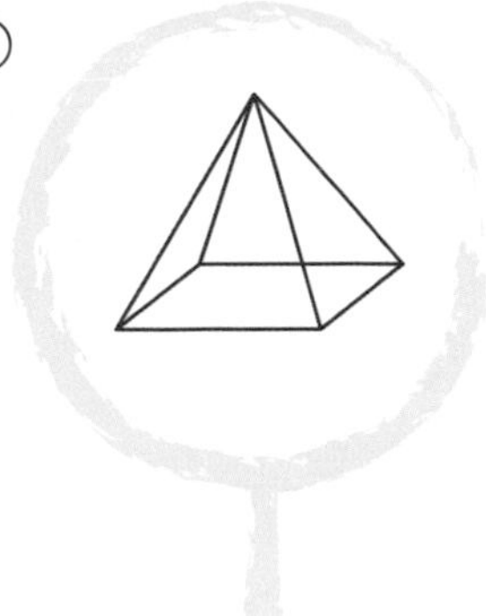

It is a _____ . It has ___ triangular faces and ___ rectangular face.

⑫

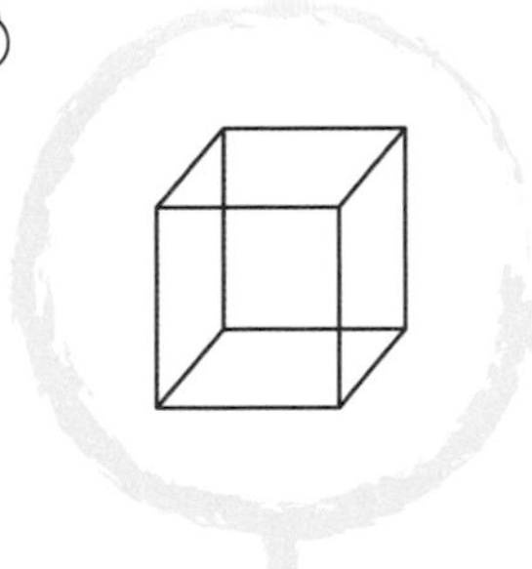

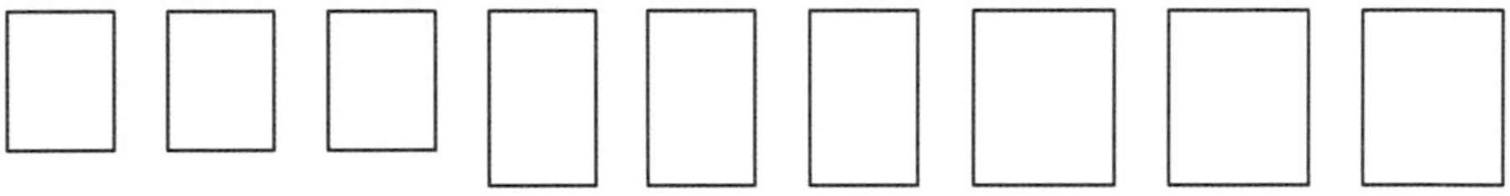

It is a _____ . It has ___ rectangular faces.

⑬

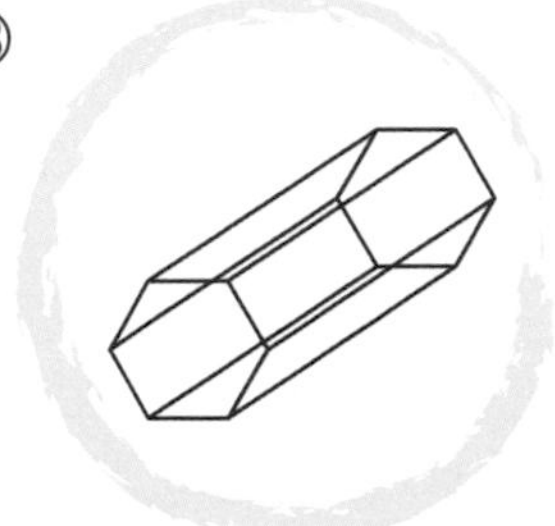

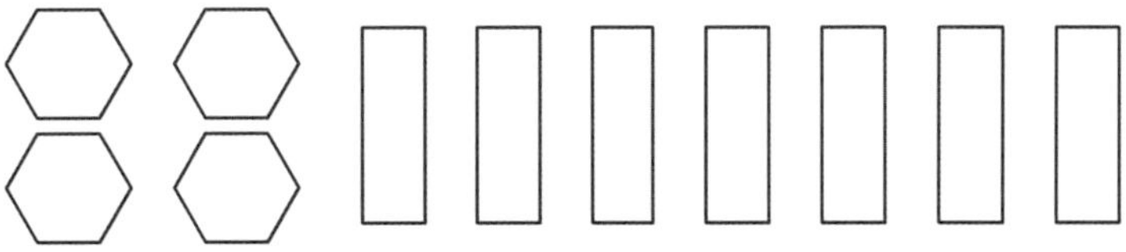

It is a _____ . It has ___ hexagonal faces and ___ rectangular faces.

Look at the solids. Answer the questions. Write the letters.

⑭ *Which solids have triangular faces?*

_____

⑮ *Which solids have rectangular faces?*

_____

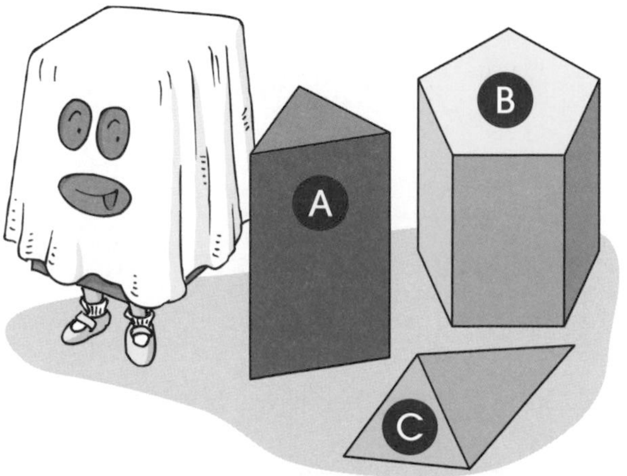

ISBN: 978-1-77149-031-3   Complete Canadian Curriculum • Grade 3

Locations of Shapes and Objects

- Describe locations of shapes and objects.
- Describe movement from one location to another.

Look at the picture. Fill in the blanks.

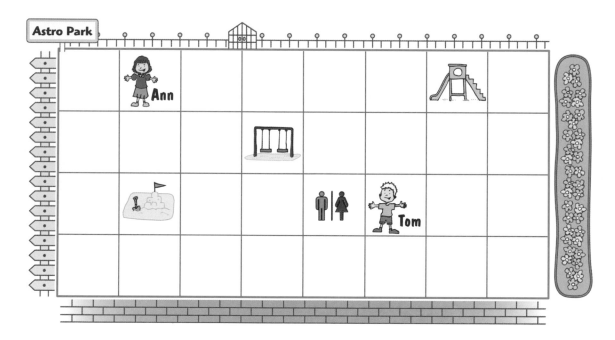

① The swings are _____ squares to the left of the flower bed.

② The slide is _____ squares up from the wall.

③ The washroom is _____ squares to the right of the fence.

④ The sandbox is _____ squares down from the gate.

⑤ Tom is _____ squares to the right of the sandbox and _____ squares to the left of the flower bed.

⑥ Ann is _____ squares to the right of the fence and _____ squares to the left of the slide.

ISBN: 978-1-77149-031-3

Mark and colour the squares in the diagram to locate the children. Then answer the question.

⑦ • Sally is 5 squares to the left of the river. Colour the squares that are the possible locations of Sally yellow.

  • Sally is 3 squares up from the buildings. Put stripes on the squares that are the possible locations of Sally.

⑧ Write "Sally" in the square to show the exact location of Sally.

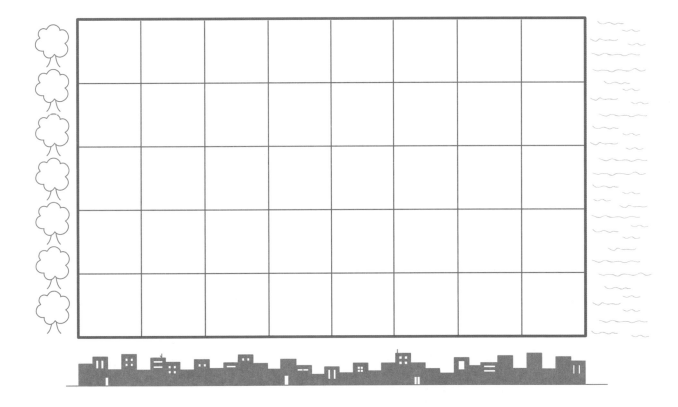

⑨ Jerry is 4 squares to the right of the trees and 5 squares up from the buildings. Write "Jerry" in the square to show his exact location.

⑩ How many squares apart are Jerry and I?

_____ square(s)

Sally

ISBN: 978-1-77149-031-3

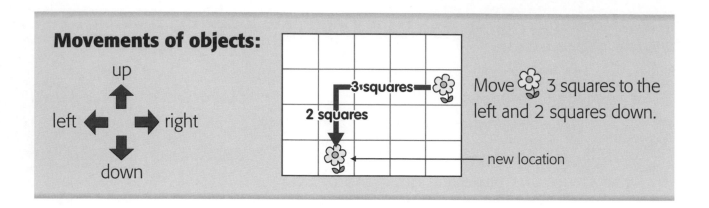

Movements of objects:

up

left ← → right

down

Move 🌸 3 squares to the left and 2 squares down.

new location

Draw lines to show the movements of the objects. Then draw the objects in the squares to show the new locations.

⑪ Move

- 🍭 3 squares to the right and 1 square down.

- 🌳 2 squares to the left and 4 squares down.

- ⭐ 3 squares to the left and 3 squares up.

- 🏠 4 squares to the right and 1 square up.

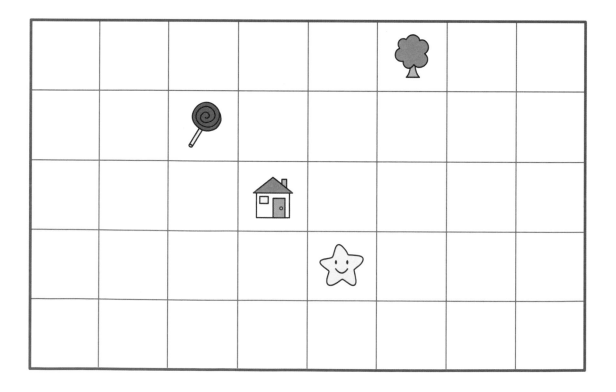

ISBN: 978-1-77149-031-3

Look at the diagram. Help each person find the shortest path to reach the destination. Then answer the questions.

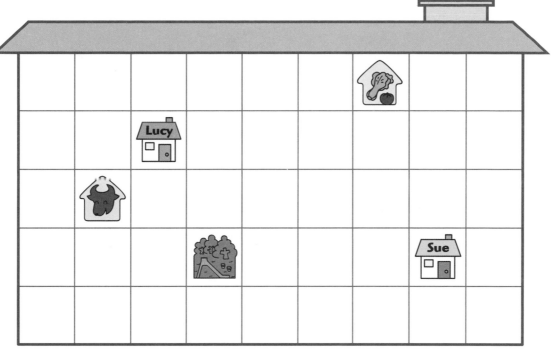

⑫ Sue wants to visit Lucy. Draw lines to show her path and describe it.

_____

⑬ Lucy's mom wants to go to the grocery store. Draw lines to show her path and describe it.

_____

⑭  _I am in the park. If I want to go to the steak house, how should I go? Draw lines and describe it._

_____

⑮ _We are in the park. We want to go to Sue's house. Draw lines to show our path and describe it._

_____

Transformations

- Identify flips, slides, and turns using objects and physical motions.

I'm sliding.

See which pairs of pictures show slides. Check ✔ the letters.

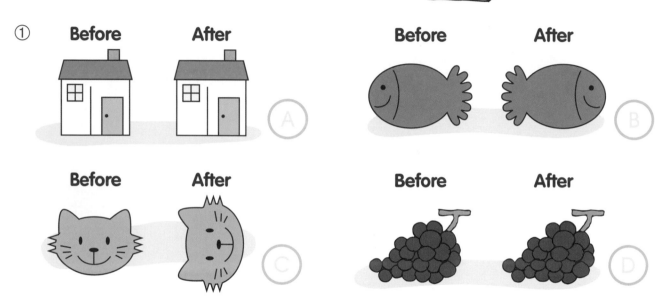

① Before   After   A

Before   After   B

Before   After   C

Before   After   D

Follow the arrow to draw the slide image of each picture.

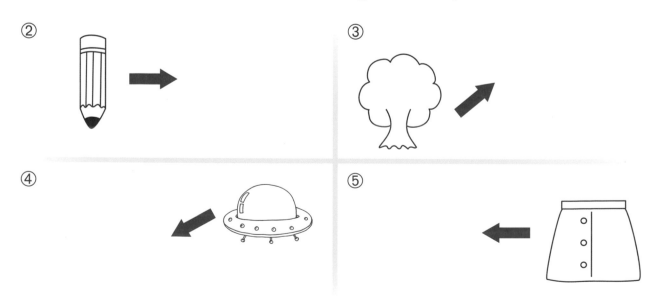

②

③

④

⑤

Which is the flip image of the picture on the left? Colour it.

Draw the missing parts of each flip image.

For each picture, which are the turn images?   Check ✔ the letters.

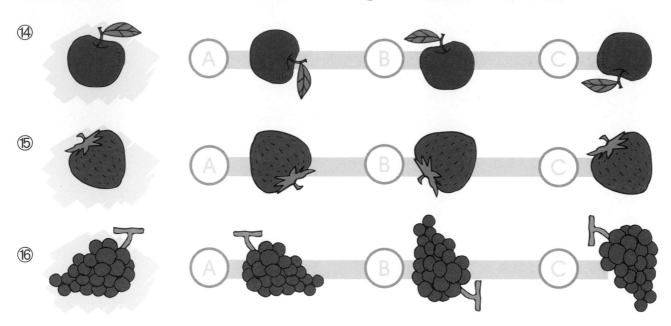

⑭ Ⓐ Ⓑ Ⓒ

⑮ Ⓐ Ⓑ Ⓒ

⑯ Ⓐ Ⓑ Ⓒ

Trace each shape with tracing paper and cut it.   Then draw the missing sides of its turn image with the help of the cut-out.

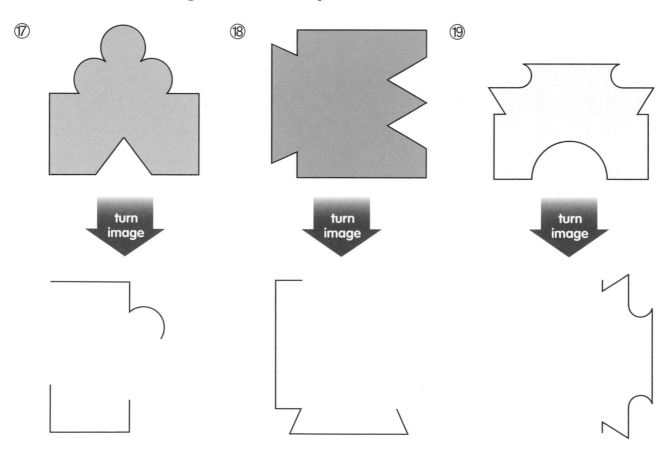

⑰ ⑱ ⑲

turn image

ISBN: 978-1-77149-031-3

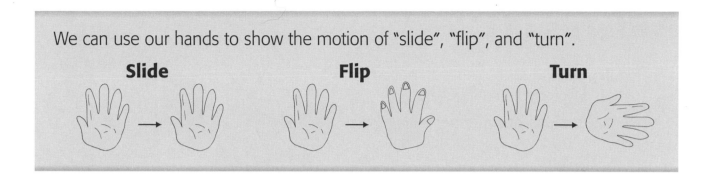

We can use our hands to show the motion of "slide", "flip", and "turn".

Slide   **Flip**   **Turn**

For each picture, tell whether the motion is a slide, flip, or turn.

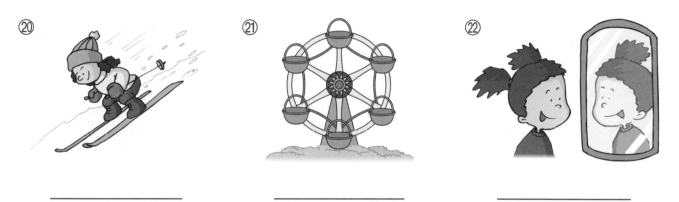

㉑   ㉒   ㉒

_____   _____   _____

Tell whether each image is a slide image, a flip image, or a turn image of each picture.

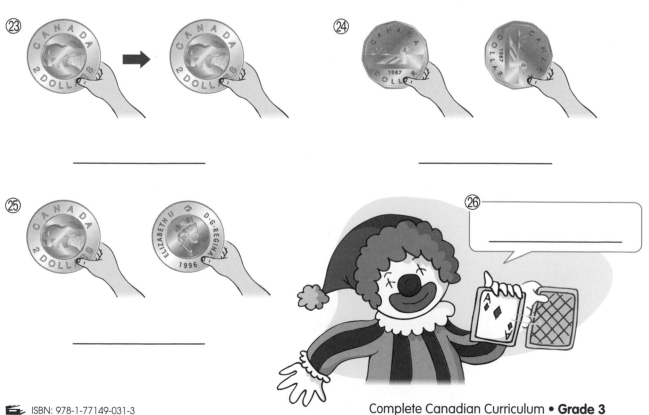

_____   _____

_____

ISBN: 978-1-77149-031-3

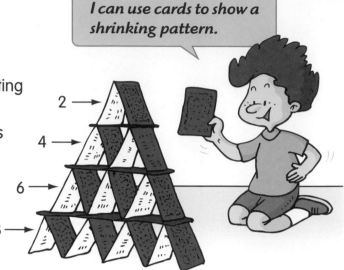

Patterns (1)

I can use cards to show a shrinking pattern.

- Identify, extend, and create a repeating pattern involving two attributes.

- Identify and describe number patterns involving addition, subtraction, and multiplication.

- Describe and extend growing and shrinking patterns.

2 →
4 →
6 →
8 →

Colour the shapes as specified. Then draw and colour the next two shapes for each pattern.

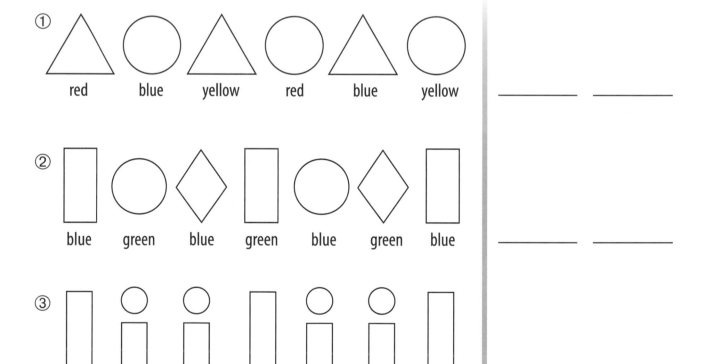

① △ ◯ △ ◯ △ ◯
   red blue yellow red blue yellow

_____ _____

② ▮ ◯ ◇ ▮ ◯ ◇ ▮
   blue green blue green blue green blue

_____ _____

③ ▮ ◯▯ ◯▯ ▮ ◯▯ ◯▯ ▮
   red green red green red green red

_____ _____

④ ⬡ ⋁ ⬡ ⋁ ⬡ ⋁
   yellow yellow green yellow yellow green

_____ _____

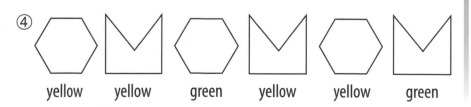

ISBN: 978-1-77149-031-3

Colour the pictures as specified. Follow the pattern in each group to draw and colour the next picture. Then fill in the blanks and circle the correct word to complete what the animal says.

⑤ red blue red blue red blue red blue red

I created this pattern by using _____ colours and circles in _____ different sizes / orientations .

⑥ yellow yellow yellow yellow yellow yellow yellow yellow

I created this pattern by using _____ patterns and a _____ in _____ different colours / orientations .

⑦ blue green blue green blue green

I created this pattern by using _____ colours and _____ different shapes, a _____ and a _____ .

24

Find the pattern in each group. Draw the missing pictures. Then write "growing" or "shrinking" on the lines.

⑧ a.

b. It is a _____ pattern.

⑨ a.

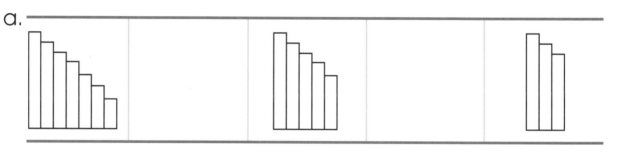

b. It is a _____ pattern.

⑩ a.

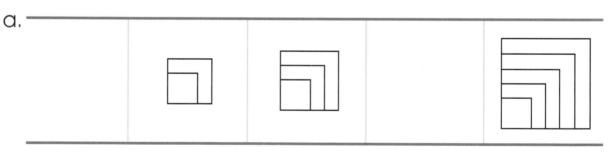

b. It is a _____ pattern.

Follow each pattern to find the next two numbers. Then tell whether each pattern is growing or shrinking.

⑪ 5   10   15   20   25   ____   ____   a _____ pattern

⑫ 30   27   24   21   18   ____   ____   a _____ pattern

⑬ 100   90   80   70   60   ____   ____   a _____ pattern

ISBN: 978-1-77149-031-3

Multiple:

the product of a given whole number multiplied by any other whole number

e.g. Multiples of 4: **4**, **8**, **12**, ...

1 x 4   2 x 4   3 x 4

Colour, mark, or circle the numbers on the hundreds chart. Then circle the correct answers.

1	2	3	4	5	6	7	8	9	10
11	12	13	14	15	16	17	18	19	20
21	22	23	24	25	26	27	28	29	30
31	32	33	34	35	36	37	38	39	40
41	42	43	44	45	46	47	48	49	50
51	52	53	54	55	56	57	58	59	60
61	62	63	64	65	66	67	68	69	70
71	72	73	74	75	76	77	78	79	80
81	82	83	84	85	86	87	88	89	90
91	92	93	94	95	96	97	98	99	100

⑭ Colour the multiples of 9 yellow and circle the multiples of 5.

⑮ The multiples of 9 run in rows / in columns / diagonally .

⑯ The multiples of 5 run in rows / in columns / diagonally .

⑰ Put a "**/**" on the multiples of 3.

⑱ *Are all the multiples of 9 also the multiples of 3?*

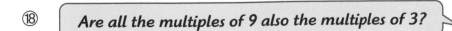

Patterns (2)

- Create a number pattern involving addition or subtraction.
- Use number sequences to represent simple geometric patterns.
- Determine the missing numbers in equations.

$25 + 9 = 30 + $

The answer is 4.

Follow the pattern rule to create a number pattern starting with the given number.

① Adding 7 each time

0 ___ ___ ___ ___ ___ ___ ___

② Subtracting 3 each time

42 ___ ___ ___ ___ ___ ___ ___

③ Adding 4 each time

20 ___ ___ ___ ___ ___ ___ ___

④ Subtracting 5 each time

40 ___ ___ ___ ___ ___ ___ ___

⑤
Make a number pattern that starts at 24 and extends by adding 6 each time.

___ ___ ___ ___ ___ ___

⑥
Make a number pattern that starts at 80 and extends by subtracting 8 each time.

___ ___ ___ ___ ___

ISBN: 978-1-77149-031-3

Follow each pattern to draw the next picture. Use a number sequence to represent the number of sticks used to make each figure. Then answer the question.

⑦ a.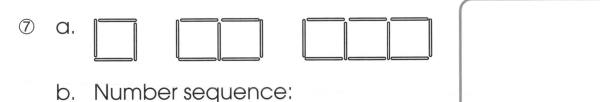

b. Number sequence:

_____ , _____ , _____ , _____

c. How many sticks are there in the 6th figure?

_____ sticks

⑧ a.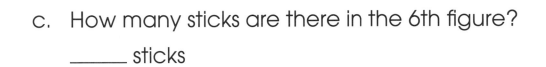

b. Number sequence:

_____ , _____ , _____ , _____

c. How many sticks are there in the 6th figure?

_____ sticks

⑨ a.

b. Number sequence:

_____ , _____ , _____ , _____

c. *How many sticks are there in the 5th figure?*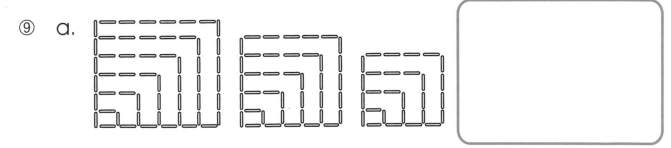

_____ sticks

ISBN: 978-1-77149-031-3

Look at each number sentence. Find the missing number.

⑩ $10 - 3 = 7$

    $3 +$  $= 10$

⑪ $4 + 20 = 24$

    $24 -$ $= 4$

⑫ $15 - 8 = 7$

    $7 +$  $= 15$

⑬ $6 + 13 = 19$

    ___ $- 6 = 13$

⑭ $9 + 16 = 25$

    $25 -$ ___ $= 16$

⑮ $30 - 18 = 12$

    ___ $+ 18 = 30$

Find the missing numbers with the help of the given equations.

$23 + 7 = 30$ $4 + 12 = 16$

$21 + 4 = 25$ $7 + 9 = 16$

$8 + 9 = 17$

$23 - 16 = 7$

$21 - 18 = 3$

$3 + 15 = 18$ $32 - 5 = 27$

$9 + 3 = 12$

$41 - 16 = 25$ $20 - 6 = 14$

⑯ $16 -$ _____ $= 9$

⑰ $25 -$ _____ $= 4$

⑱ $7 +$ _____ $= 23$

⑲   _____ $+ 16 = 41$

⑳ $18 -$ _____ $= 15$

㉑   _____ $- 3 = 9$

㉒ $3 +$ _____ $= 21$

㉓ $27 +$ _____ $= 32$

㉔   _____ $+ 14 = 20$

㉕   _____ $- 7 = 23$

㉖   _____ $- 9 = 8$

㉗ $16 -$ _____ $= 12$

ISBN: 978-1-77149-031-3

Steps to solve equations:

1st Simplify the equation.

2nd Use the guess-and-test method to find the solution.

e.g. $26 + 5 = 40 - \heartsuit$ ← Find the sum first.

$31 = 40 - \heartsuit$ ← Think: What number should be subtracted?

$\heartsuit = 9$ ←———— $40 - 9 = 31$

Simplify the equations. Then solve them.

㉘ $\heartsuit + 4 = 16 - 7$

㉙ $\star - 4 = 18 + 1$

㉚ $12 + 3 = 21 - \text{☀}$

㉛ $\text{☽} - 6 = 15 + 8$

㉜ $15 + 2 = 27 - \text{🍎}$

㉝ $18 - 3 = 10 + \text{○}$

㉞

$1 + 2 + 3 + 4 + 5 + 6 = 22 - \text{🐱}$

ISBN: 978-1-77149-031-3

Graphs (1)

- Read and describe data presented in pictographs using many-to-one correspondence.
- Make pictographs to display data with appropriate titles and labels.

> George, you have got the highest score with 550 marks!

See how many ice cream cones Mr. Winter sold yesterday. Look at the pictograph. Answer the questions.

Number of Ice Cream Cones Sold Yesterday

= 10 cones

Flavour

Strawberry

Vanilla

Chocolate

Neapolitan

① How many flavours were there? _____ flavours

② How many vanilla ice cream cones were sold? _____ cones

③ How many Neapolitan ice cream cones were sold? _____ cones

④ How many more strawberry ice cream cones were sold than chocolate ice cream cones? _____ more

⑤ If each ice cream cone cost $2, how much did Mr. Winter get from selling the ice cream cones yesterday? $ _____

ISBN: 978-1-77149-031-3

Uncle Tim recorded the number of each kind of toy left in his toy shop this week. Look at the pictograph. Answer the questions.

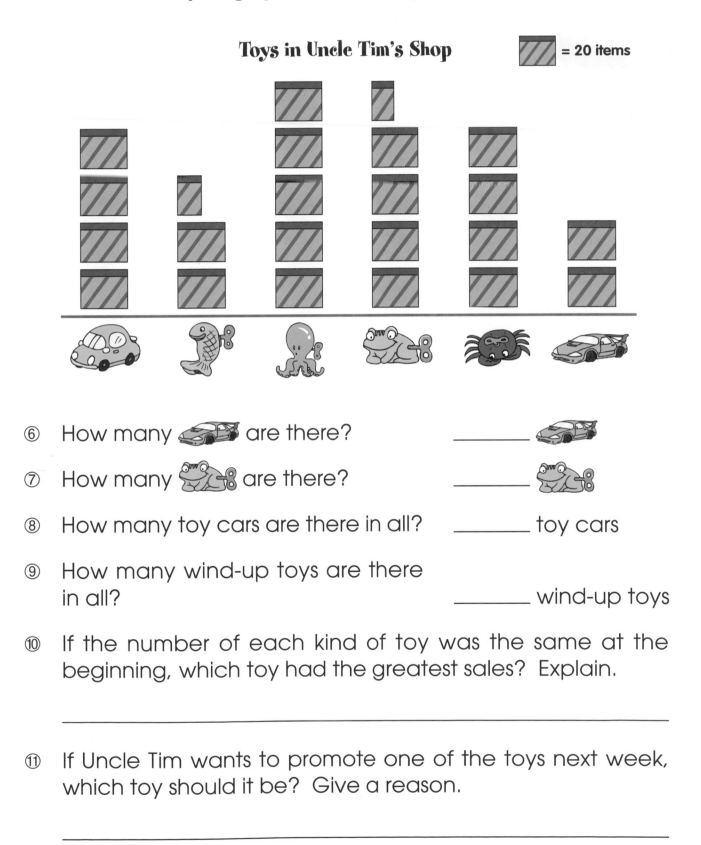

Toys in Uncle Tim's Shop   = 20 items

⑥ How many 🏎 are there?   _____

⑦ How many 🐸 are there?   _____

⑧ How many toy cars are there in all?   _____ toy cars

⑨ How many wind-up toys are there in all?   _____ wind-up toys

⑩ If the number of each kind of toy was the same at the beginning, which toy had the greatest sales? Explain.

_____

⑪ If Uncle Tim wants to promote one of the toys next week, which toy should it be? Give a reason.

_____

Judy has a collection of buttons. Help her put them into four categories and use tally marks to complete the table.

I have 2 kinds of buttons, flower and square. They have either 4 holes or 2 holes.

⑫

Number			

ISBN: 978-1-77149-031-3

Look at the table on page 108. Complete the pictograph to show the data. Then answer the questions.

 13

Each picture represents 4 buttons.

14 How many flower buttons does Judy have in all?

_____ flower buttons

15 How many buttons does she have in all?

_____ buttons

16

If I give 37 buttons to my grandma, how many buttons will I have left?

_____ buttons

Graphs (2)

The mode size of the T-shirts sold is medium.

- Read and describe data presented in a vertical or horizontal bar graph.
- Complete or make bar graphs to show the data.
- Understand and identify the mode in a set of data.

Sales of T-shirts

Read the bar graph showing the favourite insects of Mrs. Moxam's class. Then answer the questions.

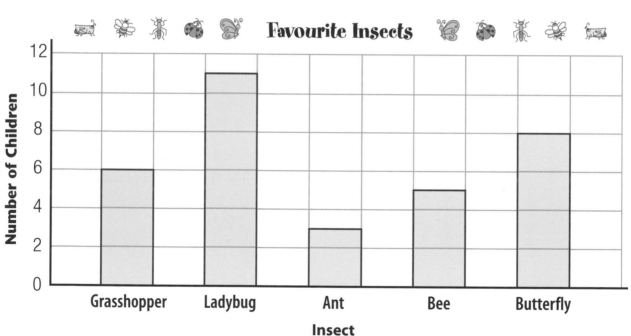

Favourite Insects

① How many children like the butterfly? _____ children

② How many children like the bee? _____ children

③ Which insect is the most popular? _____

④ Which insect is the least popular? _____

⑤ How many children are there in Mrs. Moxam's class? _____ children

ISBN: 978-1-77149-031-3

Uncle Sam has 5 grocery stores. See how long it took each store to sell 10 cartons of juice. Complete the vertical bar graph to show the data and answer the questions.

Store	A	B	C	D	E
Number of Days	30	25	15	20	10

⑥

Days Taken to Sell 10 Cartons of Juice

⑦ What is the title of the graph?

Days Taken to Sell 10 cartons of juice

⑧ How many days does each box represent?

_5_ days

⑨ Which stores took more than 3 weeks to sell 10 cartons of juice?

25 and 30

⑩ Which store had the best sales? How many cartons of juice did it sell each day on average?

_____ ; _00_ carton(s)

Judy is preparing muffins for her school's fundraising program tomorrow. Look at the table. Help her complete the horizontal bar graph to show the data. Then answer the questions.

Flavour	Carrot	Oatmeal	Raisin	Blueberry	Banana
Number	22	19	11	13	18

⑪

Judy's Muffins

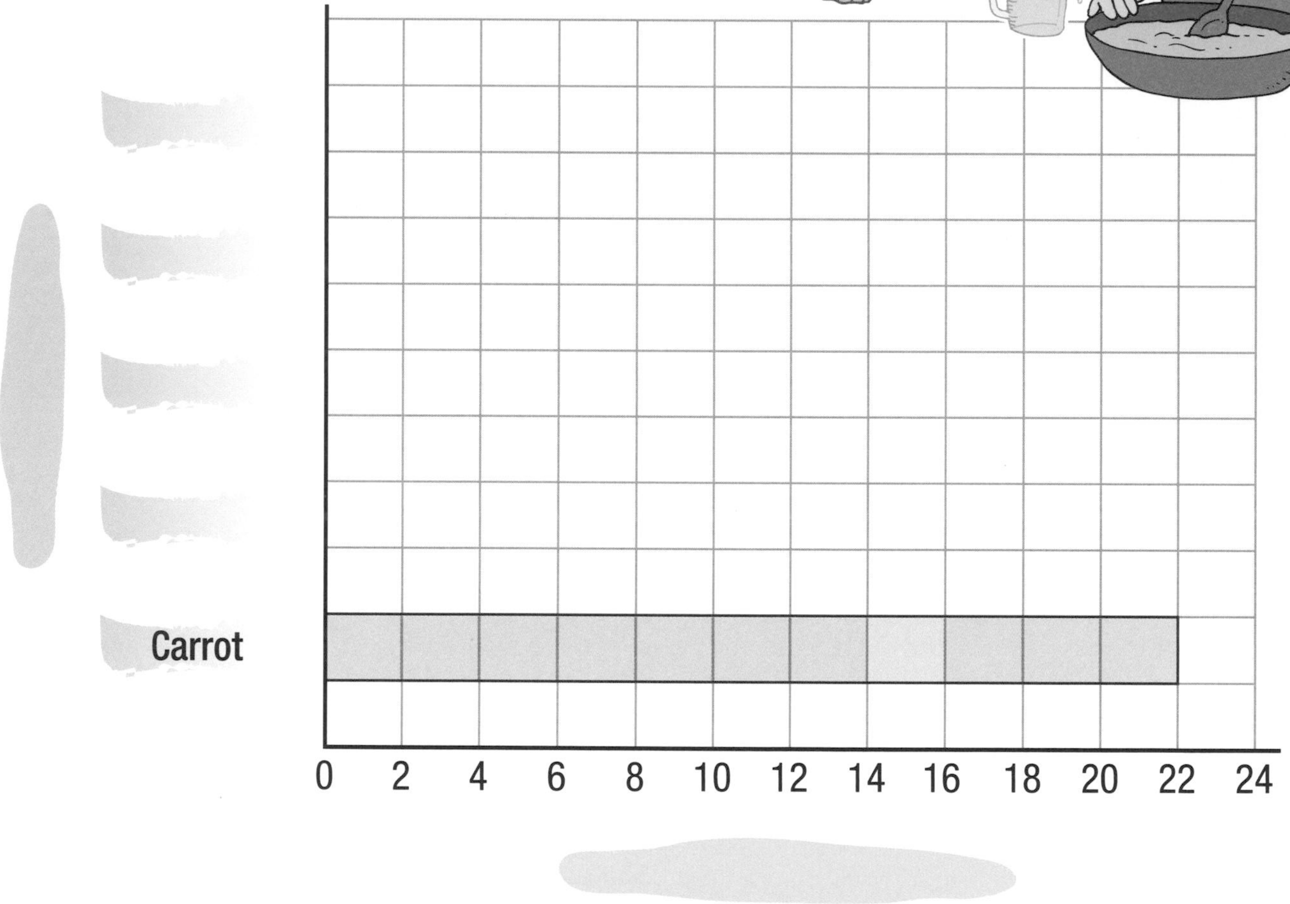

Carrot

0 2 4 6 8 10 12 14 16 18 20 22 24

⑫ How many different flavours are there? _____ flavours

⑬ How many muffins are with fruit? _____ muffins

⑭ How many muffins has she made in all? _____ muffins

⑮ If each muffin costs $1, how much will be collected from selling all the muffins? $ _____

ISBN: 978-1-77149-031-3

Mode: the value that occurs most often in a set of data

e.g. Ted's 7-day savings: 32¢, 16¢, 32¢, 18¢, 40¢, 32¢, 15¢

Since 32¢ occurs most often, the mode savings is 32¢.

Look at each set of data. Find the mode.

⑯ The heights of 12 students:

120 cm	108 cm	98 cm	120 cm
108 cm	96 cm	114 cm	125 cm
108 cm	109 cm	105 cm	111 cm

The mode height is _____ .

⑰ The weights of 15 women:

62 kg	58 kg	63 kg	70 kg	58 kg
63 kg	59 kg	58 kg	62 kg	62 kg
58 kg	61 kg	53 kg	57 kg	70 kg

Mode weight: _____

⑱ The lengths of 18 ropes:

46 cm	70 cm	52 cm	63 cm	60 cm
70 cm	54 cm	62 cm	70 cm	48 cm
49 cm	61 cm	70 cm	62 cm	70 cm
52 cm	70 cm	70 cm		

Mode length: _____

⑲ The costs of 10 rings:

| $275 | $316 | $127 | $316 | $275 |
| $117 | $98 | $275 | $400 | $400 |

The mode cost is _____ .

28

Probability

- Predict the frequency of an outcome in a simple probability experiment.
- Understand the fairness in a game and relate this to the occurrence of equally likely outcomes.

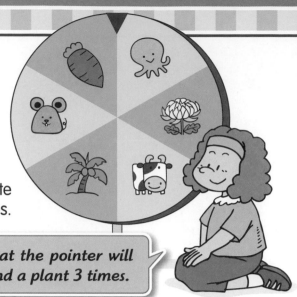

If I spin 6 times, I predict that the pointer will land on an animal 3 times and a plant 3 times.

The children are doing probability experiments. Check ✔ the best predictions.

① Draw a ball from the box 20 times.

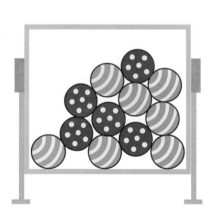

Predictions

Ⓐ – 4 times
 – 16 times

Ⓑ – 9 times
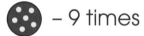 – 11 times

Ⓒ – 15 times
 – 5 times

Ⓓ  – 0 times
 – 20 times

② Pick a card from the bag 50 times.

Predictions

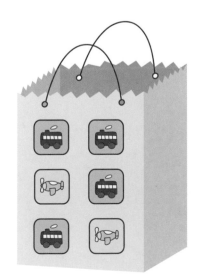

Ⓐ – 40 times
 – 10 times

Ⓑ – 34 times
 – 16 times

Ⓒ – 34 times
 – 16 times

Ⓓ – 16 times
 – 34 times

ISBN: 978-1-77149-031-3

Look at the things that the children have. Answer the questions. Then predict the results.

③ Draw a card from Elaine's collection.

Elaine's Collection

   a. What are the possible outcomes?

   _____

   b. Are the chances of drawing a 🍎 or a 🍓 the same?

   _____

④ If Elaine draws a card 50 times without looking, what results do you predict?

Prediction: 🍎 _____ times   🍊 _____ times   🍓 _____ times

⑤ Spin the spinner once. What things may the pointer land on?

_____

⑥ If Joe spins the spinner 40 times, what results do you predict?

Prediction:

🙂 ____ times   🌼 ____ times

🌳 ____ times   ☀ ____ times

ISBN: 978-1-77149-031-3   Complete Canadian Curriculum • Grade 3

If a spinner is divided into equal parts and nothing on the spinner appears more than once, it is a fair spinner.

So this is a fair spinner.

Check ✔ the fair spinners.

⑦

Draw lines on each spinner and colour it.

⑧ A 4-colour fair spinner

⑨ A 6-colour fair spinner

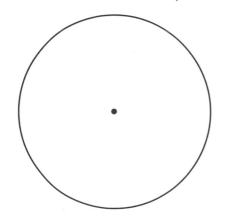

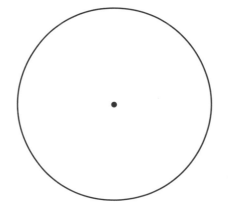

ISBN: 978-1-77149-031-3

The children are drawing marbles from a bag. Help them answer the questions.

⑩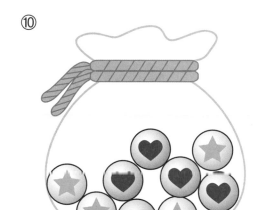

a. If Judy draws a marble, is it more likely to get a star marble?

_____

b. Is it equally likely to get a star or a heart marble? If not, take out the fewest marbles in the bag to make the game fair.

_____

⑪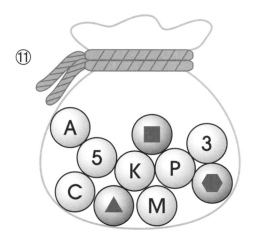

a. If Katie draws a marble, is it more likely to get a letter marble?

_____

b. Cross out ✘ the fewest marbles in the bag to make the game fair.

Colour the spinner to match what Annie says.

⑫

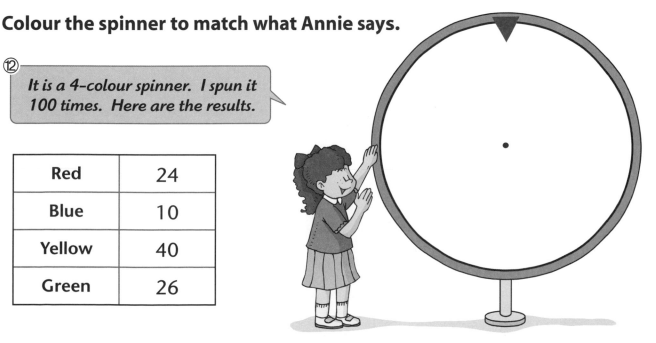

It is a 4-colour spinner. I spun it 100 times. Here are the results.

Red	24
Blue	10
Yellow	40
Green	26

ISBN: 978-1-77149-031-3

ENGLISH

ISBN: 978-1-77149-031-3

Groundhog Day

February 2 is Groundhog Day in North America. Every year on this day, we wait eagerly to see if the groundhog will come out of its burrow and find its shadow.

This idea comes from an old Scottish verse:

"If Candlemas Day is bright and clear, there will be two winters in the year."

Candlemas Day is halfway between the first day of winter (December 21) and the first day of spring (March 21). Some people used to believe that if it was sunny on this day, then the rest of the winter would be cold. But if it was cloudy on this day, then the rest of the winter would be mild and short.

If the groundhog sees its shadow, there will be six more weeks of winter. If it does not see its shadow, then we know that spring will soon be with us.

Groundhogs are the only animal to have a day named after them.

ISBN: 978-1-77149-031-3

A. **Match the pictures with the statements. Write the letters in the boxes.**

A The rest of the winter would be cold.

B The rest of the winter would be mild.

C There will be six more weeks of winter.

D Spring will soon come.

B. **You have a chance to name a day after an animal. Which day and what animal will you choose? Draw a picture of the animal and write the reason.**

ISBN: 978-1-77149-031-3

Silent Consonants

Some consonants like "**b**", "**c**", "**g**", "**gh**", "**h**", "**k**", "**l**", "**n**", "**t**", and "**w**" are silent in some words.

Examples: bri<u>gh</u>t   <u>k</u>now   ha<u>l</u>f   t<u>w</u>o

C.   Say the things. Complete the words with the correct silent consonants.

1.

s_c_issors

2.

sc_h_ool

3.

_w_reath

4.

cas_t_le

5.

sta_l_k

6.
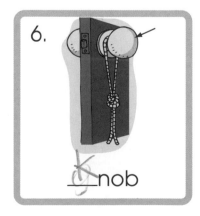
_k_nob

7.

com_b_

8.
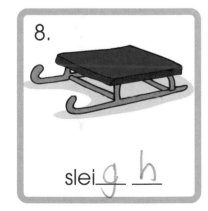
slei_g_h

ISBN: 978-1-77149-031-3

D. Read the sentences. Circle all the silent consonants.

1. The knight was frightened by the lightning last night.

2. Don't write the answers in the wrong column.

3. He designed eight Christmas cards.

4. The scientist stayed calm when he saw the ghost.

5. The rhino is blowing a whistle beside the lamb.

E. Write two words with each silent consonant.

1. **b**   lamb

2. **c**   scientist

3. **g**   eight, night

4. **gh** eight, lightning

5. **h**   rhino, frightened, ghost

6. **k**   knob, know

7. **l**   calm, stalk

8. **n**   column

9. **t**   whistle, christmas

10. **w**   write, saw   wrong

ISBN: 978-1-77149-031-3   Complete Canadian Curriculum • Grade 3   **123**

The New Student

We have a new student in our class. She sits beside me. Her name is Emelyn Marquez. She comes from the Philippines. She came here with her parents. They live with her grandparents.

Emelyn came from a town called Dupax del Sur. They plant a lot of rice there. She taught us a song about planting rice. We all did gestures to go with the song. We sang the song in English. When we finished, Emelyn sang the song in her native language. It was beautiful.

Here is how it goes:

Planting Rice Is Never Fun

Planting rice is never fun.
Bend from morn till the set of sun.
Cannot stand, cannot sit.
Cannot rest for a little bit.

Emelyn said she liked planting rice, but it was a lot of hard work. I asked Emelyn if she wanted to come over after school this week. Guess what! She just phoned me. Her mother said she can come over tomorrow. I think Emelyn and I will be best friends!

ISBN: 978-1-77149-031-3

A. **Read the story and check ✔ the correct way of planting rice in the Philippines.**

B. **Colour** Yes **for the correct sentences. Colour** No **for the wrong ones.**

1. Emelyn sits behind the writer.

Yes No

2. Some people in the Philippines grow rice.

Yes No

3. Dupax del Sur is a city in the Philippines.

Yes No

4. The writer sang the song in Emelyn's native language.

Yes No

5. Planting rice is not an easy job.

Yes No

6. The writer likes planting rice.

Yes No

7. The writer wants to be Emelyn's best friend.

Yes No

ISBN: 978-1-77149-031-3

Hard and Soft "C"

The consonant "c" usually has a **hard sound**.

Examples: <u>c</u>ome   <u>c</u>an   <u>c</u>all

When "c" is followed by "e", "i", or "y", it usually has a **soft sound**.

Examples: <u>c</u>ell   <u>c</u>ity   <u>c</u>ycle

C. Say the things. Write the letters in the correct places.

Hard "C"

B
f
c
h

Soft "C"

e
a

ISBN: 978-1-77149-031-3

Hard and Soft "G"

The consonant "**g**" usually has a **hard sound**.

Examples: go   guess   goat

When "g" is followed by "e", "i", or "y", it usually has a **soft sound**.

Examples: gesture   giraffe   gypsy

D.   Say the things. Draw lines to join the pictures to the correct signs.

Hard "G"

Soft "G"

There are many different ways to write poems. Poems do not have to rhyme. The lines of a poem can be made of many words or only a few – or even just one! Poems can tell a story and fill your head with many ideas. But some poems are about one idea, and will make you think of just one thing.

Acrostic Poems

Acrostic poems are special poems. The first letter from each line combines to spell a word. That word is like the title of the poem. Look at the two examples below.

Rain falls.
And then
I see a ribbon.
New and
Bright. Colours
Over the
Wind.

Mrs. Janet Green.
Oh, I think she is
The best.
Happy and nice
Every day.
Really, I love her a lot.

Acrostics are fun to write. Why don't you give it a try?

A. Write the title for each poem in the passage. Draw a picture to go with it.

1. _____

   Rain falls.
   And then
   I see a ribbon.
   New and
   Bright. Colours
   Over the
   Wind.

2. _____

   Mrs. Janet Green.
   Oh, I think she is
   The best.
   Happy and nice
   Every day.
   Really, I love her a lot.

B. Write the acrostic poem below.

B _____

O _____

O _____

K _____

M _____

A _____

R _____

K _____

"Y" as a Vowel (1)

When "y" comes at the end of a word with no vowel or in the middle of a word with no vowel except "e" at the end, it usually sounds like a **long "i"**.

Examples: why   try   rhyme

C. **Say the words. Help Felix the Fly get to the bread by colouring the words that use "y" as a vowel with the long "i" sound.**

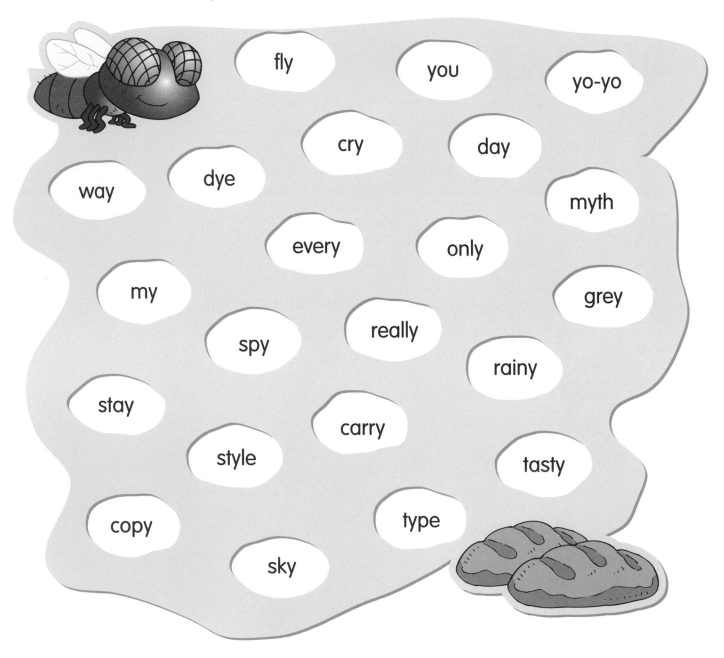

fly you yo-yo cry day way dye myth every only my grey spy really rainy stay carry style tasty copy type sky

ISBN: 978-1-77149-031-3

"Y" as a Vowel (2)

When "**y**" comes at the end of a word with another vowel in it, it usually sounds like a **long "e"**.

Examples: many   story   happy

D.   Say the words. Colour the ones that use "y" as a vowel with the long "e" sound.

1.

daisy

2.

angry

3.

monkey

4.

tray

5.

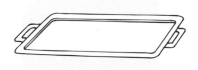

diary

6.

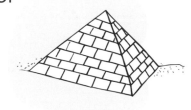

pyramid

7.

crystal

8.

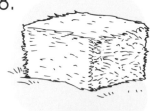

hay

9.

mummy

What Are Things Made of?

Y ou touch something plastic every day. But have you ever wondered how we get plastic? It does not grow in trees. We do not get it from animals. So, where does plastic come from?

We know how to make things from all kinds of other things found in the world around us. For example, glass is made from sand. Clay pots and china dishes are made from clay, which comes from the soil in some places. Jewellery is made from the stones we find deep under the ground.

Where do our clothes come from? We get cotton fabric from cotton balls that grow on bushes. Leather comes from the skin of animals. We also make woollen clothes from the wool of sheep.

We eat the plants we grow and the animals we raise. We get maple syrup from the sap of maple trees. Everything we use comes from the world around us.

So...where does plastic come from? We make it from oil we find in the ground!

ISBN: 978-1-77149-031-3

A. Match the pictures with the things they are made of. Write the letters.

A cotton bushes

B wool of sheep

C clay

D sand

E skin of animals

F oil in the ground

G sap of maple trees

H stones under the ground

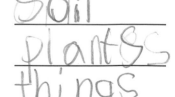

B. Change a letter in each word below to form a word you can find in the passage.

1. glow _wool_

2. boil _Soil_

3. tough _touch_

4. planes _plants_

5. would _world_

6. thinks _things_

ISBN: 978-1-77149-031-3

Long Vowel Digraphs

When two letters together form a long vowel sound, it is called a **long vowel digraph**.

"**Ai**", "**ay**", "**ei**", "**ea**", "**ee**", "**oa**", "**ow**", "**oo**", "**ew**", "**au**", and "**aw**" are all long vowel digraphs.

Examples: cl<u>ay</u>   sh<u>ee</u>p   gr<u>ow</u>   w<u>oo</u>l

C.   Say the words. Put them next to the correct long vowel digraphs.

tree   crew   day   jaw   eight
train   cause   load   eat   boot   know

1. ai _____

2. ay _____

3. ei _____

4. ea _____

5. ee _____

6. oa _____

7. ow _____

8. oo _____

9. ew _____

10. au _____

11. aw _____

ISBN: 978-1-77149-031-3

D. **Say the things. Cross out ✗ the ones that do not have long vowel digraphs.**

Some letters like "ea" in "leather" and "ow" in "cow" are not long vowel digraphs.

Today our gym teacher, Mr. Rollins, told us to do something special. At first, he told us to run one kilometre. Many of my classmates started to groan. They did not want to run.

Mr. Rollins was not happy. He said that we should be glad to have a chance to exercise at school. He said that gym class is a chance for us to keep fit.

After we ran, Mr. Rollins told us to write about why gym class is so important. He said we should be creative, so I wrote this poem.

A Special Gym Class

Ode to Gym Class

Gym class is lots of fun.
We get to run and jump and play.
I think it's my favourite time of day,
And we should all be shouting "Hooray!"

I love to eat, I know it's true.
If I didn't have gym class,
I know what I'd do.
I'd get too big to fit in my shorts.
I wouldn't want to play any sports.

I love to play what I want – what I dare.
I love to play hard, but I love to play fair.
I'd like to be voted "Most Valuable Player"!
My efforts in gym class will get me there.

ISBN: 978-1-77149-031-3

A. **Read the clues. Complete the crossword puzzle with words from the story.**

Across

A. happy
B. make a deep, sad sound
C. of great value
D. unusual
E. a kind of poem

Down

1. work out
2. best liked
3. have courage to do
4. in good health

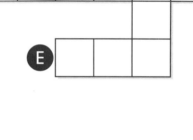

B. **Write about why gym class is important.**

Be creative!

_____

_____

_____

_____

_____

ISBN: 978-1-77149-031-3

Rhyming Words

Rhyming words are words that have the same ending sound.

Examples: fun – run   special – social

A poem may have lines ending in rhyming pairs.

C. **Say the words in each group. Cross out ✗ the one that does not rhyme with the others.**

1
do
school
true
clue

2
player
hooray
day
stay

3
fair
there
dare
tail

4
sports
shorts
efforts
escorts

5
fast
grass
class
mass

6
teacher
sculpture
richer
peaches

D. Say the things. Draw lines to match the rhyming pairs. Then write one more word that rhymes with each pair.

1.  •

2.  •

3.  •

4.  •

5.  •

6.  •

7.  •

A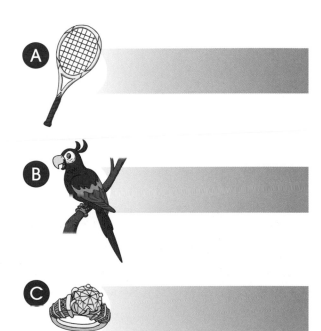

B

C

D

E

F

G

The Frank Slide

Frank, Alberta was a town at the foot of Turtle Mountain, near the border of British Columbia. It was on the Canadian Pacific Railway line. The town's main business was coal mining. It was a prosperous place.

On April 29, 1903, at 4:10 a.m., something terrible happened. Turtle Mountain broke apart. It was one of the deadliest landslides in North American history. 30 million cubic metres of limestone fell down the mountain and buried much of the town.

At that time, the population of Frank was about 600. More than 70 people died, but another 23 people who had been buried were rescued. This included 17 coal miners who were underground at the time of the slide. They rescued themselves by tunnelling upward to safety. Three quarters of the town's homes were destroyed, and two kilometres of railway line was obliterated.

The slide lasted less than two minutes, but the debris spread over three square kilometres. Scientists have long wondered how rocks could spread so far and wide in such a short time. Many believe that, in a case like this, the rock and soil flow like a thick liquid. They believe Turtle Mountain collapsed because it was made unstable by underground coal mining and erosion by weather and water.

ISBN: 978-1-77149-031-3

A. Check ✔ the correct sentences.

1. Frank is a town on Turtle Mountain.

2. Coal mining was Frank's main business in 1903.

3. Firefighters rescued 17 coal miners underground.

4. 30 million cubic metres of mud fell down the mountain during the slide.

5. The Frank Slide was one of the deadliest landslides in North American history.

6. Underground coal mining had made Turtle Mountain unstable.

B.   Match the facts. Write the letters on the lines.

> **A** the population of Frank in 1903
> **B** the day when the Frank Slide took place
> **C** the number of people rescued
> **D** the time when the slide occured
> **E** the duration of the slide
> **F** the length of railway line destroyed

1. 23   *C*

2. April 29, 1903   *b*

3. two kilometres   *f*

4. 600   *a*

5. two minutes   *e*

6. 4:10 a.m.   *D*

ISBN: 978-1-77149-031-3   Complete Canadian Curriculum • **Grade 3**   **141**

Common and Proper Nouns

A **common noun** names any person, animal, place, or thing.

Examples: miner   deer   province   rock

A **proper noun** names a specific person, animal, place, or thing. It always begins with a capital letter.

Examples: Mr. Jenkins   Bambi   Alberta   the Olympics

C. **Circle the common nouns and underline the proper nouns in the sentences.**

1. Aunt Rosaline and her family moved to Edmonton last year.

2. Her daughter Sherry told me that West Edmonton Mall is the largest shopping centre in North America.

3. You can find all types of shops in the mall.

4. Have you ever heard of Turtle Mountain?

5. There was a town called Frank at the foot of the mountain.

6. Alberta is a province to the east of British Columbia.

7. My family will take a trip to Banff next month.

8. Our neighbour will take care of our dog Mickey for us.

ISBN: 978-1-77149-031-3

D. Complete the card about yourself.

All the information you write should be proper nouns.

My name : _RUSSXIU_

My birth month : _November 12 2008_

My city : _north vancouver_

My school : _école cedardale_

My favourite book : _Dog man_

My favourite movie : _Paul Blart mall cop_

My favourite festival : _The pne_

Name of my father : _Wade winkler_

Name of my mother : _Carol-ann hart_

Name of my best friend : _Mychael_

Name of my pet (if any) : _ms. jazzy_

ISBN: 978-1-77149-031-3 Complete Canadian Curriculum • Grade 3 **143**

A **Gaggle** of Geese?

Have you ever heard of a flock of sheep, a herd of buffalo, or a litter of kittens? You probably have. But have you ever heard of a pod of seals, a pride of lions, or a colony of penguins? What about a gaggle of geese?

We use different words to talk about different groups of animals. We can use words to talk about animals that are about the same size and type. For example, we can use the word "herd" to talk about buffalo, cattle, deer, and moose. We use the word "pack" to talk about wolves and wild dogs. We can use the word "flock" to talk about sheep and birds, but when we talk about a group of crows, we call them a murder of crows. Maybe that is because farmers do not like it when crows eat their crops.

What word do we use to talk about a group of fish? If we visit an aquarium, we might say: look at the school of beautiful tropical fish! Yes...a school of fish! Do fish really go to school?

When we learn to use interesting words like these, people enjoy listening to us talk!

ISBN: 978-1-77149-031-3

A. Write the words in the correct places.

cattle   penguins   wolves   sheep   geese   fish   crows   lions   kittens   seals

1. a herd of _Cattle_
2. a school of _fish_
3. a colony of _penguins_
4. a murder of _crows_
5. a pack of _wolves_
6. a pride of _lions_
7. a flock of _sheep_
8. a litter of _kittens_
9. a gaggle of _geese_
10. a pod of _seals_

B. Draw a group of animals mentioned in the passage. Fill in the blanks to complete the title.

A _colony_ of _penguins_

Irregular Plural Nouns

For nouns ending in "y", change the "y" to "i" and add "es" to form the plural. For nouns ending in "f/fe", change the "f/fe" to "v" and add "es".

Examples: fairy → fairies   calf → calves   life → lives

Some plural nouns may be spelled the same as or completely different from their singular form.

Examples: salmon → salmon   ox → oxen

C.   Circle the correct plural form for the first words.

1.   **foot**

foots
feet
feat

2.   **deer**

deer
deeres
deers

3.   **city**

citys
cityes
cities

4.   **mouse**

mouses
mice
mousses

5.   **knife**

knives
knifes
knifees

6.   **family**

familys
famives
families

7.   **tooth**

tooths
tooth
teeth

8.   **leaf**

leaves
leaies
leafs

9.   **offspring**

offspring
offsprings
offspringes

ISBN: 978-1-77149-031-3

D. **Complete the crossword puzzle with the plural form of the clue words.**

Across

A. bunny
B. shelf
C. loaf
D. medium
E. cod

Down

1. buffalo
2. cattle
3. sheep
4. moose
5. goose

The Goat –
Our Best Friend

People say that the dog is man's best friend, but goats are very important too. In fact, people have kept goats for thousands of years – longer than they have kept dogs.

Goats are useful to us in many different ways. We can cut the hair from goats and spin it into wool. We can make clothing from the wool. One kind of wool made from goat hair is called cashmere. A cashmere sweater can be very expensive.

Goats also give milk, just like cows do! Did you know that more people around the world drink goat's milk than cow's milk? Goat's milk is easier for babies to digest. We make lovely cheese, such as feta, from goat's milk. Some people put goat's milk on their skin to keep it soft.

In many countries, goat's meat is eaten instead of beef or pork. We also use goatskin to make gloves and boots. Goatskin leather is very soft.

A female goat is called a doe or nanny. A male goat is called a buck or billy. Do you know what a baby goat is called? A kid!

With everything goats give us, we can say that the goat is also our best friend. Don't you think so?

ISBN: 978-1-77149-031-3

A. Write the names for the animals.

1.

2.

3.

B. Read the passage. Complete the diagram below with the given words.

1

hair

⬇

_____

e.g. cashmere

⬇

_____

2

_____

clothing

feta   gloves

meat   wool

leather   boots

milk

3

skin

⬇

_____

⬇

_____

and

_____

4

_____

⬇

cheese

e.g. _____

Sentence Types

All sentences begin with capital letters.

A **telling sentence** tells about someone or something. It ends with a period. An **asking sentence** asks about someone or something. It ends with a question mark. A **surprising sentence** shows a strong feeling. It ends with an exclamation mark. An **imperative sentence** tells someone to do or not to do something. It ends with a period. The subject "you" is left out.

C. **Add the correct punctuation marks at the end of the sentences. Then write the letters.**

T – telling sentence
A – asking sentence
S – surprising sentence
I – imperative sentence

1. Cashmere is made from goat hair _____

2. Do you like this cashmere sweater _____

3. Try it on _____

4. Wow, it's incredibly soft _____

5. How much is it _____

6. It is one hundred and fifteen dollars _____

7. How expensive _____

8. Let's take a look at the sweaters over there _____

9. What are they made of _____

10. I will take the blue one _____

ISBN: 978-1-77149-031-3

D. Write what they are saying.

1. Surprising Sentence

   _____

2. Telling Sentence

   _____

3. Asking Sentence

   _____

4. Imperative Sentence

   _____

5. Imperative Sentence

   _____

6. Surprising Sentence

   _____

ISBN: 978-1-77149-031-3

The Narwhal –
a Real-life Unicorn

We love unicorns, but they are not real animals. We can find unicorns only in fairy tales.

Don't be sad. There is a real-life unicorn here on Earth. It is the narwhal. A narwhal is not a horse with a long horn, but a whale!

The narwhal can be found in the waters around Canada and other northern countries. There are not very many of them, so if you see one, you are lucky! They can grow to be five metres long. They are blue-grey with white blotches. They are brown when they are born. Narwhals like to swim with their friends and talk to one another using sound waves, like other whales.

All narwhals have two teeth in their upper jaw. But the male narwhal's left tooth starts to grow outward after it is one year old. This tooth twists as it grows. It just grows and grows, and can be up to three metres long! We call it a tusk. We are not sure what it is used for.

Narwhals are amazing animals – and they are real!

ISBN: 978-1-77149-031-3

A.   Find words from the passage for the meanings below.

1. having good fortune

2. without doubt

3. very long, pointed tooth

4. very surprising

5. not imaginary

6. the biggest sea mammals

7. turns

8. large discoloured marks

1. l u c k y

2. s u r e

3. t u s k

4. a m a z i n g

5. r e a l

6. w h a l e s

7. t w i s t s

8. b l o t c h e s

B.   Complete the chart.

The Narwhal

Length: up to 1. 5 meters long

Colour: (grown-up) 2. blue and grey with 3. white blotches

(baby) 4. brown

Live in: waters around 5. canada and 6. cold places

Way of communication: 7. sound waves

ISBN: 978-1-77149-031-3

Subjects and Predicates

A sentence has two main parts – a subject and a predicate.

The **subject** tells whom or what the sentence is about. The **predicate** tells what the subject is or what the subject does.

Example: Many children │ love fairy tales.
                    (subject)   (predicate)

C.   Draw a vertical line between the subject and the predicate in each sentence.

1.   My class is doing a project on the narwhal.

2.   Mrs. Reid told us to look for information about the narwhal on the Internet.

3.   The narwhal is a whale.

4.   The left tooth of the male narwhal can grow up to three metres long.

5.   The female is slightly smaller than the male.

6.   The skin of a baby narwhal is brown in colour.

7.   You may see a narwhal in the Arctic seas.

8.   Fish, squid, and shrimp are what narwhals eat.

9.   I think a narwhal really looks like a unicorn.

ISBN: 978-1-77149-031-3

D.   Fill in the blanks with the correct subjects.

the fairy tale   Bruce   we
the main character
our teacher   the unicorn

1. _____ told us a fairy tale.

2. _____ in the story is called Bruce.

3. _____ met a brave unicorn in a forest.

4. _____ is called Anston.

5. _____ has a happy ending.

6. _____ all enjoyed listening to this story.

E.   Write predicates to complete the sentences.

1. My sister _____ .

2. The movie _____ .

3. The theme song _____ .

4. Tim and Matt _____ .

5. The whales _____ .

6. Everyone _____ .

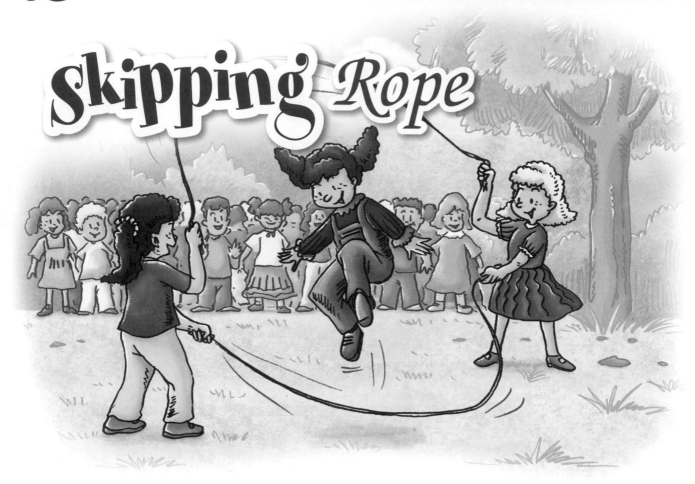

Skipping Rope

Skipping rope is fun to play for boys and girls. It is also a good form of exercise. You can skip by yourself or skip with friends. You can skip fast or slowly. You can skip in an easy way or a difficult way. Skipping is a great sport!

When you are skipping with friends, try skipping while you all say this chant. The skipper can also do some actions to match the words:

Teddy Bear, Teddy Bear, turn around.
Teddy Bear, Teddy Bear, touch the ground.
Teddy Bear, Teddy Bear, touch your head.
Teddy Bear, Teddy Bear, go to bed!

Here's another chant. Jump in and then say:

Apples! Peaches! Bananas! Plums!
Tell me when your birthday comes!

You then skip "pepper" (really fast skipping) and shout out the months of the year: January, February, March... You jump out when you come to the month of your birthday. Try not to get caught in the skipping rope before then!

ISBN: 978-1-77149-031-3

A. Circle the words in the word search.

- the fruits mentioned in the passage
- the months mentioned in the passage

a	J	e	s	p	b	a	n	a	n	a	s	J	p	a	c
p	a	C	F	e	b	r	u	a	r	y	b	a	l	p	p
p	n	e	M	a	c	u	m	p	l	M	a	n	u	F	l
e	o	a	n	c	s	a	s	p	e	a	n	u	S	e	u
k	c	y	h	e	r	p	l	u	m	s	a	e	o		
	h	F	e	d	y	l	e	p	M	a	r	c	h		
	a	s	f	t	u	s	e	a	e	y	s				

B. Fill in the blanks with words from the passage.

1. Skipping is a kind of _____ .

2. You can skip with your _____ .

3. You can skip while saying a _____ .

4. The _____ can do some actions while skipping.

5. Be careful not to get _____ in the skipping rope.

ISBN: 978-1-77149-031-3

Commas

Commas can be used to:

· separate items in a list.

Example: Blue, purple, and pink are my favourite colours.

· introduce and follow quotations.

Examples: Ben said, "Skipping is good for you."

"Skipping is good for you," said Ben.

C.   Add commas where needed.

1.   There are four seasons in Canada. They are spring summer fall and winter.

2.   June July and August are the summer months in Ontario.

3.   I like skipping swimming cycling and rock climbing.

4.   Sarah asked "Would you like to skip with me?"

5.   "Let's ask Jerry to join us" I said.

6.   She reminded me "Don't forget to take your skipping rope with you."

7.   We sell all kinds of fruits: apples oranges bananas peaches cherries mangoes – you name it.

ISBN: 978-1-77149-031-3

Quotation Marks

Quotation marks are used in pairs. They can be used to:

· contain the exact words of a speaker.

Example: "Your skipping rope looks nice," I told Liz.

· draw attention to a term that is used in a special way in the context.

Example: We skipped "pepper" and shouted out the months.

D. Check ✔ if the quotation marks are used correctly in the sentences.

1. Is Oshawa one of the "bedroom communities" of Ontario?

2. "How many times can you skip in a minute? he asked me."

3. Our coach always reminds us, "Practice makes perfect."

4. "Halifax" is the capital city of Nova Scotia.

5. This lake "swallows" all the water from the river.

6. The berries are the "jewels" of this dessert.

7. Dad said, "When the sun sets," we'll have to leave.

I Love Haiku!

I am a poet. I write all kinds of poems: acrostic poems, rhyming poems, non-rhyming poems... But my favourite kind of poem is called haiku.

Haiku is a Japanese word. It means "short verse". Haiku poems are very short! People have been writing them for centuries. They are made with only three lines. The first and last lines should have five syllables. The middle line should have seven syllables.

A man named Basho from Japan wrote the first haiku poem. His most famous poem is about a frog. This is how you say his poem in Japanese:

Furu ike ya
Kawazu tobikomu
mizu no oto

In English, it means:

There is an old pond
A frog goes jumping in it
The sound of water

Writing a short haiku is not easy. It takes practice to write a poem about something in only three lines!

ISBN: 978-1-77149-031-3

A. Check ✔ the poem that is a haiku.

1. *Chicken wings*
   Chicken wings
   We all love them fried ☐
   Yummy!

2.

   One two three
   Apple trees ☐
   Growing tall in the green green meadow

3. *Summertime is great*
   Let's go swimming at the beach ☐
   Do you love it not?

B. Change the underlined words in the sentences to make them correct.

1. The writer loves writing <u>stories</u>. _____

2. Haiku is a kind of <u>long</u> verse. _____

3. There are <u>four</u> lines in a haiku. _____

4. Basho was a man from <u>England</u>. _____

5. Basho's most famous haiku is about a <u>toad</u>. _____

ISBN: 978-1-77149-031-3

Syllables

A **syllable** is an individual sound segment in a word. Words can have one or more syllables.

Examples: frog (1 syllable)   water (2 syllables)

favourite (3 syllables)   kindergarten (4 syllables)

C.   Say the things. Write the number of syllables in the boxes.

1.

2.

3.

4.

5.

6.

7.

8.

9.

ISBN: 978-1-77149-031-3

D.   Say the words. Write them on the correct lines.

> acrostic   famous   Japanese   sound
> competition   lollipop   information
> book   bright   stationery   pizza   author

1 Syllable _____

2 Syllables _____

3 Syllables _____

4 Syllables _____

E.   Use "/" to separate the syllables in these words.

If the word has a double consonant, each letter in the double consonant belongs to a different syllable.
Example: puz/zle

1. s y l l a b l e

2. g a r a g e

3. a f t e r n o o n

4. c o l o u r f u l

5. c a r r y

6. e x c i t i n g

7. i n v i s i b l e

8. n e c e s s a r y

ISBN: 978-1-77149-031-3

Why Do We Sneeze?

Sometimes our body does things we do not ask it to do. Sneezing, coughing, blinking, and even yawning are examples of *involuntary movements* or *reflex actions*. What makes our body do these things?

These involuntary actions are a response to a *stimulus*. Believe it or not, when we do these things, our body is trying to protect itself. If an irritant such as pollen from plants gets into our nose or nasal passages, our body sneezes to get it out. If we breathe in dust, our body coughs to remove it from our lungs or windpipe. We blink in order to keep our eyes clean and moist and to prevent dust and other objects from settling on them. A yawn is our body's way of making us put more oxygen into our bloodstream.

What tells our body to take care of us the way it does? These involuntary movements occur because our brain is sending out signals. There is a system of nerves, the *central nervous system*, that covers our entire body: from the brain, down the spinal cord inside our spinal column (the column of bones that goes down our back), to the very tips of our fingers and toes. When a body part senses certain things, like a mosquito bite, a message is sent to our brain. Then the brain sends a message back to tell it to itch.

Without these reflex actions, we would not be able to live very long.

ISBN: 978-1-77149-031-3

A. **Read the sentences. Complete the crossword puzzle with words from the passage.**

- **3** actions or **C** movements are things that our body does without our asking.

- Our body responds to a **4** on its own in order to **A** itself.

- Our body sneezes or **5** to get rid of an **1** .

- **D** is a way to keep our eyes clean and moist.

- We **2** to put more oxygen into our bloodstream.

- Our body parts send messages to our **B** through the central **E** system.

Subject Pronouns

A **subject pronoun** acts as the subject in a sentence.

"I", "you", "we", "they", "he", "she", and "it" are subject pronouns.

Example: Our body is amazing. <u>It</u> does things to protect us.

B.   Fill in the blanks with the correct subject pronouns for the underlined words to complete the sentences.

1. <u>Our eyes</u> are very important to us. _____ enable us to see.

2. <u>Mom and I</u> have an appointment with Dr. Amo. _____ will have our eyes checked.

3. <u>Our central nervous system</u> is very complicated. _____ covers our whole body.

4. <u>Tommy</u> has got some mosquito bites on his legs. _____ feels very itchy now.

5. Kingsley has left <u>you</u> a message. _____ don't have to call him back.

6. <u>Betsy</u> did not sleep well last night. _____ kept yawning the whole morning.

7. Mom has bought <u>me</u> some cough syrup. _____ will have to take some before bed.

ISBN: 978-1-77149-031-3

Object Pronouns

An **object pronoun** acts as an object that receives the action of the verb or to whom or what the verb is directed in a sentence.

"Me", "you", "us", "them", "him", "her", and "it" are object pronouns.

Example: Miss Carter told <u>us</u> about our body's reflex actions.

C. Check ✔ if the underlined object pronouns are correct. Correct the wrong ones and write them on the lines.

1. Lester has given <u>her</u> a diary. I write in it every night.

    _____

2. Mrs. Carlos has made some cream puffs for us. I have put <u>it</u> in the fridge.   _____

3. I gave <u>him</u> the key yesterday. Where have you put it?   _____

4. The riddle was not difficult. Hilda could solve <u>it</u> very quickly.   _____

5. Martha is having a swimming class now. We'll meet <u>her</u> in the afternoon.   _____

6. Is the actor here yet? I really want to see <u>us</u>.   _____

7. Dad has promised to take <u>him</u> to the zoo when we finish the project.   _____

Girls' Festival *in Japan*

March 3

Dear Sammy,

Today is a special day. We call it *Hina Matsuri*. "Hina" means "doll" and "matsuri" means "festival". We also call this day "Girls' Festival". It is a special day for us girls. On this day, our families wish us success and happiness. We put special dolls on display in our homes. My doll set has 15 dolls and it used to be my grandmother's! It is very beautiful.

We also have peach blossoms in our house for Girls' Festival. Yesterday, my mother took me to the flower market to buy some. Peach blossoms are a lovely pink colour. I love pink, do you?

I like to wear my kimono on Hina Matsuri. I am going to have a little tea party at my house today too. My grandmother will make some sushi for us to eat. Do you like sushi?

Happy Girls' Festival, Sammy! I wish you success and happiness!

Sayonara (this means goodbye)!

Your friend,

Kiyoka

ISBN: 978-1-77149-031-3

A. Circle the things related to Girls' Festival.

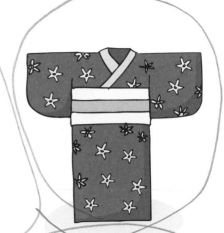

B. Draw lines to match the two parts.

1. hina

2. matsuri

3. Hina Matsuri

4. peach blossom

5. kimono

6. sayonara

Girls' Festival

goodbye

a kind of pink flower

festival

doll

a kind of Japanese clothing for girls and women

Possessive Nouns

A **possessive noun** shows possession.

For a singular noun or a plural noun not ending in "s", add an apostrophe and an "s" at the end of the noun.

Example: Miss Reid's folder is yellow. The children's folders are blue.

For a plural noun ending in "s", add only an apostrophe.

Example: The students' performance was outstanding.

C.   Circle the correct possessive nouns to complete the sentences.

1.   Girls's / Girls'   Festival is on March 3 every year.

2.   Kiyoka's / Kiyoka'   doll set is awesome.

3.   It was her   grandma's / grandmas'   doll set.

4.   The   dolls's / dolls'   clothes are beautiful.

5.   Her   sister's / sisters's   kimono is too big for her.

6.   Her   friends' / friends's   parents will also join the tea party.

7.   Mr. and Mrs.   Tanaka's / Tanaka'   home is also decorated with peach blossoms.

8.   Their   daughters's / daughter's   favourite doll is the empress.

ISBN: 978-1-77149-031-3

Possessive Adjectives

A **possessive adjective** describes a noun that follows it. It tells who possesses or is related to the noun.

"My", "your", "our", "their", "his", "her", and "its" are possessive adjectives.

Example: You have to put <u>your</u> books away.

D. Fill in the blanks with the correct possessive adjectives.

1. Yumi and I are saving money to buy a doll set. We will put _____ doll set in the living room.

2. _____ parents will wish me success and happiness at Girls' Festival.

3. Mom likes making sushi. _____ sushi is delicious.

4. Dad will drive _____ car to the flower market to get some peach blossoms.

5. Our dog likes the scent of peach blossoms. It always wags _____ tail when it gets close to the plant.

6. My friends will all wear _____ kimonos to the tea party.

7. Will you tell _____ friends about Girls' Festival?

A Visit to the Seniors' Centre

My mom works on Saturdays, so every Saturday morning my babysitter, Jenny, takes me somewhere interesting. Once she took me to the aquarium, and then she made me do a project about my favourite fish.

Today, Jenny took me to a seniors' centre. There were a lot of old people there. Some of them were in wheelchairs. Some of them could not see or hear very well. Jenny introduced me to some of the people. Then she asked me if I would read the newspaper to them. I spoke loudly so they could hear me well. They said my reading was excellent. I felt proud.

Later, Jenny and I had lunch with them. I sat at a table with four people. During lunch, they told me about their lives. One man had been a soldier in World War II! He fought in France. The two ladies at my table had grown up in other countries. Mrs. Ip grew up in China and Mrs. Guleed is from Somalia. They told me a little bit about life in their old countries. I thought it seemed hard.

After lunch, Jenny played the piano. Some of the people sang along to the music. The people at the seniors' centre were very interesting and very kind to me. I told Jenny that I would like to go back to the seniors' centre next Saturday.

A. Put the events in order. Write the letters in the boxes.

A The writer had lunch with the people.

B The writer read the newspaper to some people.

C A man and two women told the writer about their lives.

D Jenny introduced the writer to some people at a seniors' centre.

E Jenny played the piano and some people sang along.

D → B → A → C → e

B. Answer the following questions.

1. What did Jenny ask the writer to do after their trip to the aquarium?

   the Seniors centre

2. Why did the writer read the newspaper loudly?

   beacause Some of the Coudnt hear well

3. Why did the writer want to go back to the seniors' centre again?

   beacause the writer had fun with the old people

Demonstrative Pronouns

A **demonstrative pronoun** shows or points to someone or something.

Use "this" or "these" for someone or something near you.
Use "that" or "those" for someone or something farther away.

Example: <u>These</u> flowers are lilacs and <u>those</u> over there are daffodils.

C. Fill in the blanks with the correct demonstrative pronouns.

1. Jenny looked at the sketchbook in front of her and said, "Is _____ the project I asked you to do?"

2. Jenny pointed to the building at the far end of the road and said, "_____ is where we are going today."

3. Let's go and talk with _____ people over there.

4. "_____ is today's newspaper," Jenny said as she handed the newspaper to Victor.

5. Could you pass me _____ fork?

6. "_____ vegetables are delicious," Victor said as he started eating.

Possessive Pronouns

A **possessive pronoun** tells who possesses something or is related to someone.

"Mine", "yours", "ours", "theirs", "his", and "hers" are possessive pronouns.

Example: Those are our bikes.
          Those bikes are <u>ours</u>.

D.   Rewrite the sentences using possessive pronouns.

1.   This is my book.

   _____

2.   These are Jerry's stickers.

   _____

3.   Is this your lunch box?

   _____

4.   Those are Lisa's shoes.

   _____

5.   That is our puppy.

   _____

6.   These are Mr. and Mrs. Newman's pictures.

   _____

Dear Ms. Naughton,

My name is Emi. I am a grade three student at Primrose School. You used to be the principal of this school. My teacher, Mrs. Rao, told us to write a letter to you today. She said you are retired now, so you need things to do. Is it true? Are you bored? What do you do now? My grandpa likes to play golf. Maybe you should try it.

Love,
Emi King

A Letter to – and from –
Ms. Naughton

Dear Emi,

Thank you so much for your lovely letter. I have been getting so much mail this week. Mrs. Rao is correct. I am retired now. I miss my students and teachers very much.

I am not bored, Emi, but my life is very different. I do volunteer work at the hospital twice a week. I also go for a long walk every day with my friends. I am doing some interesting work at the library, too. And I am thinking about writing a book about being a principal for 30 years – I have a lot of funny stories to tell! When the weather gets warmer, I will try to do some golfing. My son is a good golfer and he can teach me.

Thank you again for your thoughtful letter, my dear.

Love,
Margaret Naughton

ISBN: 978-1-77149-031-3

A. **Complete the following about Ms. Naughton.**

What Ms. Naughton is doing:

1. _____

2. _____

3. _____

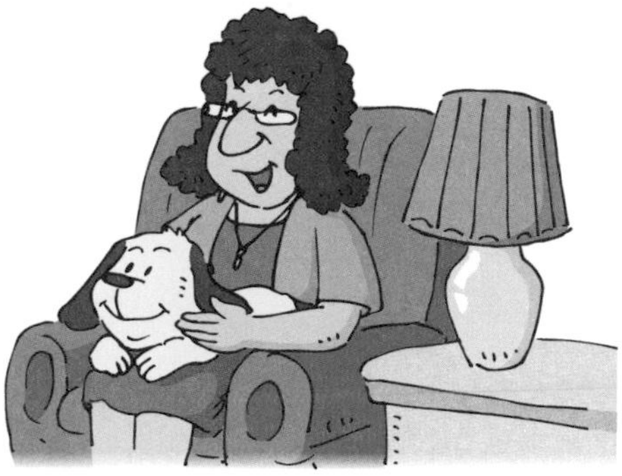

What Ms. Naughton is planning to do:

4. _____

5. _____

B. **Imagine you are another student at Primrose School. Write a letter to Ms. Naughton and suggest what other things she can do.**

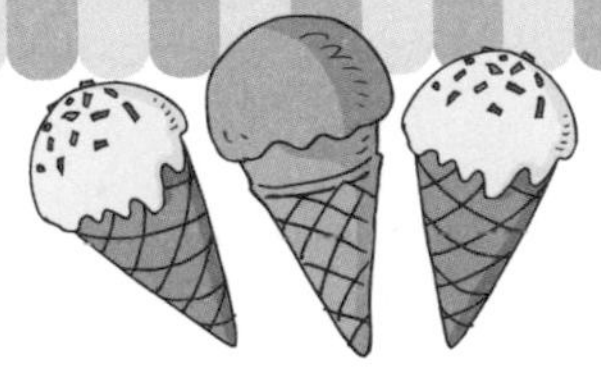

Dear Ms. Naughton,

_____

_____

_____

_____

_____

_____

_____

_____

Subject-Verb Agreement

The **verb** must **agree** with its **subject** in a sentence.

If the subject is singular, a singular verb should be used.

Example: <u>Ms. Naughton</u> <u>is</u> retired now.

If the subject is plural, a plural verb should be used.

Example: <u>The children</u> <u>write</u> letters to her every month.

C. Circle the correct verbs to complete the sentences.

1. Ms. Naughton help / helps at the library every Saturday.

2. She invite / invites an author to read stories to children every week.

3. Some authors wear / wears funny costumes.

4. Others use / uses interesting props as they read / reads .

5. Ms. Naughton then ask / asks the children to draw a book cover for the story.

6. Each week, she and the author choose / chooses the best design and put / puts it on a beautifully decorated board.

7. There is / are now 11 pictures on the board.

   ISBN: 978-1-77149-031-3

D. **Check ✔ if the underlined verbs are correct. Correct the wrong ones and write them on the lines.**

1. Emi and her family <u>live</u> just a block away from Primrose School. _____

2. Emi's little sister, Liz, also <u>go</u> to that school. _____

3. The playground at the school <u>are</u> big. _____

4. Liz <u>likes</u> to play with Emi and her friends at recess. _____

5. Emi's friends also <u>enjoys</u> playing with her. _____

E. **Change the subject of each sentence to plural. Rewrite the sentence with the correct verb form. Make other changes where needed.**

1. The kitten drinks the milk happily.

   _____

   _____

2. The child is looking at the ladybug.

   _____

3. The pastry tastes sweet and delicious.

   _____

4. The girl puts away her book.

   _____

I had a great day yesterday. My parents took my brother and me to the Sugar Shack. We go there every spring.

My dad said that the weather would be perfect for a good sugaring-off. For the past week there were sunny days and cold, frosty nights. Dad said this kind of weather would get the sap running in the maple trees. He was right!

There were red, silver, and sugar maple trees as far as I could see, and most of them had little wooden buckets hanging on them. We collected the watery sap that dripped out of the maple trees through spigots bored into the tree trunks. This is the old-fashioned way. People in many other places use tubes and vacuum pumps to collect the sap now.

The Sugar Shack

Then we went to a large campfire in the snow. A woman poured the sap we collected into a big iron pot. A man was stirring and stirring. We watched the sap cook. Slowly it got thicker and darker. It was turning into delicious sweet-smelling maple syrup!

When it was done, we sat at a picnic table outdoors and ate plates of pancakes, sausages, ham, baked beans, and scrambled eggs with our maple syrup. My parents put maple syrup in their coffee, too! We ate as much as we could. Then we went for a long walk in the maple woods.

ISBN: 978-1-77149-031-3

A. Circle the things the family ate on the picnic at the Sugar Shack.

baked beans

bacon

sausages

ham

corned beef

fried eggs

Maple Syrup

waffles

pancakes

scrambled eggs

B. Find words from the passage that mean the same as the words below.

1. small

2. correct

3. excellent

4. ready

5. gathered

6. method

7. pails

8. outside

9. tasty

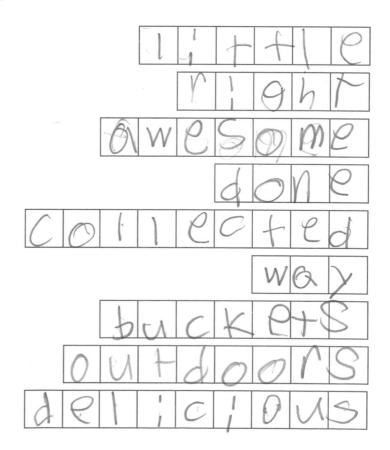

1. little
2. right
3. awesome
4. done
5. collected
6. way
7. buckets
8. outdoors
9. delicious

Past Tense Verbs

Most **past tense verbs** are formed by adding "d" or "ed" to the base form. Some are formed by repeating the last letter before adding "ed". Others remain the same or have completely different spellings.

Examples: dance → danced   pour → poured
drip → dripped   put → put
go → went

C. Complete the crossword puzzle with the past form of the clue words.

Across

A. cost
B. catch
C. let
D. collect
E. have
F. tan

Down

1. buy
2. watch
3. pat
4. stir
5. will
6. shut

D. Fill in the blanks with the past form of the given verbs.

For some verbs ending in "y", change the "y" to "i" before adding "ed".

Yesterday morning, Mom (promise) 1._____ to make pancakes for us as afternoon snacks, so after school, my brother and I (hurry) 2._____ home.

When we (arrive) 3._____ home, we (be) 4._____ delighted to see the pancakes on the kitchen table. I (grab) 5._____ the maple syrup we (buy) 6._____ from the Sugar Shack and (pour) 7._____ some on my pancakes. My brother (do) 8._____ the same to his after me. The golden brown fluid (spread) 9._____ all over our pancakes. We (devour) 10._____ our treats at once. I (eat) 11._____ so fast that I nearly (choke) 12._____ . My brother (look) 13._____ scared at first. When he (see) 14._____ that I (be) 15._____ all right, we (burst) 16._____ into laughter together.

The Amazing Coconut

Do you know what an amazing fruit the coconut is? Maybe you have seen small, round, and brown coconuts in the fruit section of the supermarket. Maybe you have made coconut macaroons, and needed to buy a bag of dried, shredded, white coconut meat. We call this coconut meat *copra*. It is a tasty and healthy snack.

Coconuts grow on palm trees. But the small, round coconuts you see in the supermarket grow inside larger pods, or husks. The husk is a tough fibre called *coir*. We use coir to make ropes, yarn, and carpets. Coir is even used to make aquarium filters, flowerpots, soundproofing materials, and mattresses!

Coconut oil comes from copra. This oil is used in making some snack foods and is quite a healthy oil to eat. Coconut oil is also used in suntan lotions and other cosmetics that we put on our skin.

Many people love coconut milk. You can buy it in cans or make it yourself by adding a cup of boiling water to a bag of dried coconut and putting it into the blender, but you must strain out the bits after.

There is coconut water inside a coconut. It has more vitamins and fewer calories than milk or orange juice. And best of all...coconut water is delicious!

A. Read the passage. Match the things made from the different parts of the coconut.

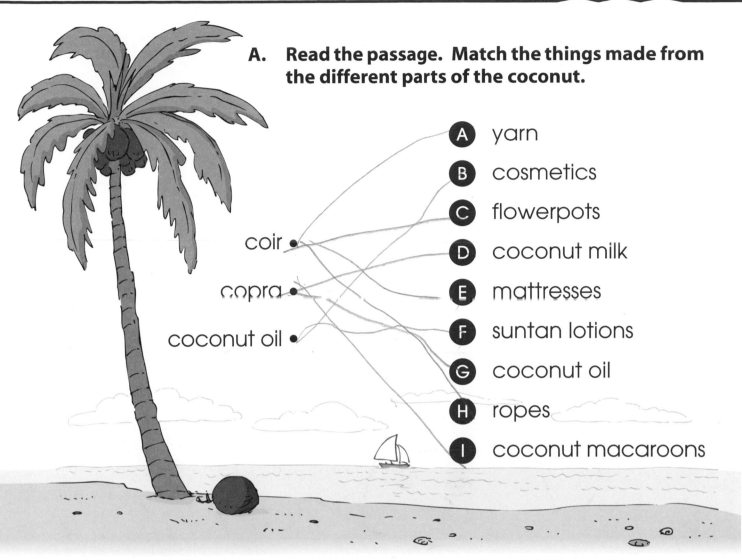

coir •

copra •

coconut oil •

A yarn

B cosmetics

C flowerpots

D coconut milk

E mattresses

F suntan lotions

G coconut oil

H ropes

I coconut macaroons

B. Complete the recipe.

Coconut Milk

DRIED COCONUT

Ingredients: 1 bag of dried coconut
1 cup of boiling water

Steps:

1. _boil water_

2. _add it to dried coc onuts_

3. _blend it_

ISBN: 978-1-77149-031-3   Complete Canadian Curriculum • **Grade 3**

Adjectives

An **adjective** describes a noun.

We use adjectives to add interest and detail to our writing.

Example: Mom bought a coconut from the superstore.

Mom bought a <u>small</u>, <u>round</u> coconut from the <u>new</u> superstore.

C.   Circle the adjectives in the sentences.

1.   The coconut is an amazing fruit.

2.   It has white meat inside a large, hard husk.

3.   A young coconut is green with tender meat inside.

4.   The water inside a coconut is healthy and refreshing.

5.   The coconut is very useful and can be used to make many things.

6.   Coir can be used to make strong ropes.

7.   The brown pots are also made from this tough fibre.

8.   The dried, shredded meat can be used to make delicious macaroons.

D. Fill in the blanks with the correct adjectives.

bright   wet   early   slimy   stuffy

crowded   colourful   tall   big   cold

1. A _big_ coconut fell from the _tall_ tree.

2. The _slimy_ snail is moving slowly on the _wet_ mud.

3. The heat from the _bright_ sun warms the _cold_ water.

4. _colourful_ tulips start blooming in _early_ spring.

5. The air is _stuffy_ in the _crowded_ room.

E. Add adjectives to the sentences to make them more interesting.

1. The children played happily in the water.

   _____

   _____

2. We went to the restaurant for dinner.

   _____

   _____

3. The birds are chirping in the tree.

   _____

   _____

Shooting Stars

Shooting stars are not stars – and they don't shoot! They are rocks, called meteors, that come toward the Earth from far away in space. These meteors can be any size, large or small.

A meteor flies through space at a very high speed, up to 200 000 kilometres per hour! When things go this fast through the air around the Earth, everything becomes very hot. The air around the meteor gets so hot it glows blue-white. This blue-white streak in the sky is what we see, and it is why we call it a "shooting star".

As a meteor shoots through the sky, it breaks into pieces. Usually this "shooting star" will disappear in less than a second. But some meteors are larger and do not break up completely. Some bits of rock will crash into the Earth. When this happens, we call them meteorites. Most meteorites fall into the ocean.

Seeing a shooting star is an amazing thing. We think it is lucky to see one. The truth is, shooting stars happen often, but they move so fast that we often miss them if we are not looking carefully.

Have you ever seen a shooting star? If not, why not take the time to sit back and watch the sky the next time the stars are shining bright and clear? If you watch carefully and concentrate, you will surely see a shooting star. Don't forget to make a wish!

 ISBN: 978-1-77149-031-3

A. Read the sentences. Circle the answers in the word search.

- Shooting stars are ___ that fly through ___ at very high speeds.

- These rocks are called ___ .

- The ___ air around a fast flying meteor forms a blue-white ___ .

- ___ are bits of meteors that crash into the ___ .

- Seeing a shooting star is something ___ . You can make a ___ when you see one.

- You need to ___ if you want to see a shooting star.

q	m	E	a	r	h	e	c	i	d	h	m	e	t	o	l
m	e	t	e	o	r	s	o	q	c	r	e	c	k	j	b
o	r	d	s	c	k	p	n	s	h	a	t	n	a	s	p
h	o	e	t	k	E	a	r	t	h	E	e	h	o	c	f
j	k	a	r	s	p	c	s	r	n	a	o	s	m	e	d
l	e	m	e	c	o	n	c	e	n	t	r	a	t	e	g
s	p	a	o	e	c	t	i	a	z	g	i	c	o	t	k
h	t	z	b	a	e	s	v	k	l	r	t	e	i	r	p
b	c	i	s	g	t	p	g	h	a	m	e	t	t	e	o
r	o	n	s	t	r	a	q	j	w	i	s	h	o	c	m
e	n	g	i	p	m	c	o	n	c	t	r	o	c	s	f
n	t	k	d	i	E	e	a	t	h	p	h	t	i	k	j
i	s	t	a	e	k	n	b	a	m	a	s	e	l	g	c

Adverbs

An **adverb** describes a verb. It tells how an action takes place.

Most adverbs are formed by adding "ly" to the adjective. Others are irregular.

Example: The rock did not break up <u>completely</u> and fell <u>fast</u> into the ocean.

B.   Check ✔ if the underlined words in the sentences are adverbs.

1. If you look <u>carefully</u>, you can see quite a number of shooting stars on a clear night.

2. People <u>often</u> scream when they see a shooting star.

3. That star looks so <u>lonely</u> in the night sky.

4. We'll <u>surely</u> see the full moon tonight.

5. I tried <u>hard</u> to concentrate but I still could not see a shooting star.

6. That's a <u>lovely</u> story about the stars.

7. We <u>usually</u> stay up to watch the stars when we go camping.

8. The weather <u>soon</u> cleared up and the stars started twinkling again.

ISBN: 978-1-77149-031-3

C. Change the adjectives in parentheses ( ) to adverbs to complete the sentences.

1. Jane asked her dad (eager) _eagerley_ when he would get her a telescope.

2. Mary and Sandra are working (patient) _patientley_ on a jigsaw puzzle of different groups of stars.

3. The plane soared (high) _high_ and disappeared behind the clouds.

4. Terry arrived (late) _late_ and missed the meteor shower.

5. The leaves danced (graceful) _gracefully_ in the light breeze.

D. Write sentences of your own with the given adverbs.

1. stealthily

the panther stealthily stalked its preye

2. gladly

Russyl gladly helped his mom make soup

3. hard

a box fell and hit the ground hard.

The Circus School

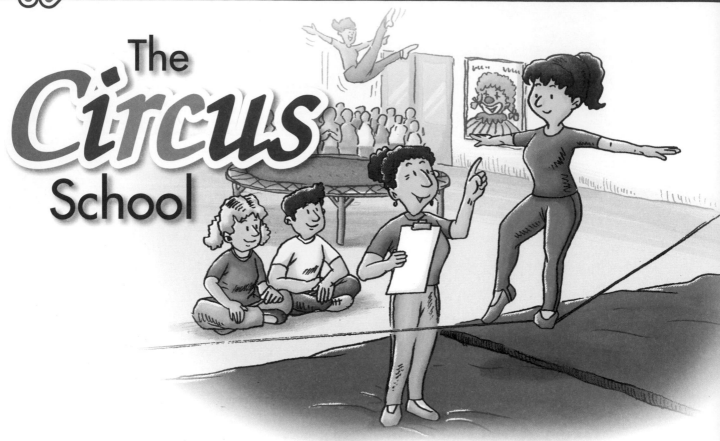

Aunt Jamilla is a student at the National Circus School in Montreal. She has very busy days. She has to take classes about anatomy and about nutrition. She is also taking French lessons, and music and rhythm lessons. She does a lot of stretching all day long. She says stretching is very important, especially for circus performers. She takes classes about learning to balance. She can balance on balls, on chairs, on a tightrope, and on a slack wire, too.

In her "acrobatics" class, Aunt Jamilla uses a trampoline, ladders, chairs, and something called a teeterboard. In her class on "aerials", she learns to move on a trapeze. She is also learning how to climb ribbons and swing around on them, like doing a dance in the air.

In her clowning arts class, Aunt Jamilla learns how to fall without getting hurt. She also learns how to "talk" with her body. She is also learning to juggle – not only with her hands, but with her feet!

Soon, Aunt Jamilla will finish her classes. Then she will have her Diploma of Collegial Studies in Circus Arts. With her experience, she will be able to find a job. It is Aunt Jamilla's dream to perform with the famous Cirque du Soleil someday. It is my dream to watch her do it.

A. Write what classes Aunt Jamilla takes at the National Circus School.

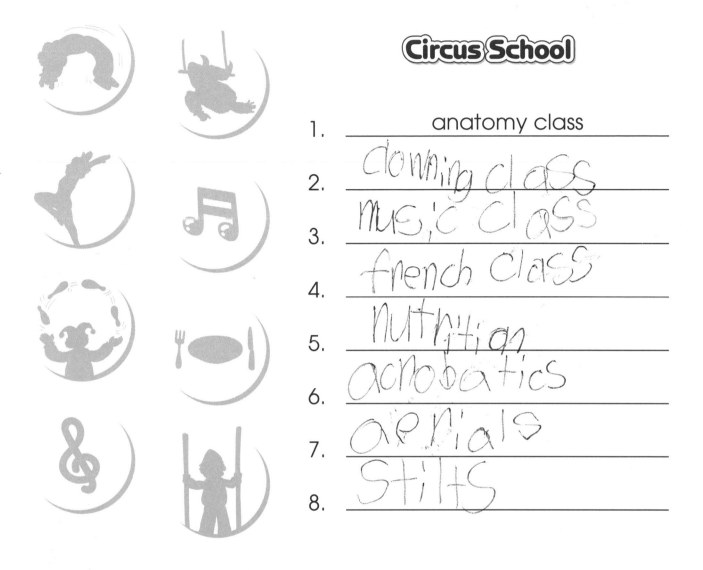

Circus School

1. _anatomy class_
2. clowning class
3. music class
4. french class
5. nutrition
6. acrobatics
7. aerials
8. stilts

B. What would you want to learn most at a circus school? Why?

_____

_____

_____

_____

_____

ISBN: 978-1-77149-031-3

Prepositions

Some **prepositions** tell where something happens. Others tell when something happens.

Examples: Aunt Jamilla takes classes <u>at</u> the National Circus School. (where)

She started her studies there <u>in</u> 2014. (when)

C. **Circle the prepositions. Then write the groups of words in the correct places.**

Where

on chairs

in the sky

inside the box

at sunset

beside the doll

at Christmas

behind the house

When

at two o'clock

in the morning

on weekends

in 2015

above Lydia

ISBN: 978-1-77149-031-3

D. Circle the correct prepositions to complete the sentences.

1. **At / On** my birthday last year, my parents held a party for me. They invited a clown to the party. The clown show started 2. **at / in** three o'clock. My friends and I sat 3. **in / on** the carpet to watch the performance.

The clown had a few balls of different colours 4. **in / inside** her hands. She juggled the balls and we were amazed to see that they formed a colourful arc 5. **above / in** the air.

The clown then took out a box the size of a small toaster oven from 6. **in / under** the table. She showed us that there was nothing 7. **between / inside** it. She put the box 8. **in / on** the middle of the table and said, "Abracadabra". Then she slowly pulled a teddy bear out of the box. My friend Anson whispered to me that there must be a hidden part 9. **at / over** the bottom of the box. But the clown continued to pull teddy bears

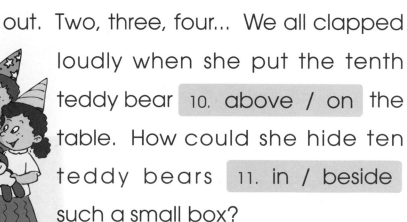

out. Two, three, four... We all clapped loudly when she put the tenth teddy bear 10. **above / on** the table. How could she hide ten teddy bears 11. **in / beside** such a small box?

ISBN: 978-1-77149-031-3   Complete Canadian Curriculum • **Grade 3**

My Brother Loves to Dance

My brother Toller is a very good dancer. He is 12 years old and has been dancing for about six years. He has won many awards. He loves being a dancer, but it wasn't always this way.

One day, a new student named Morris joined Toller's class. When he found out Toller was a dancer, he picked on my brother and called him names. This made other classmates do the same. It was a difficult time for Toller. He stopped going to dance class. He was unhappy.

Toller's dance instructor came to visit us. She wanted to know why Toller had stopped going to dance class. My parents and I were shocked; Toller hadn't told us he had stopped! We all sat together and talked it out. Toller explained that he was being teased at school. The instructor asked him what was making him sad. He was sad mainly because he wanted to keep dancing.

We worked out a plan and role-played it together. My father pretended to be Morris. When he teased Toller about being a dancer, Toller replied, "Yes, I am a dancer. I'm good at it, too. You are good at teasing and bothering people. You need to find something else to do." It didn't take long before Toller finally told Morris this. The other classmates stopped copying Morris. Soon, Morris didn't have many friends. He stopped bothering Toller.

Toller danced hip hop for the talent show at school last week. Everyone cheered when he finished...even Morris. I am proud of my brother.

ISBN: 978-1-77149-031-3

A. Circle the correct answers.

1. Toller has been dancing for about __ years.
   A. twelve   B. (six)   C. two

2. Toller was __ when Morris called him names.
   A. happy   B. shocked   (C. sad)

3. Toller's __ visited the writer's family to see why Toller had stopped going to dance class.
   A. class teacher   B. principal   (C. dance instructor)

4. __ was good at teasing others.
   (A. Morris)   B. Toller   C. The writer

5. Toller danced __ for his school talent show.
   A. samba   (B. hip hop)   C. tap-dance

B. Rewrite the sentences so that they are correct.

1. Toller has not won any awards.
   Toller has won many awards

2. The writer pretended to be Morris in the role play.
   _____
   _____

3. Everyone jeered when Toller finished his dance.
   everyone cheered when toller finished his dance

Contractions

A **contraction** is a short way of writing two words. One or more letters are replaced with an apostrophe.

Examples: I am → I'm
            was not → wasn't

C.   Draw lines to match the words with their contractions.

1. did not   shouldn't

2. I have   doesn't

3. does not   there's

4. there is   didn't

5. she is   we'll

6. we will   she's

7. should not   he'd

8. he had   I've

D.   Fill in the blanks with the contractions of the given words.

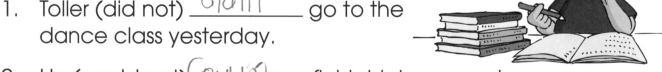

1. Toller (did not) _didn't_ go to the dance class yesterday.

2. He (could not) _couldn't_ finish his homework.

3. He (had not) _hadn't_ missed any dance classes before.

4. (He will) _he'll_ never miss his dance class again.

5. (He would) _he'd_ like to be a professional dancer in the future.

Abbreviations

An **abbreviation** is the shortened form of a word or words.

Examples: Doctor → Dr.
Tuesday → Tue.
Royal Canadian Mounted Police → RCMP

E. Circle the correct abbreviations for the words.

1. Mister   Ms. / Mrs. / (Mr.)

2. kilometre   ki / (km) / kilo

3. Boulevard   Bl. / Bv. / (Blvd.)

4. November   (Nov.) / No. / Novem.

5. number   num. / (no.) / nb.

6. British Columbia   Br.Co. / B.Co. / (B.C.)

7. Mountain   (Mt.) / Mo. / Mot.

F. Rewrite the sentences using abbreviations.

1. Toller will join a dance competition on October 23.

_____

2. It will take place in a school on Berry Drive.

_____

3. He will go on a trip to Prince Edward Island afterwards.

_____

Lacrosse
Canada's National Summer Sport

Lacrosse is the oldest game in North America. It has been played by the native people of North America for more than 500 years. The first game took place in 1840, and it soon became very popular. In 1859, the government of Canada named lacrosse Canada's national game. In 1994, lacrosse was given the title of Canada's national summer sport.

Lacrosse can be played indoors or outdoors. Women's field lacrosse is played with two teams of 12 players. Men's field lacrosse teams have ten players. The players must pass and catch a rubber ball using netted sticks, and try to score goals by hurling the ball into the other team's goal area.

In the men's game, contact between players is allowed, so protective gear such as helmets and padding is worn. Women's lacrosse does not permit such contact between players. It is based more on the skills of ball control and passing, like the original version of lacrosse.

In the 1930s, box lacrosse was created. There are six players on a team. Box lacrosse requires players to think fast and be quick. It is more popular than field lacrosse in Canada.

Another type of lacrosse called inter-lacrosse is a non-contact sport. It is popular with children and teenaged players.

Lacrosse is one of the fastest growing sports in Canada. Why not give it a try?

    ISBN: 978-1-77149-031-3

A.   Put the events in order. Write 1 to 4 on the lines.

3 Lacrosse was named Canada's national summer sport.

2 Lacrosse was named Canada's national game.

4 Box lacrosse was created.

1 The first game of lacrosse was played.

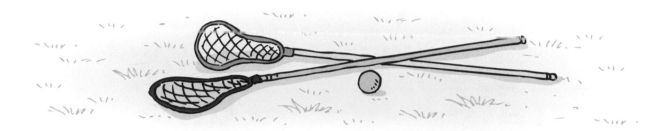

B.   Write "T" for the true sentences and "F" for the false ones.

1. Lacrosse can only be played outdoors.

2. There are 12 players on a men's team in field lacrosse.

3. The players score goals by kicking the ball into the net.

4. No contact between players is allowed in women's lacrosse.

5. The original version of lacrosse is based on the skills of ball control and passing.

6. Players in box lacrosse have to think fast and be quick.

7. Field lacrosse is more popular than box lacrosse in Canada.

8. Children can take part in inter-lacrosse.

F
F
F
F
T
T
F
T

ISBN: 978-1-77149-031-3

Prefixes

A **prefix** is a group of letters added to the beginning of a word that changes the meaning of the word.

The prefix "re" means "to do again".
The prefix "un" means "not" or "opposite of".

Examples: write → <u>re</u>write

happy → <u>un</u>happy

C. Cross out ✗ the words that do not use "re" or "un" as a prefix.

re

un

re		un	
react	result	under	uncertain
reach	rewind	unkind	uncover
retrieve	retake	unit	unstable
repeat	rebuild	unless	uncle
rename	restart	unable	unseen

D. Add "re" or "un" to the given words to complete the sentences.

1. Field lacrosse is (popular) _____ in Southeast Asia.

2. The government is planning to (develop) _____ this district.

3. You have to (set) _____ your watch to local time.

4. I didn't see that part clearly. Can you (play) _____ it?

5. It is (wise) _____ to take action now.

Suffixes

A **suffix** is a group of letters added to the end of a word that changes the meaning of the word.

The suffix "al" means "of" or "related to". The suffix "ful" means "full of". The suffix "less" means "without".

Examples: origin → origin<u>al</u>

meaning → meaning<u>ful</u>

meaning → meaning<u>less</u>

E.   Read the clues and complete the crossword puzzle.

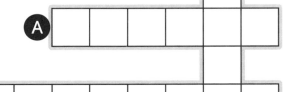

Across

A. full of joy
B. of a nation
C. without colour
D. of a region

Down

1. related to education
2. full of hope
3. without care

Rupinder
the Reporter

Rupinder is a member of the newspaper club at his school. His club publishes the school newspaper once a month. Rupinder is a reporter for the paper. His job is to find things to write about. The students at his school like reading his articles.

This month, Rupinder wrote about his classmate, Toller. Toller has won many awards for his amazing dancing. He is famous in their city because he is such a good dancer. Rupinder's article focused on how hard Toller practised to become a good dancer.

Last month, Rupinder wrote a story about his school's "green program". His school has new hand dryers in the washrooms, so they don't use paper towels anymore. They also have recycling bins at school. No paper cups are allowed in the staff room or cafeteria anymore.

Right now, Rupinder is working on an article about bullying at school. He notices bullies like to keep things secret, but he is going to make sure it is not a secret anymore!

Rupinder loves his job with the school newspaper. When he grows up, he wants to be a famous journalist.

ISBN: 978-1-77149-031-3

A. Check ✔ the main idea of each paragraph.

Paragraph One

☑ Rupinder is a reporter for his school newspaper.

☐ B There is a newspaper club at Rupinder's school.

Paragraph Two

☐ A Rupinder wrote about Toller this month.

☑ B Toller practised hard to become a good dancer.

Paragraph Three

☐ A No paper cups are allowed in Rupinder's school.

☑ B Rupinder wrote about his school's "green program" last month.

Paragraph Four

☑ A Bullies like to keep things secret.

☐ B Rupinder is working on an article about bullying at his school.

Paragraph Five

☐ A Rupinder wants to work for his school newspaper when he grows up.

☑ B Rupinder wants to be a famous journalist when he grows up.

ISBN: 978-1-77149-031-3 Complete Canadian Curriculum • Grade 3

Compound Words

A **compound word** is formed when two words are put together to form a new word of a different meaning.

Example: news + paper = newspaper

B. **Unscramble the letters to form compound words. Circle the words in the word search.**

n a y + r o e m   w t e r a + l a f l   i a r n + w b o

t o f o + i n p r t   s h w a + o o r m   y e k + a d b r o

l u e b + a y j   a t e r f + o n n o   a s c l s + t a m e

c	s	m	a	t	c	p	a	m	y	m	o	t	h	c
l	o	o	f	j	v	r	i	n	t	l	g	c	b	i
a	p	j	t	a	w	a	t	e	r	f	a	l	l	w
s	c	k	e	y	x		h	a	o	m	a	u	a
e	l	o	r	w					o	a	s	e	t
r	a	i	n	j					t	o	k	j	e
g	s	m	o	t					p	e	e	a	n
b	s	d	o	d					r	t	y	y	b
n	m	v	n	l	n	w	s	r	a	i	n	b	o	w
w	a	s	h	r	o	o	m	j	p	n	l	o	k	n
a	t	e	r	n	o	f	a	q	e	t	h	a	b	z
k	e	y	b	j	n	r	a	n	y	m	o	r	e	f
g	d	k	a	s	c	i	t	r	e	b	k	d	i	a

ISBN: 978-1-77149-031-3

C. Draw lines to match the pictures to form compound words. Write the words in the boxes.

1.

2.

3.
   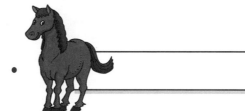

4.

5.

D. Draw two pictures to form a compound word. Write the word on the line.

+ $\quad$ = _____

A Special Project

One day my mother asked me if I wanted to do a special crocheting project with my friends. I said yes. I invited four friends over for a pyjama party. I told them to bring their crochet hooks. My mother taught us how to make crocheted squares.

We started to crochet big squares. There were five of us, and we each made four squares. My mom had bought different colours of wool: peony pink, sky blue, buttercup yellow, lime green, and lavender. My mom made four squares, too.

Then my mom showed us how to sew four squares into a row. We made small, careful stitches using white wool. Then we sewed the six rows together. It turned into a large rainbow-coloured blanket. My mom took a photograph of all of us with our blanket.

That night, we all tried to sleep under the blanket, but it was a bit too small! The next morning, we took a bus to an orphanage. My mom said the children there do not have any parents. The lady who runs the orphanage was kind. We gave her the blanket we made and she thanked us. She took us to a playroom. We played with some of the babies for a little while. They were sweet.

We were glad to meet the babies and give them our blanket.

     ISBN: 978-1-77149-031-3

A. Give short answers to the questions.

1. What did they need to make crocheted squares?

   _____yarn_____

2. How many crocheted squares did they make?

   _____4 each_____

3. What did they use to sew the squares together?

   _____wihte wool_____

4. What did they make with the crocheted squares?

   _____a blanket_____

5. Where did they go the next day?

   _____the orphanage_____

B. Crocheted squares can be sewn together to make different things. Write one thing that you would like to make with crocheted squares. Draw a picture to go with it.

   _____

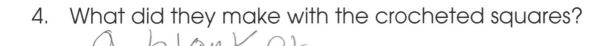

Commonly Confused Words

We may confuse words that have similar spellings or sound alike.

Examples: bought – brought
sew – sow

C. Circle the correct words to complete the sentences.

1. My mom is crocheting a big
| circle |
| cycle |
.

2. She wants to make a
| vary |
| very |
big
| cloth |
| clothe |
to cover the table.

3. She puts the wool on the small table
| beside |
| besides |
the
| coach |
| couch |
.

4. Oh
| dear |
| deer |
! The stitches here are too
| lose |
| loose |
.

5. Adrian, could you
| pass |
| past |
the wool to me?

6.
| Its |
| It's |
very beautiful, Mom.

7. Mom likes having a
| desert |
| dessert |
after crocheting.

D. **The underlined words are wrong in the sentences. Write the correct words on the lines.**

1. I think crocheting is <u>quiet</u> interesting. _____

2. Wait at the <u>curd</u> before crossing the road. _____

3. He <u>pores</u> the juice into a big jug. _____

4. I helped Mom <u>sat</u> the table. _____

5. This is a <u>nine-story</u> building. _____

6. Mrs. Hopewell is talking to the school <u>principle</u>. _____

7. Kim made a <u>bald</u> move in joining the contest. _____

8. The zebra has black and white <u>strips</u>. _____

E. **Write sentences with the words to show the difference in meaning between the words in each pair.**

1. diner / dinner

   _____

   _____

2. forth / fourth

   _____

   _____

Durian
King of the Fruits

Fruit is always a delicious treat. In Canada, we grow a lot of apples, pears, cherries, and cranberries. But Canada is too cold to grow certain fruits.

Have you ever tasted a durian? It is grown in warm places like Malaysia and Thailand in Southeast Asia. The name "durian" comes from the Malay word *duri*, meaning "thorn".

The durian is often called "King of the Fruits" because it is big and dangerous looking, and has a very strong smell. One durian can grow up to 40 centimetres long and 30 centimetres wide. It can weigh up to five kilograms. It is an oval shape and the outside is a hard, greenish-brown husk. It is covered with prickly thorns.

But the most amazing thing about the durian is what is inside. When you open it up, a very strong smell comes out. Some people love this smell but others hate it! In Singapore, you are not permitted to bring a durian into your hotel room or onto city trains. Some airlines will not let you carry a durian onto the airplane.

Despite the smell, the flesh inside is quite tasty. It is yellowish in colour, and tastes a little bit like custard. Animals such as squirrels, wild pigs, and orangutans love it.

    ISBN: 978-1-77149-031-3

A. Write the words in the correct places.

cherries

Malaysia

cranberries

Thailand

Singapore

wild pigs

durians

squirrels

pears

orangutans

Canada

Fruit

_____

_____

_____

_____

Animal

_____

_____

_____

Place

_____

_____

_____

_____

_____

B. Complete the chart.

The Durian

Shape: 1._____   Weight: up to 2._____ kg

Length: up to 3._____ cm   Width: up to 4._____ cm

Colour: husk – 5._____ ; flesh – 6._____

ISBN: 978-1-77149-031-3

Synonyms and Antonyms

Synonyms are words that have similar meanings.

Examples: cold – chilly

Antonyms are words that have opposite meanings.

Examples: cold – hot

C. **Circle the synonyms and underline the antonyms of the shaded words.**

1. big

large

small

huge

2. love

hate

like

dislike

3. fast

speedy

slow

swift

4. delicious

yummy

tasty

flavourless

5. cloudy

overcast

sunny

bright

6. balmy

pleasant

warm

stormy

7. interesting

boring

absorbing

amusing

ISBN: 978-1-77149-031-3

D. **Fill in the blanks with synonyms for the given words.**

1. It is too (cold) _____ to grow durians in Canada.

2. We are planning a (holiday) _____ in Thailand.

3. Why is your room so (messy) _____ ?

4. This dish is too (spicy) _____ for me.

5. Don't bring a durian into this hotel. It is
    not (allowed) _____ .

6. The first train (departs)
    _____ at six thirty
    in the morning.

E. **Rewrite the sentences with antonyms
for the underlined words.**

1. I <u>seldom</u> try exotic fruits.

    _____

2. This store <u>opens</u> on Sundays.

    _____

3. The <u>old</u> lady is choosing a <u>small</u> durian.

    _____

ISBN: 978-1-77149-031-3

The Story of Honey

Honey is made by bees. They make honey for wintertime when flowers are not blooming and nectar is not available. Lucky for us, there are so many bees to make honey that there is plenty for us too.

Honeybees live and work together in colonies. A colony of honeybees includes a queen bee, drone bees, and worker bees. The queen is the largest bee in the colony, and she lays all the eggs for the colony. The drones help the queen make eggs.

Worker bees are the smallest bees. One colony can have as many as 60 000 worker bees. Their job is to collect nectar from flowers to make honey. They also make the honeycomb from beeswax to store the honey. Drones may live up to eight weeks and worker bees live about five to six weeks. A queen bee may live up to five years.

There are many kinds of honey and they taste different, depending on the flowers the bees take the nectar from. The average worker bee makes about 1/10 of a teaspoon of honey in its lifetime! A honeybee will visit 50 to 150 flowers on one trip. To make half a kilogram of honey, the bees must tap two million flowers and fly over 40 kilometres. Half a kilogram of honey is what 300 bees can make in their lifetime!

It takes a lot of work to make honey. No wonder it tastes so good!

    ISBN: 978-1-77149-031-3

A. Complete the chart.

Queen·Bee

A Honeybee Colony

- the <u>1.   </u> bee
- Number: <u>2.   </u>
- Job: <u>3.   </u>
- Lifespan: up to <u>4.   </u>

Drone Bee

- Job: <u>5.   </u>
- Lifespan: <u>6.   </u>

7. <u>   </u>

- the smallest bee
- Number: as many as <u>8.   </u>
- Jobs: <u>9.   </u>

  <u>10.   </u>

- Lifespan: <u>11.   </u>

Similes

A **simile** is a comparison of two things that have something in common. The two things are linked by "as" or "like".

Examples: He is hardworking like a worker bee.

These candies are as sweet as honey.

B. Check ✔ if the sentences use similes.

1. The city is as busy as a bee colony.

2. The honeycomb is like a storeroom.

3. The beehive is as big as a basketball.

4. My parents like to add honey to their coffee.

5. Little Sharon smiled as she tasted the honey.

6. Honey is as tasty as maple syrup.

7. Mr. Gibson works as a beekeeper.

8. Would you like to try some?

9. The flowers are colourful like a rainbow.

ISBN: 978-1-77149-031-3

C.   Complete the similes with the given words.

a hotel   snails   a ball   birds   a stone   coffee

1.   The full moon is as round as _____ .

2.   The cars are moving slowly like _____ .

3.   This chocolate is bitter like _____ .

4.   The coconut is as hard as _____ .

5.   Her house is as luxurious as _____ .

6.   The children sing sweetly like _____ .

D.   Rewrite the sentences using similes.

1.   The little girl is beautiful.

   _____

2.   This flashlight is bright.

   _____

3.   The phone is ringing loudly.

   _____

ISBN: 978-1-77149-031-3

Hello around the World

In Canada, most people say *Hello* and *Bonjour* when we greet people. Have you ever wondered what people say in other countries? Japanese people bow and say *Konnichiwa*. In China, they say *Ni hao*. In Thailand, *Sawatdee* is said. In Korea, they say *Anyong haseyo*. In Kenya, *Jambo* is the Swahili word for "Hello".

People in Egypt, Iraq, Syria, Qatar, and Oman greet each other by saying *Salam,* which is an Arabic word. Many languages are spoken in India, but in Hindi – one of the most common languages there – people say *Namaste*. In Malaysia and Indonesia, people say *Apa kabar*.

There are a lot of countries in Europe and a lot of languages, too! In Italy, people say *Bongiorno* (which means "good day"). In Denmark, people say *Goddag*, and in the Netherlands, people say *Goede dag*. In Spain, Mexico, and Cuba, people speak Spanish. They say *Hola*. In Germany, people say *Guten tag* (good day) or *Hallo*. Over in Russia, people say *Privyet*.

In Hawaii, people say *Aloha*, which means hello, goodbye, and love. In Israel, people speak Hebrew. When people greet each other there, they say *Shalom*. It means hello, goodbye, and peace.

It is fun to greet people in their native language. Why not give it a try?

 ISBN: 978-1-77149-031-3

A.   Draw lines to match the greetings with the countries.

Kenya •   • Konnichiwa

China •   • Aloha

Israel •   • Jambo

Thailand •   • Bonjour

Canada •   • Ni hao

Germany •   • Hola

Japan •   • Hallo

Hawaii •   • Hello

Korea •   • Bongiorno

India •   • Anyong haseyo

Spain •   • Guten tag

Italy •   • Shalom

• Namaste

• Sawatdee

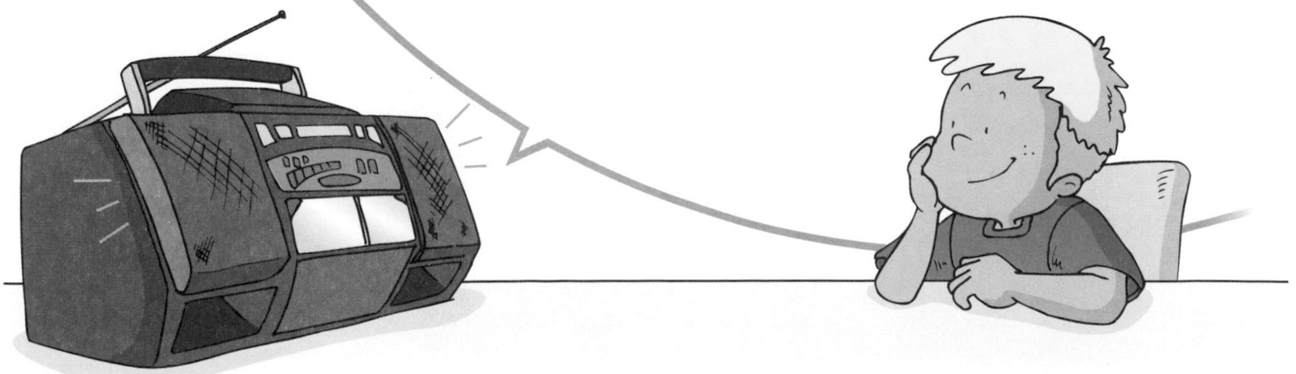

Conjunctions

A **conjunction** like "and", "or", or "but" can be used to join words or sentences.

Example: In Canada, some people say "Hello". Others say "Bonjour".

In Canada, some people say "Hello" <u>and</u> others say "Bonjour".

B. Check ✔ if the underlined words are correct. Correct the wrong ones and write them on the lines.

1. My sister is fluent in Spanish <u>or</u> I just know a little Spanish. _____

2. We can either learn the language ourselves <u>and</u> take a course on it. _____

3. The tourist kept speaking Japanese <u>and</u> I did not understand what he was saying. _____

4. You can watch the English version <u>or</u> the French version of the film. _____

5. Macy wants to learn a language <u>and</u> she has not decided which one to learn. _____

6. "Hello", "Hola", <u>and</u> "Hallo" sound similar.

_____

7. "Aloha" means hello, goodbye, <u>or</u> love.

_____

Aloha!

Hello!

ISBN: 978-1-77149-031-3

C. Fill in the blanks with "and", "or", or "but".

1. Who is your class teacher this year, Miss Sheldon _____ Mrs. Winsor?

2. This computer is old _____ it still functions well.

3. You can stay here _____ come with me.

4. Toronto is a big city _____ there are lots of high-rise buildings in downtown Toronto.

5. This storybook is interesting _____ it is full of colourful pictures too.

6. Ray wants to fly his kite _____ there is no wind.

D. Join the sentences using "and", "or", or "but".

1. I tried to call Tracy. Her line was busy.

   _____

   _____

2. I will get some snacks. You can prepare the drinks.

   _____

   _____

3. Put your shoes in the box. Leave them on the rug.

   _____

   _____

My Brother, the Babysitter

My big brother Colin is a babysitter. He is 15 years old. He always looks after me, and now he looks after my friends and classmates too.

Colin likes his job. He tries very <u>hard</u> to be a good babysitter. Last year, he took <u>special</u> classes at a babysitter school. He learned many important things there. He learned to ask the parents a lot of questions before they went out, like "Where are you going?", "When will you be <u>back</u>?", and "What is your cellphone number?" He also asks about fire exits and fire meeting <u>points</u>. Sometimes the parents do not know the answers so they make the rules together.

Colin keeps a list of all the important phone numbers, such as the numbers of the police department, the fire department, the family doctor, and another adult who lives nearby.

Colin knows how to help someone who is choking. He also knows what to do if someone gets cut or burned. He does not use the oven or the stove when he is babysitting.

The best thing Colin does when he is babysitting me is that he plays with me! His head is filled with ideas about fun things to do. My friends tell me that my brother is a great babysitter. I think so too.

ISBN: 978-1-77149-031-3

A. Check ✔ the correct meanings of the underlined words as they are used in the passage.

1. special

| A | not common |
| B | designed for a particular purpose |

2. back

| A | rear part of something |
| B | return |

3. hard

| A | with great effort |
| B | not soft |

4. points

| A | places |
| B | marks |

B. Answer the following questions.

1. How can you tell that Colin tries very hard to be a good babysitter?

_____

2. Write one question that Colin might ask the parents.

_____

3. Why does Colin avoid using the oven and the stove when he is babysitting? Give your opinion.

_____

_____

Forming Questions (1)

We can use "do", "does", "is", or "are" or their past form to begin a question.

Examples: <u>Is</u> your brother a babysitter too?

<u>Did</u> he take special babysitting classes?

C. Fill in the blanks with the correct words to form questions.

do   does   did   is
are   was   were

1. _____ your sister look after you when your parents are not at home?

2. _____ the children need babysitting?

3. _____ Sara good at looking after children?

4. _____ his parents there when you arrived at their place?

5. _____ you interested in learning to be a babysitter?

6. _____ you do well in last year's babysitting course?

7. _____ Carla five when you started babysitting her?

Forming Questions (2)

Words like "what", "when", "where", "which", "who", "why", and "how" can also be used in asking questions.

Examples: <u>Who</u> is Amy's family doctor?

<u>Which</u> number should I call first?

D. You will be babysitting Billy. Write the questions that you will ask his parents with the given words.

1. What

2. When

3. Where

4. Why

5. How

Most mammals, like dogs and whales, and people too, give birth to living babies. When the babies are born, they drink milk from the mother's body and grow quickly.

But marsupials are a unique kind of mammal. They are sometimes called "pouched mammals". This is because the mother has a pouch somewhere on her body. Marsupial babies are born differently from most other mammals. When they are born, they are still very tiny and unformed. They are born blind and hairless. The tiny marsupial baby crawls through its mother's fur to find her pouch. It is a dangerous journey.

Once the baby finds the pouch, it stays there and drinks milk until it is big and strong enough to live as a real baby animal. It starts to explore the world, but goes back into its mother's pouch when it wants to. The young marsupial continues to drink its mother's milk for a long time – even when it becomes too big to fit in its mother's cozy pouch!

Marsupials

There are many kinds of marsupials, but most of them live in Australia. Kangaroos, koalas, and wombats are the most well-known kinds of marsupials. There is only one kind of marsupial living in North America. It is called the opossum. They live mostly in forested areas and prairie grasslands. They are about the size of a cat. They hunt mostly at night, looking for small rodents, as well as insects, worms, fruits, seeds, and nuts.

 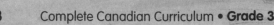

A. Put the sentences in order. Write 1 to 5.

____ The baby stays in the pouch.

____ A baby marsupial is born.

____ The baby finds its mother's pouch.

____ The baby goes out to explore the world.

____ The baby goes back to its mother's pouch.

B. Rewrite the sentences so that they are correct.

1. Marsupial babies are born blind with lots of hair.

_____

_____

2. The baby has to find its father's pouch on its own.

_____

_____

3. Most marsupials live in North America.

_____

_____

4. The opossum is about the size of a kangaroo.

_____

_____

Paragraphs

A **paragraph** is a group of sentences that express the same idea.

A good paragraph has a **topic sentence** which is usually the first sentence and introduces the main idea, and **supporting sentences** that add details to that idea.

C. **Put a line through the sentence that does not belong in each paragraph in the passage below.**

The Opossum

The opossum is a marsupial. The mother has a pouch, like a kangaroo. You cannot find other kinds of marsupials in Canada. It has a triangular head and a pointed nose. Its fur is grey, but its ears and tail are furless. It can hang from a tree limb on its long tail.

The opossum is a mammal. The mother gives birth to living babies. The opossum baby is very tiny when it is born. It is just the size of a honeybee. Honeybees are hard-working insects. It climbs through its mother's fur to her pouch. It stays there for about 60 days. Then it becomes strong enough to leave the pouch and see the world outside.

Opossums eat a wide variety of things. They like looking for food at night. They eat worms, snails, insects, and small animals like rodents. A spider is not an insect. They also eat the seeds, fruits, and nuts of different plants. They will even eat pet food.

ISBN: 978-1-77149-031-3

D. Write a topic sentence for each paragraph below.

1. _____

I met her when I was four. She was my neighbour and we were in the same kindergarten class. Although her family has moved, we still see each other often. I tell her my little secrets and she shares hers with me. We will stay best friends forever.

2. _____

You can find it on the Canadian flag. It has been on the penny since 1937. Tourists visiting Canada like to buy souvenirs with the maple leaf on them. People around the world will surely think of Canada when they see a maple leaf.

3. _____

My alarm clock did not work so I got up late. I missed the school bus and had to take the city bus instead. On the way, the bus broke down. It was just two blocks away from school so I decided to walk the remaining distance. When I was near my school, it suddenly rained heavily. I was soaked to the skin. To make matters worse, I found that I had left my bag on the bus. It was probably the worst day of my life.

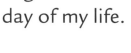

ISBN: 978-1-77149-031-3

SOCIAL STUDIES

ISBN: 978-1-77149-031-3

Communities between 1780 and 1850

The people of early Canada lived very differently from how we live today. Their experience of living in Canada was not the same as ours.

A. **Read about these groups of First Nations peoples. Then write about their similarities and differences.**

The Wendat

longhouse

The Wendat and the Anishnawbe were both First Nations groups, yet they lived differently from each other.

The Wendat lived together in large walled villages all year round. Several Wendat families lived in one longhouse. The Wendat took care of the land and they grew corn, squash, and beans.

The Anishnawbe moved each season to be close to the animals they hunted. They lived in small camps of dome-shaped homes that were called wigwams. These homes were made of natural materials. One family lived in each wigwam.

The Anishnawbe

wigwam

The Wendat and the Anishnawbe were both spiritual peoples connected to nature. Their clothing was made from tanned animal skins from the animals they hunted.

ISBN: 978-1-77149-031-3

Similarities

What group did they belong to?
In what way were they spiritual?
What did they wear?

The Wendat and the Anishnawbe

- both were 1._____

- 2._____

- 3._____

Differences

What type of house did they live in?
Did they move frequently?
Did they hunt or farm?

The Wendat

- many families lived together in a

  4._____

- 5._____

  _____

- 6._____

  _____

The Anishnawbe

- each family lived in their own

  7._____

- 8._____

  _____

- 9._____

  _____

B. **These two boys lived in early Canada, but they had different backgrounds. Match the descriptions with the correct boys.**

A His father was a European man and his mother was a First Nations woman.

B His father was a slave in the south, but Canada gave his family freedom to settle in Upper Canada.

a Métis boy

an African-American boy

Roles: Then and Now

Men, women, and children from the beginning of the nineteenth century had different roles in their communities than those we have today.

A. Read about the roles of these First Nations peoples. Match the roles with the correct people. Then write about the roles in your own family.

A "I respect the adults in my father's clan because it is my clan too. From my parents, I learn the skills I will need to survive and be a useful member of my community."

B "I take my older boys hunting and fishing. We work together to protect our family and community."

C "My daughters and I collect wild berries, nuts, and vegetables. We prepare the meat too."

We have different roles.

Our Family Roles

My dad: _____

My mom: _____

Myself: _____

ISBN: 978-1-77149-031-3

B. **Read about a day in the life of a girl living in Upper Canada in 1803. Then write a short diary entry to show how your day is different from hers.**

Dear Diary,

It was another long, hard day. My brothers, sisters, and I helped on the farm from morning until night. We dug up the soil because it had to be turned to be ready for planting.

Mother's dress was finally worn out so she decided to pull the stitching out and make new dresses from it for my sister and me. We carded wool and now we can dye it with the rhubarb and dandelions we collected.

Yours,
Anna Adams
1803

You can write about what you did at school and your chores at home.

Dear _____

_____

_____

_____

_____

_____

_____

_____

_____

Yours,

Early Canadian Travel

Early Canadians had different ways of travelling. They did not have the same ways of getting around as those we have today.

A. **Name the different means of travel. Then choose the best choices for the early Canadians. Write the letters.**

snowshoes　canoe　horse and cart

A

_____

B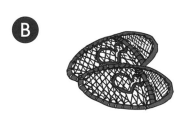

_____

C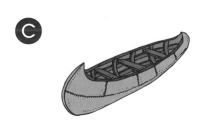

_____

1.

◯ a European fur trader

2.

◯ a First Nations person

3.

◯ early settlers

ISBN: 978-1-77149-031-3

B. Fill in the blanks.

Birchbark Canoes – an Important Means of Transportation

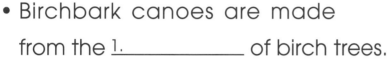

large   heavy   bark
lightweight   Fur Trade

- Birchbark canoes are made from the 1._____ of birch trees.

- Birch trees are ideal for making canoes because the bark comes off the trees in 2._____ pieces.

- The canoes are 3._____ , easy to construct, and able to carry 4._____ loads.

- Birchbark canoes were used by the traders in the 5._____ as they travelled around Canada hunting for fur.

C. Answer the question.

Back then, people used toboggans to carry people and small loads from place to place. What do we mainly use toboggans for today?

_____

_____

Adapting to the Climate

Canada's climate was a challenge to early Canadians. They did not have the same resources as we do today, but they learned to adapt to the climate.

A. Label the map. Then fill in the blanks.

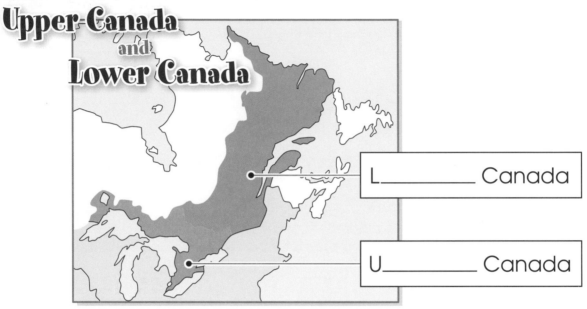

Upper Canada and Lower Canada

L_____ Canada

U_____ Canada

log   shelters   Upper   Lower   warm

The early settlers of 1._____ Canada had to survive colder winters than those in 2._____ Canada. They did not have the sturdy, warm homes that we have today, so they worked hard to build their 3._____ . They cleared the land to build 4._____ homes so that they could stay 5._____ in winter. It was a lot of hard work and they faced many challenges.

ISBN: 978-1-77149-031-3

B. **Match the sentences with the pictures to show how early settlers survived the winter. Write the letters.**

Challenges

Solutions

1. The cold froze their water. ◯

2. They could not travel easily to get food in the winter. ◯

3. They needed something to keep their bodies warm. ◯

A boiled water

B quilted blankets

C dried food

C. **List three details to show what an early settler, Susanna Moodie, wrote about the cold.**

The morning of the seventh was so terribly cold that everything liquid froze in the house. The wood that had been drawn for the fire was green, and it lit too slowly to stop the shivering of women and children; I grumbled about the fire out loud, where I tried to thaw frozen bread and to dress crying children...

How do we keep warm today?

• _____

• _____

• _____

_____

_____

_____

ISBN: 978-1-77149-031-3

Early Settlers' Challenges

Early Canadian settlements did not have the same support and resources that we have today. Most of them were isolated from other towns and early settlers faced many challenges.

A. An early settler had a series of challenges to overcome before having a home in Canada. Fill in the blanks and put the pictures in order.

Settling in Canada

 grant   log   ship   land

A

arriving safely by _____

B

building a _____ house

C

clearing the _____

D

A land grant is land given to the people by the government.

receiving a land _____

A series of challenges early settlers went through:

ISBN: 978-1-77149-031-3

B. **Read to see what type of support or resource each early settler needs. Write the letters.**

Support or Resource

A *a general store*   **B** *a teacher*

C *an officer of the law*   **D** *a doctor*

1. "My mother teaches me how to read while we rest from our work on the farm." ◯

2. "Thieves have stolen my chickens. I must block off the pen to prevent it from happening again!" ◯

3. "My little sister is very sick. We've given her soup but we do not know what else to do." ◯

4. ◯

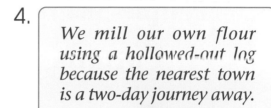

We mill our own flour using a hollowed-out log because the nearest town is a two-day journey away.

C. **Compare your lifestyle with that of early settlers. Write about what people do today.**

Water

Early settlers: Water was collected from springs or rivers.

People today: _____

Light

Early settlers: Candles and oil lamps were used for lighting.

People today: _____

Canadian Identity

Our Canadian identity, or who we are as Canadians, has been shaped by the people who came before us.

A. Fill in the blanks.

People Shaping Canada

English culture French
multicultural bilingual two

The French settled in Nova Scotia, bringing their culture and the 1._____ language to Canada. The British arrived in Newfoundland, and brought the 2._____ language from Britain. Today, Canada is 3._____ . It has 4._____ official languages.

Soon, more people from other countries came to Canada, each time bringing a new 5._____ . All of these different cultures have become part of the Canadian identity, making us a 6._____ country, which means we have many cultures.

B. **Look at the pictures of early Canadians. Connect them to the correct Canadian celebrations we have today. Write the letters.**

A — *We are no longer slaves. We are free now!*

B — *Jesus died and rose again for you.*

C — *Your traditional uses of plants are amazing!*

D — *I'm thankful that we have arrived safely.*

◯ Easter   ◯ Black History Month

◯ Thanksgiving Day   ◯ National Aboriginal Day

What is your favourite Canadian celebration? Why?

_____

_____

The Original Inhabitants

The original inhabitants of Canada were the First Nations peoples. For thousands of years, they have lived on the land we now call Canada.

A. **Read the paragraph. Write about the food sources of the original inhabitants and match the tools with the correct groups.**

The First Nations peoples got their food from the land. Some groups, like the Wendat, were good at farming. They planted crops such as corn, squash, and beans. Other groups, like the Anishnawbe, were great fishermen and hunters. They caught fish and hunted deer, buffalo, and rabbits.

Tools

snare

hoe

fishing net

wooden spade

Food Sources

The Wendat

Method: by _____

Food: _____

_____

Tools: _____

The Anishnawbe

Method: by _____

Food: _____

_____

Tools: _____

ISBN: 978-1-77149-031-3

B. **Fill in the blanks to complete what the people say. Then answer the question.**

sleds   rivers   children   hunting   baskets   women

Men: We play an important role in families. We are responsible for 1._____ and fishing. We also clear the land for our homes and crops. We make canoes and 2._____ .

Children: The girls usually follow the 3._____ and help with everyday chores like sewing and cooking meals. The boys follow the men to learn how to hunt and fish in the lakes and 4._____ .

Women: We take care of family life. We tend the crops, collect food, and cook meals. We also make household items like mats, 5._____ , and pots, as well as tools like fishing nets. We are the primary caretakers of the 6._____ .

7.   Do you think the life of the First Nations peoples was difficult? Explain.

_____

_____

Moving Out

When the European settlers arrived, they needed land to live on. The First Nations peoples agreed to move to different areas to make room for the new settlements.

A. **Answer the questions with the help of the map.**

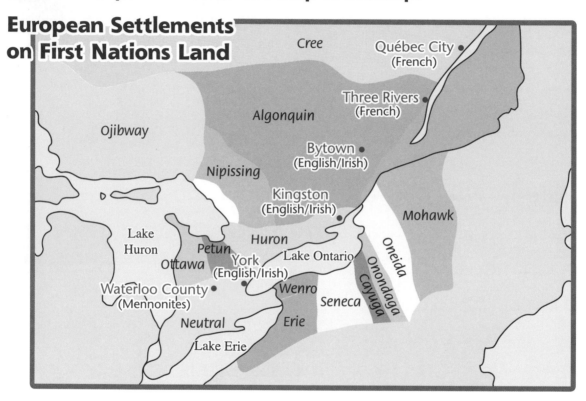

European Settlements on First Nations Land

Cree
Québec City (French)
Three Rivers (French)
Algonquin
Ojibway
Bytown (English/Irish)
Nipissing
Kingston (English/Irish)
Mohawk
Lake Huron
Huron
Oneida
Petun
Ottawa
York (English/Irish)
Lake Ontario
Onondaga
Cayuga
Waterloo County (Mennonites)
Wenro
Seneca
Neutral
Erie
Lake Erie

1. List three First Nations tribes that lived near Lake Ontario.

_____

_____

_____

2. Name the English/Irish settlements.

_____

_____

_____

3. Name the First Nations peoples and Europeans who lived in:

       Waterloo County   Three Rivers

_____ _____   _____ _____

B. **Fill in the blanks. Then circle "T" if the statement is true or "F" if it is false.**

money   land   reserves
agreements   farming

When the European settlers arrived, they looked for land to settle. The First Nations peoples signed 1._____ stating that they would give parts of their 2._____ to the settlers. The settlers then used this land for housing and 3._____ . In return, the First Nations peoples received 4._____ and protection, and lands called 5._____ were set aside for their use.

6. The agreements stated that the First Nations peoples would give up all of their land.   T / F

7. The settlers built their homes on the land given by the First Nations peoples.   T / F

8. The First Nations peoples got money and protection from the Europeans.   T / F

9. Reserves were areas where the First Nations peoples and the settlers lived together.   T / F

Settling the Land

Europeans saw that Canada was a beautiful country that was rich in resources. They came to settle in the land and make new homes for themselves.

A. **Imagine that you are a European looking for a new place to settle. What kind of land would you want? Check the letters.**

My new land should:

(A) have water nearby for drinking and watering crops.

(B) be surrounded by beautiful mountains for scenery.

(C) be flat with fertile soil for farming.

(D) have trees nearby to be used for building.

(E) have a nice environment for growing flowers.

(F) have easy access to a waterway.

B. **The map shows early settlements in Upper Canada. From what you learned in (A), explain why you think the settlers chose these areas.**

Water is one of our basic needs!

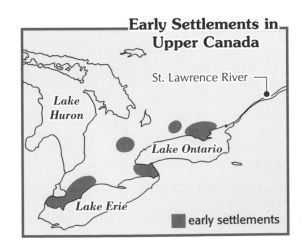

Early Settlements in Upper Canada

St. Lawrence River

Lake Huron

Lake Ontario

Lake Erie

■ early settlements

_____

_____

_____

ISBN: 978-1-77149-031-3

C. **Put the sentences in order to show how settlers started their settlements.**

(A) received tools for building and clearing land

(B) built homes and farm buildings, sowed seeds

(C) cleared land and chopped trees

(D) received land grants

(E) harvested crops

Many settlers, like me, became farmers when we settled in Canada.

Starting a Settlement

☐ — ☐ — ☐ — ☐ — ☐

D. **Write "Men", "Women", or "Children" to show how different family members helped in early Canada.**

Farm life was difficult for settlers. Everyone in the family had to help and the farm required a lot of hard work. Men were usually responsible for the physically demanding tasks. Women usually took care of food and household chores. Children helped by gathering or collecting things.

1.

2.

3.

- planting crops
- cooking food

- gathering food
- feeding farm animals

- ploughing fields
- chopping wood

10

Changing the Environment

The new people who came to Canada had a significant impact on the land and the people already living there.

A. Read the passage. Then fill in the blanks.

Trading Post

The Europeans learned that the First Nations peoples not only provided fresh food for trading, but they also had valuable fur. As the Europeans wanted to sell fur in Europe, they set up trading posts along the St. Lawrence River to trade with the First Nations peoples. They also cleared land to build homes and farms. As a result, many animals lost their habitats.

With more and more trading posts being set up, the First Nations peoples were forced to move elsewhere to settle and find food. They could no longer live near rivers where fish and other resources were abundant. Their way of life changed because hunting was no longer just for food, but it was also for fur to trade with the Europeans in exchange for goods such as pots, cloth, and metal tools. As fur became harder to find in some areas, conflicts broke out among various First Nations groups who were all scrambling for hunting grounds.

ISBN: 978-1-77149-031-3

Impacts of the Europeans

- set up _____ posts to trade goods
- cleared _____ for their homes and _____

Lifestyle

- _____ out of their land because of growing European settlements

- had to find new areas to _____ animals for food and fur due to overhunting

Conflict

- fought for _____ grounds

- had to hunt for more _____ to trade

Natural Environment

- lands were _____ to build new settlements

- _____ populations dropped due to hunting and destroyed habitats

B. **Put the pictures in order from 1 to 3 to show how a new European settlement affected First Nations communities.**

11

Hardships

Life became complicated when the Europeans came to Canada. Both the First Nations peoples and the Europeans faced hardships. They faced diseases, shortage of resources, and conflicts.

A. Read the paragraph. Then complete the diagram.

Europeans travelled to Canada by ship. While travelling, many of them caught scurvy, a disease caused by not eating enough fruits and vegetables. The First Nations peoples gave the Europeans their cure for scurvy, which was a tea they made with crushed cedar and spruce needles. Unfortunately, the First Nations peoples themselves caught diseases such as small pox, measles, and diphtheria from the Europeans. Many First Nations peoples died because they did not have any cures for these new diseases.

showed the Europeans their cure for
1. _____

the First Nations

suffered from scurvy because of the lack of fruits and
2. _____ in their diet

caught new diseases from the Europeans and many First Nations peoples
4. _____

the Europeans

brought 3. _____ such as small pox and measles to the First Nations peoples

ISBN: 978-1-77149-031-3

B. **Fill in the blanks to complete the paragraph. Then answer the questions.**

animals   fur   metal   overhunting

Trading soon began between the First Nations peoples and the Europeans. The Europeans traded clothing and 1._____ goods such as pots and knives, and the First Nations peoples traded 2._____ . Trading fur quickly led to 3._____ and soon, animals began to disappear. This had a significant impact on the First Nations peoples because they needed 4._____ for food, clothing, and tools.

5. How did the decreasing animal populations affect the First Nations peoples?

_____

_____

6. The areas where the First Nations peoples could hunt were reduced. Why do you think this caused conflicts among the different First Nations tribes?

_____

_____

12

Getting along Together

People from different cultures lived together in early Canada. Sometimes they helped one another, but other times, they did not get along.

A. Write the letters to show what each group shared with the other.

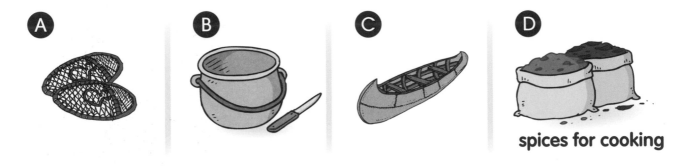

(A) (B) (C) (D) spices for cooking

(E) new ways of planting and harvesting

(F) hunting and trapping methods

(G) travel routes in Canada

(H) natural medicine

(I) education

(J) religion

What They Shared

The First Nations

The Europeans

ISBN: 978-1-77149-031-3

B. **Fill in the blanks to complete the letter. Then answer the questions.**

*In early Canada, not everybody got along with one another. The **Black Loyalists**, for example, had a hard time living amongst the other settlers. The Black Loyalists were slaves who fought for Britain during the American Revolution. In return, they were promised land and freedom. After the war, many of them went to Nova Scotia.*

equal   lower   poor   land
last   Sierra Leone (a place in Africa)

Dear John,

It is hard starting a new life in this place. First, I had to wait over a year to receive the 1._____ *I was promised. And when I finally received it, the land was in* 2._____ *condition; it was dry, rocky, and infertile.*

The other settlers are not welcoming. They do not treat me as an 3._____ . *I am the* 4._____ *to receive food and supplies. And my wages are much* 5._____ *than theirs.*

Life is not easy here. I am going on a boat that will take me to 6._____ . *Perhaps life will be better there.*

Richard

7. Write two examples of how the Black Loyalists were treated unfairly.

_____

_____

13

Mapping Ontario

A map can show us a lot about the land that it represents. A map of Ontario gives information about its different regions.

A. Look at the map of North America. Answer the questions.

1. Trace to show the boundaries of Canada's provinces and territories.

ARCTIC OCEAN

PACIFIC OCEAN

CANADA

High Level
Inukjuak

ALBERTA
Edmonton

QUÉBEC

ONTARIO

2. Match the following with the labelling styles.

Thunder Bay
Québec City

Toronto

ATLANTIC OCEAN

cities   oceans
countries provinces
capital cities

UNITED STATES

a. _____ : largest, black capital letters in bold

b. _____ : large blue capital letters

c. _____ / territories: medium-sized black capital letters in bold

d. _____ : red dots

e. _____ : black dots

ISBN: 978-1-77149-031-3

3. Why are there different styles of letters on maps?

_____

4. Rewrite each name using the correct style of letters.

China

_____

Nova Scotia

_____

Indian Ocean

_____

Northwest Territories

_____

Barrie (a city in Ontario)

_____

B. Look at the map of Ontario. Then answer the questions.

1. Name the cities and draw the symbols used to indicate them.

The capital city of Canada

_____ ; ☐

The capital city of Ontario

_____ ; ☐

A city in Ontario

_____ ; ☐

Fort Severn

ONTARIO

Neskantaga

Moosonee

Thunder Bay   Timmins

Sault Ste. Marie

Ottawa ★

LAKE HURON

Toronto

LAKE ONTARIO

Windsor

LAKE ERIE

2. Lake Superior is northwest of Lake Huron. Use the correct style of letters to label it on the map.

14

Ontario's Landforms

Ontario has different landforms, each with its special characteristics and unique physical features that favour different human activities.

A. **Colour to complete the map to show Ontario's landforms. Answer the questions.**

Landform Regions of Ontario

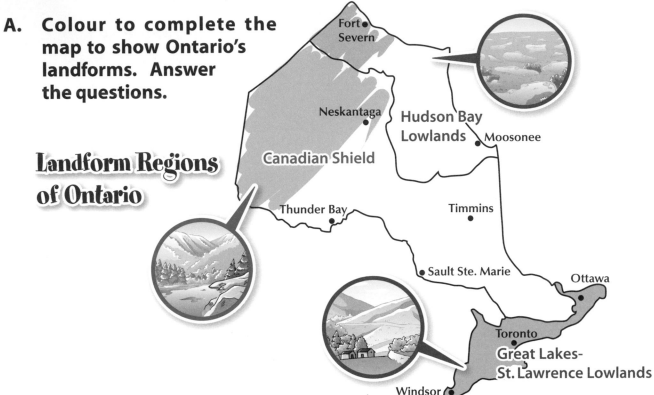

Fort Severn

Neskantaga

Hudson Bay Lowlands · Moosonee

Canadian Shield

Thunder Bay

Timmins

· Sault Ste. Marie

Ottawa

Toronto

Great Lakes-St. Lawrence Lowlands

Windsor

1. How many landforms are there?

_____

2. Which region is

   a. the largest?

   _____

   b. the smallest?

   _____

3. Name a city that is located in each region.

   Hudson Bay Lowlands:

   _____

   Canadian Shield:

   _____

   Great Lakes-St. Lawrence Lowlands:

   _____

ISBN: 978-1-77149-031-3

B. **Read about the characteristics of the landforms. Fill in the blanks.**

Landforms in Ontario

Canadian Shield	marshes	mining
minerals	fishing	fertile	plains
agriculture	bedrock	polar bears

Hudson Bay Lowlands

- many lakes, rivers, and 1._____

- animals: caribou and 2._____

- human activities: hunting and 3._____

. . . .

4._____

- ancient 5._____ and forests

- lots of 6._____ like gold and silver

- animals: black bears, lynx, and moose

- human activities: 7._____ and logging

. . . .

Great Lakes-St. Lawrence Lowlands

- many hills and flat 8._____

- 9._____ soil

- animals: raccoons, deer, and beavers

- human activities: 10._____ and manufacturing

ISBN: 978-1-77149-031-3

15

Where People Live

People are drawn to live in different areas of Ontario. Some people live in Northern Ontario and some live in Southern Ontario. Each region has its own unique features.

Look at the map. Answer the questions.

Most Populated Cities, Reserves, and Land Use in Ontario in 2011

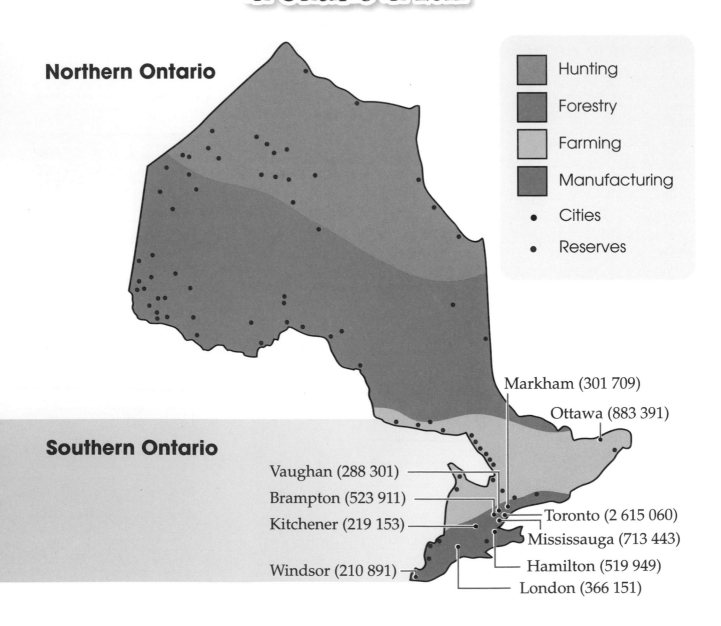

Northern Ontario

Legend:
- Hunting
- Forestry
- Farming
- Manufacturing
- • Cities
- • Reserves

Markham (301 709)

Ottawa (883 391)

Southern Ontario

Vaughan (288 301)

Brampton (523 911)

Kitchener (219 153)

Toronto (2 615 060)

Mississauga (713 443)

Hamilton (519 949)

Windsor (210 891)

London (366 151)

ISBN: 978-1-77149-031-3

1. The three most populated cities in Ontario and their populations:

_____ | _____ | _____

Population: Population: Population:

2. Write about the land use. Then fill in the blanks with the given words.

populated   natural   wilderness   winter

Northern Ontario

Land use:

_____

_____

Features:

remote _____

more _____ resources

Southern Ontario

Land use:

_____

_____

Features:

densely _____

relatively shorter and warmer

_____

3. Where are the most populated cities located? Do you know why?

_____

_____

4. Where are the reserves located? Do you know why?

_____

_____

16

Enjoying Ontario Today

Ontario is a big and beautiful province with many valuable features. There are many things people can do on this land.

A. Look at the beautiful parks in Ontario. Fill in the blanks to complete the descriptions.

Toronto   skiing   variety   Thunder Bay   hiking   recreational

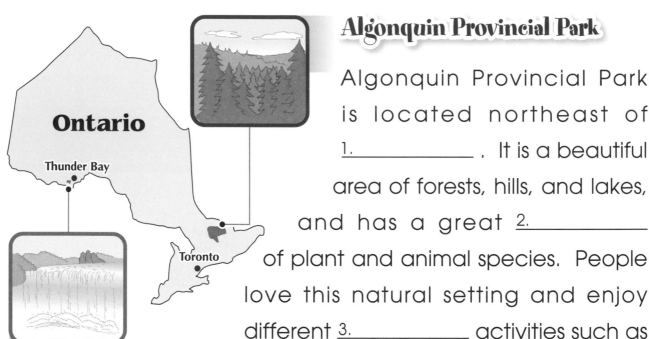

Algonquin Provincial Park

Algonquin Provincial Park is located northeast of 1._____ . It is a beautiful area of forests, hills, and lakes, and has a great 2._____ of plant and animal species. People love this natural setting and enjoy different 3._____ activities such as camping, hiking, and horseback riding.

Kakabeka Falls Provincial Park

Kakabeka Falls Provincial Park is southwest of the city of 4._____ . It has the second highest waterfall in Ontario. The waterfall is steep and powerful. People enjoy 5._____ in summer and cross-country 6._____ in winter there.

ISBN: 978-1-77149-031-3

B. **Ontario is a great place that supports different activities. Fill in the blanks and match the activities with the places in Ontario.**

Activities in Ontario

A transporting goods by ship

B growing crops and raising cattle

C growing grapes

D downhill skiing

E snowmobiling

Places in Ontario

Blue Mountain   North Ontario forests

Niagara vineyards   Thunder Bay Port

Lake Ontario

1.

farmland
near _____

2.

_____

3.

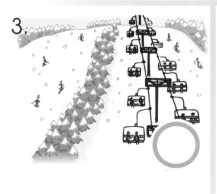

_____

4.

_____

5.

_____

Working in Ontario Today

Different areas in Ontario offer different kinds of jobs. People have many choices of work in Ontario.

A. Read what the people say about their jobs. Name their jobs. Then match them with the correct places in Ontario.

chef   tour guide   factory worker

Places in Ontario

1.

I take tourists close to the Falls. They like to see the beautiful nature this place has to offer.

_____ ; ◯

A

Dryden

2.

I work at a paper mill. We get wood from the many forests in our area.

_____ ; ◯

B

Niagara Falls

3.

I work in a restaurant. My city is diverse and people can try many different cuisines.

_____ ; ◯

C

Toronto

ISBN: 978-1-77149-031-3

B. **Look at the graph of Eric's work hours for his three different jobs throughout the year. Then answer the questions.**

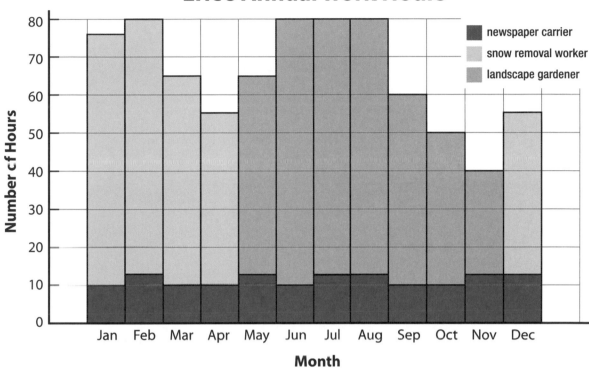

Eric's Annual Work Hours

1. How many months of the year did Eric work as

   a. a newspaper carrier?

   _____ months

   b. a snow removal worker?

   _____ months

   c. a landscape gardener?

   _____ months

2. Which of Eric's jobs are dependent on the seasons?

   _____

   _____

3. Think of a job that can only be done in

   a. summer _____

   b. winter _____

ISBN: 978-1-77149-031-3

Ontario's Valuable Land

People depend on Ontario's land for many reasons. It is used for housing, farming, commerce, industry, transportation, and recreation.

A. Fill in the blanks. Then draw lines to match the different types of land use in Ontario with the pictures.

commercial   agricultural   residential
recreational   transportation

Land Use

1. _____ •
   farming

2. _____ •
   business

3. _____ •
   sports and leisure

4. _____ •
   travel

5. _____ •
   housing

commercial buildings in Toronto

apple orchard in Newmarket

Wasaga Beach in Simcoe County

Burlington townhouse development

Highway 11/17 in Thunder Bay

ISBN: 978-1-77149-031-3

B. **Colour the Oak Ridges Moraine green. Then fill in the blanks to complete what Sarah Winterton says about Ontario's Greenbelt.**

People make good use of the valuable land in Ontario. They work together to protect its green spaces from development. Conservation areas are protected lands that provide natural habitats for plants and animals.

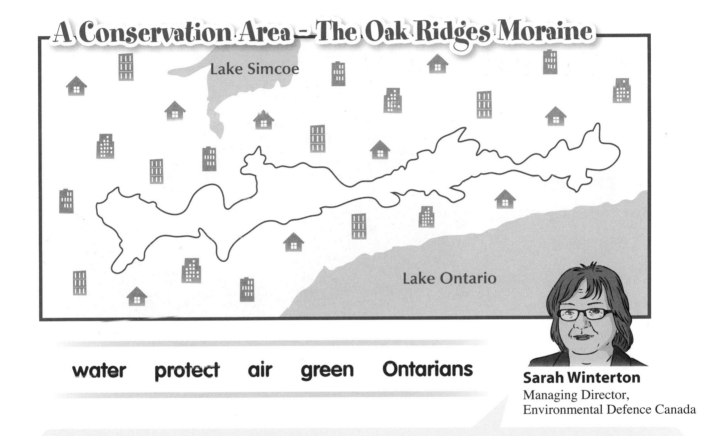

A Conservation Area – The Oak Ridges Moraine

Lake Simcoe

Lake Ontario

water   protect   air   green   Ontarians

Sarah Winterton
Managing Director,
Environmental Defence Canada

Ontario's Greenbelt* plays a vital role in protecting our 1._____ spaces, wetlands, drinking 2._____ , and working farmland. Thanks to the new urban river valley designation, the Greenbelt can now permanently 3._____ urban river valleys. This will enable the Greenbelt to grow and continue to clean our 4._____ and water, and connect millions of 5._____ to the jewel that is Ontario's Greenbelt.

*The Oak Ridges Moraine is a part of Ontario's Greenbelt.

Using Our Land

The natural resources in Ontario are valuable. We must be responsible in the ways and amounts that we use them.

A. Read about the boreal forest. Then fill in the blanks.

The Boreal Forest

habitat
quarters
west
dominant
wood
recreational

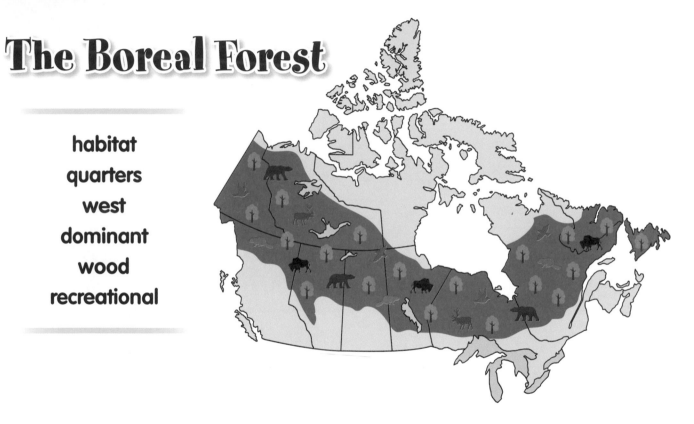

The boreal forest is the 1._____ forest region in Canada. It runs across Canada from 2._____ to east and makes up more than three 3._____ of the country's total forest area. The boreal forest plays the important role of providing a 4._____ for different animal and plant species. It also provides resources for valuable 5._____ products. The boreal forest offers many job opportunities and 6._____ activities.

ISBN: 978-1-77149-031-3

B. **Read about deforestation.
Then answer the questions.**

Deforestation means clearing a section of a forest and using that area for things such as logging, building roads, growing crops, and raising cattle.

1. What are the reasons for deforestation?

   To reduce the damaging effects of deforestation, people either let the area regenerate on its own or plant seedlings if natural regeneration cannot occur.

   _____

   _____

2. When deforestation takes place, how does it affect each of the following?

   animals: _____

   plants: _____

   people: _____

3. What will happen if, one day, all forests are cleared?

   _____

   _____

4. What are people doing to lessen the effects of deforestation?

   _____

   _____

Using Our Resources

When we use Ontario's resources, we impact our environment. As residents of Ontario, we have the responsibility of keeping it clean and healthy.

Read about mining. Then answer the questions.

Mining in Ontario

Mining is an important industry in Ontario. People get many precious resources such as gold, copper, and nickel through mining. However, mining has negative impacts on the environment. Building new roads and power lines changes the landscape around the mining sites. Plants and wildlife lose their habitats when forests are cleared. Mining also produces lots of toxic chemicals that contaminate our water and soil.

Since mining causes so many environmental issues, our government has imposed different regulations to monitor all mining activities and ensure that the mining companies do not damage the surrounding environment too much. Mining companies are required to make plans for mine reclamation even before their mining sites begin to operate. They have to rehabilitate their mining sites afterwards by covering landfills with soil and restoring vegetation to the site. This action will bring the site back to life and may allow the land to be restored to its original state.

1. What do people get from mining?

   _____

2. What are the negative environmental impacts of mining?

   on land: _____

   on plants and wildlife: _____

   on water and soil: _____

3. What do mining companies do to help bring a mining site back to life?

   Step 1 _____

   Step 2 _____

4. Put the pictures in order to show the change at a mining site.

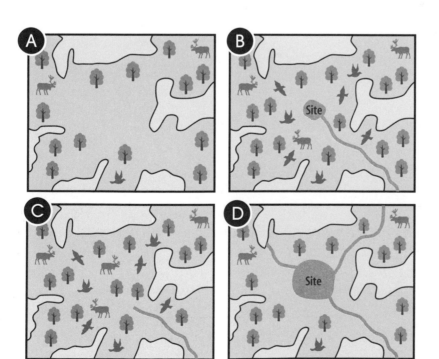

From **Mining** to **Rehabilitation**

21

Developing the Land

As our cities grow, land is further developed to meet the needs of people. This growth affects our environment, so people work hard to minimize the impact.

A. Look at the map of the Greater Toronto Area. Trace the boundary of the City of Toronto. Then answer the questions.

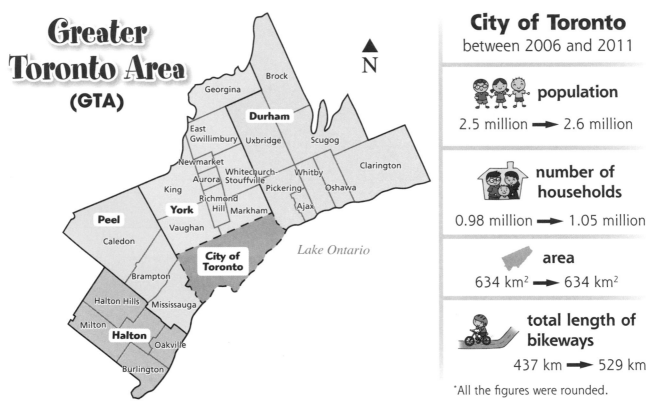

Greater Toronto Area (GTA)

Brock
Georgina
Durham
East Gwillimbury
Uxbridge
Scugog
Newmarket
Whitechurch-Stouffville
Whitby
Clarington
Aurora
Pickering
Oshawa
King
Richmond Hill
York
Markham
Ajax
Vaughan
Peel
Caledon
City of Toronto
Lake Ontario
Brampton
Halton Hills
Mississauga
Milton
Halton
Oakville
Burlington

N

City of Toronto
between 2006 and 2011

population
2.5 million ➝ 2.6 million

number of households
0.98 million ➝ 1.05 million

area
634 km² ➝ 634 km²

total length of bikeways
437 km ➝ 529 km

*All the figures were rounded.

1. Name two neighbouring cities of the City of Toronto.

_____

2. *Since all the cities on the map are already developed with homes and businesses, it is difficult for Toronto to expand into those cities. Do you think it is possible for Toronto to grow further to its south? Why?*

_____

ISBN: 978-1-77149-031-3

3. Write how the City of Toronto changed in the following areas between 2006 and 2011.

- population: _____
- no. of households: _____

- area: _____
- total length of bikeways: _____

4. What did the City of Toronto do to encourage people to ride bikes in order to reduce traffic congestion and air pollution?

_____

B. Label the different means of transportation in the City of Toronto. Then answer the question.

1. **airplane   train   bike   car   subway**

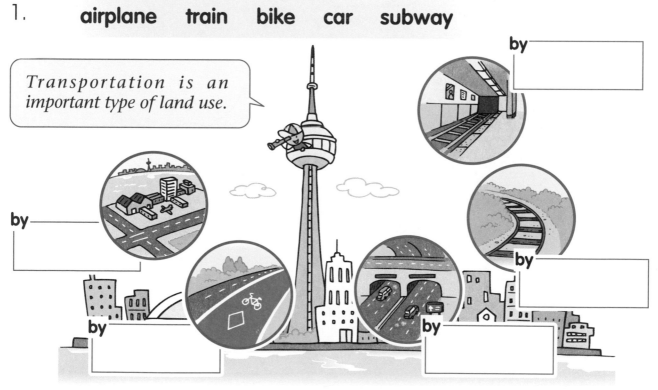

Transportation is an important type of land use.

by _____
by _____
by _____
by _____
by _____

2. Some people carpool to commute. Why do you think this is a good idea?

_____

22

Local Governments

Ontario is divided into many municipalities. Municipalities can be cities, towns, townships, villages, counties, or reserves. The Ontario government and municipal (local) governments work together to deal with issues in Ontario.

A. **Fill in the blanks to complete the names of the municipalities in Ontario. Then answer the questions.**

1.

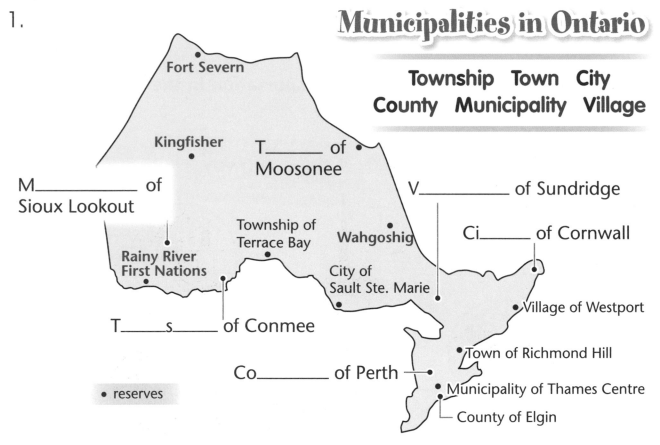

Municipalities in Ontario

Township   Town   City
County   Municipality   Village

- Fort Severn
- Kingfisher
- T_____ of Moosonee
- M_____ of Sioux Lookout
- V_____ of Sundridge
- Township of Terrace Bay
- Wahgoshig
- Ci_____ of Cornwall
- Rainy River First Nations
- City of Sault Ste. Marie
- T_____s_____ of Conmee
- Village of Westport
- Co_____ of Perth
- Town of Richmond Hill
- Municipality of Thames Centre
- County of Elgin

• reserves

2. Name two reserves in Ontario.

_____

3. *Research your community. Which municipality do you live in?*

_____

B. Fill in the blanks to tell about the roles of the Ontario government and municipal governments. Then write which government is responsible for each service.

> mayor   province   local   police   streets   premier   health

Provincial Government of Ontario

- takes care of the needs of the _____ ,

  such as education, _____ , culture,

  natural resources, tourism, transportation,

  and First Nations relations

- the head of the government: p_____

Municipal Government

- handles _____ issues and needs,

  such as fire, ambulance, and _____

  services, parks and recreation facilities,

  water supply, _____ and roads,

  public transportation, and municipal land use

- the head of the government: m_____

The government responsible for:

Education

_____ government

_____ government

Transportation

_____ government

Reserves have band councils. A band council represents a First Nations group and is chaired by a chief. Bands can be grouped together into larger regional groups called tribal councils and these councils govern their own reserves.

23

Municipal Lands

Towns and cities have different types of land use. Land use depends on the needs of the community.

A. Read the passage. Label the two municipalities on the map. Then complete the chart and answer the questions.

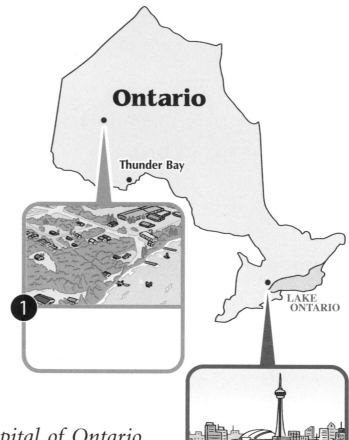

The **Township of Pickle Lake** is northwest of Thunder Bay and is one of the most northerly communities in Ontario. Pickle Lake, with just over 400 residents, is a remote township that is accessible by Highway 599. It is surrounded by many lakes and forests. There are gold and copper mining sites in Pickle Lake. Some fun things to do in Pickle Lake are fishing and animal-watching, such as watching moose, caribou, and black bears.

The **City of Toronto** is the capital of Ontario and the most populous city in the province. It is located northwest of Lake Ontario. Toronto, with a population of over 2.5 million, has a huge commercial area with many businesses operating in the downtown area. The Toronto Transit Commission (TTC) serves as the main public transportation system, providing bus, streetcar, and subway services. There are also many highways and expressways running through the city. In Toronto, people enjoy various indoor and outdoor activities, such as indoor rock-climbing, biking, and hiking.

3.

Land Use		Pickle Lake (a little / a lot / none)	Toronto
	Residential		
	Commercial		
	Mining		
	Recreational		
	Transportation		

4.

How does population affect the types of land use in a community?

_____

_____

B. Different types of communities have different types of housing. Draw the suitable type of housing for each place.

City of Toronto

Township of Pickle Lake

ISBN: 978-1-77149-031-3

24

Municipal Jobs

Different types of communities offer different types of jobs. These jobs depend on the characteristics of each community.

A. **Read the newspaper. Identify the different kinds of jobs. Then write the letters.**

JOBS

A **Taxpayer Services Advisor**

works for Canada Revenue Agency answering business enquiries on tax issues

B **ESL Teacher**

teaches English to elementary school students

C **Park Warden**

protects natural, cultural, and historical resources of the park

D **Mineral Resources Specialist**

implements mineral development programs and resource management

E **City Planner**

works closely with the city council to design and implement city plans

F **Mine Geologist**

does underground mapping to identify the locations of minerals

Jobs in

Education: _____   Mining Industry: _____

Government: _____   Recreational Industry: _____

B. Read (A) again. Then answer the questions.

1. Which jobs are dependent on natural resources?

    _____

2. In which place is each job offered? Why do you think so?

    Job B

    around **Pickle Lake / Toronto**

    because _____

    _____

    Job D

    around **Pickle Lake / Toronto** because _____

    _____

C. Look at the map in (B) again. Then suggest three places for each person.

I want to be a financial advisor. Where can I go for this type of job?

I love the wilderness. Where can I go for more job opportunities related to nature?

_____   _____

_____   _____

_____   _____

ISBN: 978-1-77149-031-3

ISBN: 978-1-77149-031-3

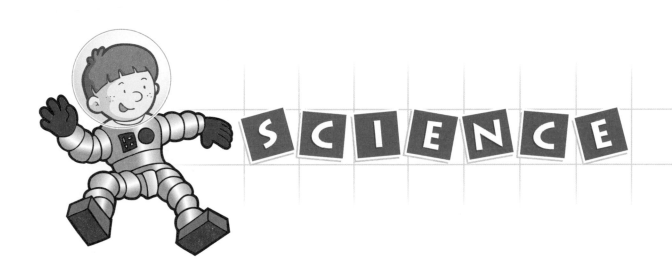

SCIENCE

ISBN: 978-1-77149-031-3

1

Plants

- Different parts of a plant work together to make a healthy plant.
- Different kinds of plants have parts that do the same job, but they may not look alike.
- A tree can be described as broadleaf or coniferous.

A. Write the correct part of a plant on the line.

stem   flower   roots   leaves

This is the 1._____
It is sweet, not sour
Making seeds for new plants
Is the flower's power

These are the 2._____
The greens that breathe
Food for the plant
Is what they achieve

This is the 3._____
That's holding them
Food up and food down
From end to end

These are the 4._____
Like spongy boots
They take water and food
To send up to the shoots

B. Label the parts of the plant.

stem
leaf
root
flower

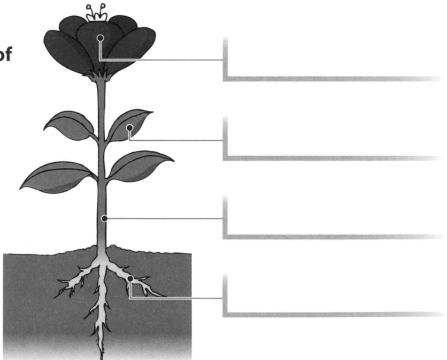

ISBN: 978-1-77149-031-3

C. Unscramble the words to name the parts of a tree. Then draw lines to match the names with the parts.

1. arbk   b_____ •

2. nuktr   t_____ •

3. veales   l_____ •

4. troos   r_____ •

5. abrchnse   b_____ •

D. Match each description with the correct type of tree. Write the letter.

Broadleaf Tree

Coniferous Tree

A most have leaves that change colour in the fall

B often have needle-shaped leaves

C deciduous trees belong to this group

D most are evergreen

E seeds found in cones

F have wide, flat leaves

 **Science Fact**

Trees are the largest kind of plant. While some trees will never be as tall as you, there are others that are taller than a 15-storey building!

Leaves and Flowers

- Although leaves have different shapes and sizes, they do the same job.
- Each part of a flower has a different job to do.

A. **Draw the other half of each leaf. Then match the leaf with the name of the plant. Write the letter.**

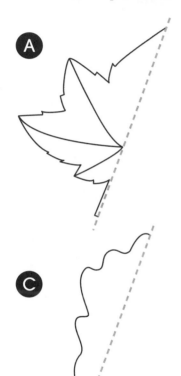

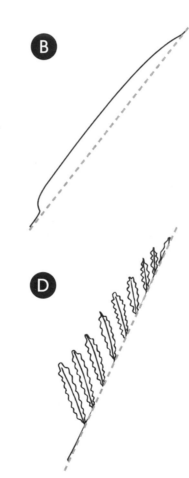

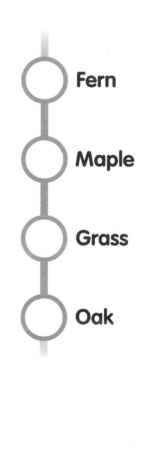

Ⓐ

Ⓑ

Ⓒ

Ⓓ

Fern

Maple

Grass

Oak

B. **Match the descriptions with the plants above. Write the names of the plants on the lines.**

1. These long and narrow leaves grow outward all season. _____

2. The leaves of this plant unfold from a coiled position when they first appear. _____

ISBN: 978-1-77149-031-3

C. Use the flower clues and the given words to complete the names of the parts of the flower. Then answer the questions.

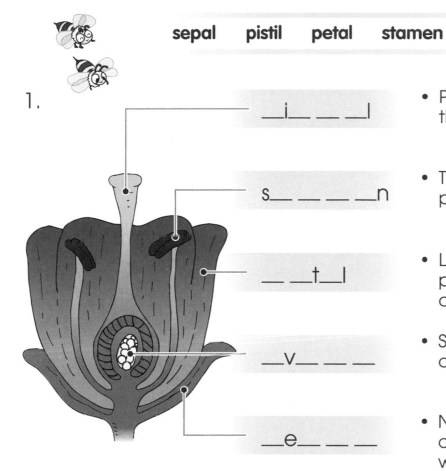

sepal   pistil   petal   stamen   ovary

1.

__i__ __ __l

- Pollen reaches the ovary through this stalk.

s__ __ __ __n

- This is the pollen-producing part.

__ __t__l

- Like a colourful leaf, this protects the flower and attracts pollinators.

__v__ __ __

- Seeds form here if pollination occurs.

__e__ __ __

- Now at the flower's base, it covered the flower when it was just a bud.

2.

Which part of the flower is at the base of the pistil and is a place for seed development?

_____

3.

Which part of the flower is usually green and protects the bud?

_____

Science Fact

Some plants have special leaves that are not flowers but look like them. The true flowers of the dogwood tree and poinsettia are barely visible inside their colourful imposters.

poinsettia

The Needs of Plants

- Plants need air, light, and water to live and be healthy.
- Plants have adapted ways of getting what they need from their environment.

A. **The children are talking about what plants need.** **Unscramble the letters to find the answers.**

1.

   It goes in and out of the plant through special parts of the leaf. Without it, leaves cannot use light to make food. What is it?

   r i a

   _____

2.

   It enters plants through their roots in the ground. It helps take nutrients to all parts of the plant. What is it?

   a w t r e

   _____

3.

   It comes from the sun. Leaves use it to make food. What is it?

   t g h l i

   _____

Experiment

Completely cover a plant leaf by folding a piece of black construction paper over it. Attach a piece of tape to keep it closed. After a few days look underneath the paper.

What does the leaf look like? Of the three things a plant needs, what could not reach that part of the leaf?

ISBN: 978-1-77149-031-3

B. **Write the correct words to complete the sentences. Then show where each plant belongs. Write the letter.**

1.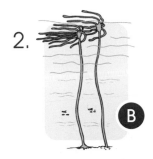

   Cacti have thin _____ that retain water,
   <u>leaves/flowers</u>
   and _____ stems that store water.
   <u>thin/thick</u>
   Because of this, they do not need a regular
   source of water.

2.

   Bull kelp has an air-filled bulb that will
   _____ on the ocean's surface. This is
   <u>float/walk</u>
   how the leaves get _____ .
   <u>water/sunlight</u>

3.

   These plants grow in clumps close to the
   _____ . They protect themselves from
   <u>ground/tree</u>
   cold and wind this way.

4.

   The trillium grows, flowers, and dies within the
   first few weeks of spring before emerging tree
   _____ completely shade the forest floor.
   <u>roots/leaves</u>

| alpine | desert | water | woodland |
| ○ | ○ | ○ | ○ |

Science Fact

Plants can "move". The leaves of a houseplant move to face a window, and sunflowers follow the daily movement of the sun.

Plants: Pollination

- When the pollen from one plant's stamen reaches the pistil of another, pollination occurs. The pollinated plant can now produce seeds capable of growing into new plants.
- Animals and wind are the pollinators of some plants.

A. Find the most likely pollinator for each plant. Write the answer on the line.

hummingbird   wind
moth   bee   butterfly

1. Because this pollinator works in the evening, easily seen white flowers are a favourite.

   _____

2. This pollinator likes to land on the bright flower clusters of this plant.

   _____

3. This pollinator is attracted to bright pumpkin flowers which are yellow like itself.

   _____

4. The silk of the corn plant is slightly sticky at pollination time. It makes it easier to "catch" the pollen.

   _____

5. The fuchsia's pollinator must reach the nectar through the long, narrow blossom.

   _____

ISBN: 978-1-77149-031-3

B. **Fill in the blanks with the given words. Then find the examples of flowers for each kind of pollination.**

animals   wind
small   colours

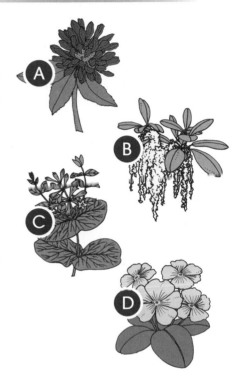

Animal pollination:

• The flowers pollinated by _____ always have bright _____ , strong scents, and sweet nectar.

• Examples: _____

Wind pollination:

• The flowers pollinated by_____ are always _____ and not colourful.

• Examples: _____

C. **Find the correct word to match each description.**

stamen	pistil	pollen	scent	nectar	seed

1. _____ – tiny grains made by the stamen

2. _____ – the part of the flower that makes pollen

3. _____ – the part of the flower that receives pollen

4. _____ – what develops when pollination occurs

5. _____ – the smell that attracts animals to flowers

6. _____ – a rewarding drink for pollinating animals

 **Science Fact**

Pollination is not just good for flowers. Honey is made from the nectar collected by honeybees while they pollinate.

Seed Dispersal

Seed dispersal.

- Seeds spread themselves around so they do not all grow in the same area. This is called seed dispersal.
- Plants have developed different ways of dispersing their seeds.

A.   Match the seed with the method of dispersal. Write the letter.

A Like parachutes, they are carried by a breeze.

B Eaten by animals, they are eventually deposited far away.

C The seeds are forcefully expelled from the pod.

D Floating to its new home, it is carried away by ocean currents.

E It hitches a ride with a furry animal or a fuzzy shoe.

F With its helicopter wings, it spins to the ground.

G Rolling like a wheel, its seeds travel far.

ISBN: 978-1-77149-031-3

B. **Put the sentences in the correct order to show how the seeds are dispersed. Write 1 to 3. Then tell what method each plant uses to disperse its seeds.**

1

○ A ripe berry drops onto the water, floating to its new home.

○ Water levels rise around a maturing cranberry bush.

○ The water recedes, the berry seed germinates, and a new cranberry bush sprouts.

by _____

2

○ Fluffy hairs on the seeds allow even a small breeze to carry them away.

○ Fireweed seedlings grow far from the parent plant.

○ Pods of the fireweed split open to release tiny seeds.

by _____

3

○ Acorns fall from oak trees in fall.

○ A new oak tree sprouts in spring.

○ A squirrel packs a few in its cheeks, but drops one or two along the way.

by _____

Science Fact

Very large seeds often depend on gravity for dispersal. They can gain distance from the parent plant by rolling down slopes and mountainsides.

6

Plants: Life Cycles

- All plants have similar cycles of growth and reproduction.
- While some plants can live for hundreds of years, others complete their life cycle within a year.

A. Draw pictures to complete the life cycle of a pumpkin with the help of the pictures on the left.

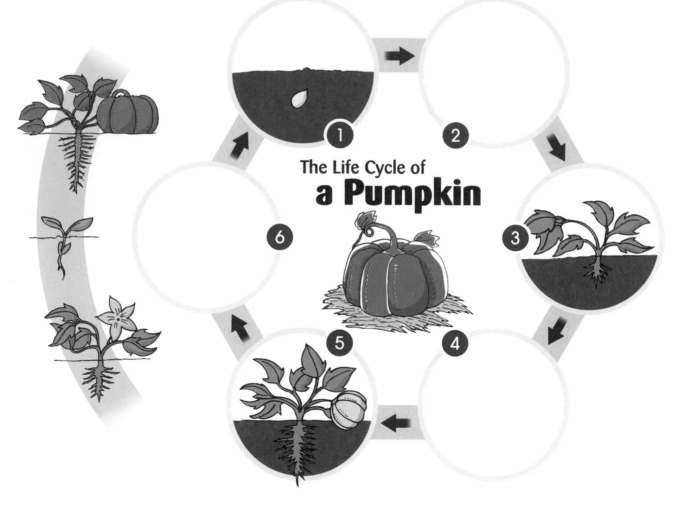

The Life Cycle of **a Pumpkin**

B. Put the life cycle of a flower in the correct order. Write the letters.

Life Cycle of a Flower

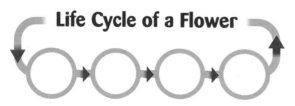

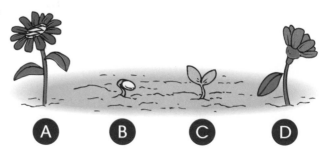

ISBN: 978-1-77149-031-3

C. Fill in the blanks with the correct words to complete the life cycle comparison.

months	years
maple tree	leaves
flowers	sunflower

Life Cycles of  and

1. It takes many _____ for a maple tree to grow to maturity and produce seeds. A sunflower completes its life cycle within a few _____ .

2. The maple tree and the sunflower grow many _____ before their _____ and seeds form.

3. The maple tree and the sunflower both start as small seeds, but the _____ grows to be much larger than the _____ .

D. Draw lines to give examples of these kinds of plants.

Annual plants •

Biennial plants •

Perennial plants •

• A pumpkin plant sprouts and dies within one year.

• Many plants, including trees, can live for many years.

• Parsley and foxgloves are examples of plants that live for two years.

Olive trees grow slowly but can live a very long life. Some do not bear fruit until they reach 30 years or older, but then they produce olives for hundreds of years.

7

Uses of Plants

For external use only.

- We use plants for many different things, from medicine to furniture and clothing.
- How we use particular plants or their parts depends on their characteristics.

A. **Circle the words that describe the characteristics of the plants. Then match the plants with the things that can be made with them.**

1. The hard wood of the oak tree makes sturdy floors. _____

2. Rope is made from the strong fibres of the sisal plant. _____

3. Sweet juice from the sugar cane gives us sugar for tea and for baking. _____

4. The soft, light wood of the pine tree is ideal as a building material. _____

5. The stem of the rattan palm is flexible and strong, making it ideal for making baskets. _____

6. The soft, fine hairs of cotton plants are made into fabric for clothing. _____

7. The flexible substance that oozes from the rubber tree makes rubber for bike tires. _____

ISBN: 978-1-77149-031-3

B. **Fill in the missing letters to match each part of the pine tree with the product that it makes.**

needles bark trunk sap

1 for fragrance

n__ __ __l__ __

2  tannins — used in leather-making

__ __r__

3 for making matches

__r__ __k

4 for cleaning paint from brushes

__ __p

C. **Read what Lucy says. Then unscramble the word to see what the things are made from.**

Although these products are all made from different plants, they are made from the same part of a plant. What is it?

e s d e

the _____

Science Fact

Plants are more than useful to us; all other living things, including humans, cannot live without them. They give us oxygen to breathe, and are the base of all our food sources.

8

Endangered Plants or Invasive Plants

- When new plants take over a land, they may become invasive plants because they make native plants struggle for survival.
- Endangered plants are those that need protection in order to survive.

A. **Find the reasons for the loss of habitat of plants. Check ✔ the correct letters.**

(A) vehicles driving off-road

(B) fertilizing fields

(C) over-picking flowers

(D) trampling on plants

(E) spraying pesticides

(F) watering plants

(G) planting saplings in a new field

(H) clearing land for growing crops

(I) new species taking over a field

(J) clearing land for animals to graze

(K) clearing land for houses, shopping malls, or other buildings

ISBN: 978-1-77149-031-3

B. Write "Invasive" or "Endangered" to complete the titles. Then colour the flowers as specified.

E_____ Plants

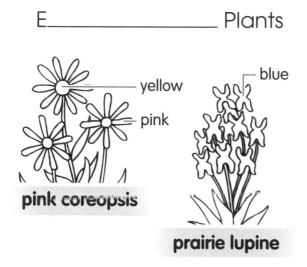

pink coreopsis

prairie lupine

I_____ Plants

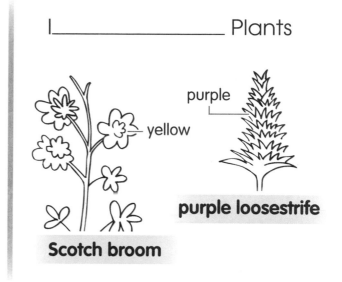

purple loosestrife

Scotch broom

C. Fill in the blanks with the given words to complete the paragraph.

extinct   endangered   invasive
habitat   protected   native

Every time a forest or meadow is cleared for human development, some plants lose their 1._____ . If a plant is rare, or its habitat is special, it may be in danger of becoming 2._____ . There are many 3._____ plants in Canada. Some are 4._____ by laws, and many conservation groups are trying to save them from extinction. They remove the 5._____ plants and grow more 6._____ plants in their place.

Science Fact

Many invasive plants are very beautiful, and sometimes useful to humans. Scotch broom is admired while it is in bloom, and Himalayan blackberries are a sweet treat in late summer.

Himalayan blackberries

9

Rainforests

- *Rainforests are the habitat of many plants and animals. They have heavy rainfall and hot or mild temperatures.*
- *Almost all rainforests are found in regions around the equator. These are tropical rainforests.*

A. **Look at the plants found in the different layers of the rainforest. Match each description with the correct plant and layer. Write the letter and the name of the layer.**

1. This tree is one of the few that burst through the canopy. It is assured of sunshine, and space to spread its leaves.

   _____ ; _____

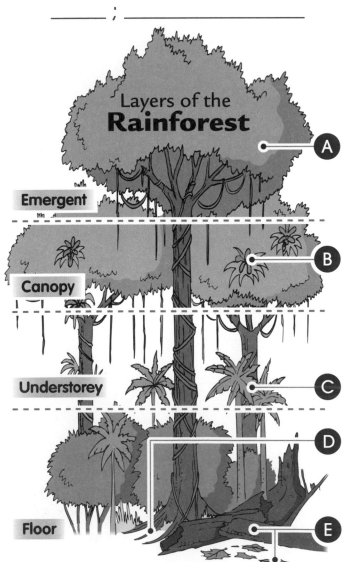

2. Tall trees send down buttress roots for extra support.

   _____ ; _____

3. Fallen logs and dead leaves feed the soil that nourishes the forest.

   _____ ; _____

4. An orchid grows on a branch to get its share of sunshine.

   _____ ; _____

5. The palm is a tree that grows in shade, below the forest canopy.

   _____ ; _____

ISBN: 978-1-77149-031-3

B. **Fill in the blanks with the given words to complete the passage.**

canopy   birds   rainfall   seeds   vines   layer   animals
understorey   plants   forest floor   dense   fruits

The Rainforest Canopy

An amazing variety of 1._____ and 2._____ live in rainforests. Most animals are found in the 3._____ , enjoying the 4._____ and 5._____ , and the sun when it shines. 6._____ easily fly from treetop to treetop, but this 7._____ is so 8._____ that even flightless animals have no trouble getting around. The busy canopy weathers almost daily 9._____ , acting like a leaky umbrella to the 10._____ and 11._____ . It also shades the plants below, causing 12._____ and smaller trees to struggle to reach light.

Science Fact

Canada is home to a temperate rainforest. It stretches along British Columbia's mild west coast.

10

Force as a Push or Pull

Pull harder!

- A force is a push or pull that one thing exerts upon another.
- Forces can be of two types: pushes and pulls of objects that make contact, and those that are at work from a distance.

A. Identify the force(s) in each picture. Write "Push", "Pull", or "Both Push and Pull" on the line.

1.

_____

2.

_____

3.

_____

4.

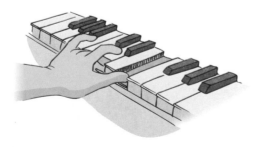

_____

5.

_____

ISBN: 978-1-77149-031-3

B.   Fill in the blanks with "g", "t", "v", or "r" to complete the "force" words.

1.

___ra___ity

2.

s___a___ic

elec___ ___ici___y

3.

ma___ne___ism

C.   Identify the type of force in each picture.

Types of Forces

- **Direct Contact** or **From a Distance**
- **Push** or **Pull**

1. _____ ; _____

2. _____ ; _____

3. _____ ; _____

4. _____ ; _____

Science Fact

When you are standing still on the ground, you are exerting a
force downward on the ground. The ground is exerting a force
of the same size upward on you.

ISBN: 978-1-77149-031-3

11

Forces and Movement

- Forces acting upon objects that are not moving occur in pairs: equal in size but opposite in direction. They are balanced.

- Unbalanced forces that act upon an object will result in movement or a change in movement of that object.

A. Draw an arrow in each picture to balance the force.

ISBN: 978-1-77149-031-3

B. Put the pictures in order. Write 1 to 3. Then colour the one that shows where the forces become unbalanced.

1.

2.

3.

Science Fact

Walking is controlled falling. While standing still, you are balanced. When you lift one foot and push with the other foot, you become unbalanced. Balance is returned when you put your foot down again. You have moved forward.

ISBN: 978-1-77149-031-3

Gravity

- Gravity is a pulling force on things.
- The heavier or bigger the object is, the greater the force of gravity.

Who just hit me?

It was "gravity".

A. Draw an arrow if the picture shows gravity at work; otherwise, write "No Gravity" on the line.

1.

_____

2.

_____

3.

_____

4.

_____

5.

_____

ISBN: 978-1-77149-031-3

B. **Look at the planets. Put them in order from the one with the greatest gravity to the one that has the least. Write their names on the lines. Then answer the questions.**

1.

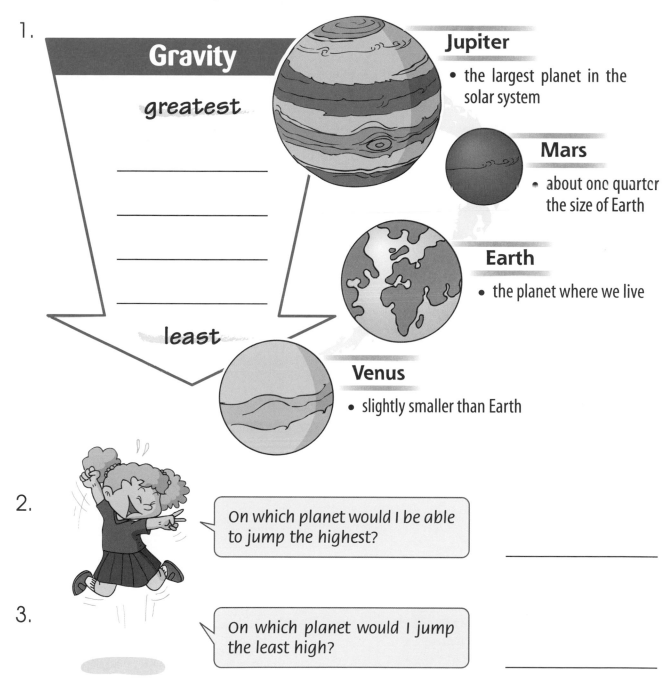

Gravity

greatest

_____

_____

_____

_____

least

Jupiter
- the largest planet in the solar system

Mars
- about one quarter the size of Earth

Earth
- the planet where we live

Venus
- slightly smaller than Earth

2. On which planet would I be able to jump the highest?

_____

3. On which planet would I jump the least high?

_____

Science Fact

In order to function properly, a ballpoint pen needs the force of gravity. In space or on the space station, it would not work.

ISBN: 978-1-77149-031-3

13

Friction

more fricton

- Friction is a force that is produced when two objects rub against each other. Its direction is opposite to the direction of movement.
- Sometimes friction is a good thing for us, but sometimes it is not. Sometimes we can even change the amount of friction.

It's easy to drive on a muddy road when you have tires with deeper tracks.

A. Describe the amount of friction in each picture. Write the word in bold on the line.

FRICTION – great force of friction   **friction** – small force of friction

1.

_____

2.

_____

3.

_____

4.

_____

B. **Help the magazine editors answer the letters dealing with friction problems. Fill in the blanks with the given words.**

1

Dear Editors,
I know to use an environmentally friendly car wash detergent and a soft cloth to clean my car, but sometimes I can't get all the dirt off. What can I do?

Thanks,
Jim-Bob McGillioutty

Use a _____ sponge to
       rough/soft

_____ friction.
increase/reduce

2

Dear Editors,
What can I do to increase the friction that is needed to clean my teeth?

Yours truly,
Sofie Cannie

Use a brush with _____
                    softer/harder
bristles.

3

Dear Editors,
The chain on my bicycle is old and I think it is making it hard for me to pedal. Any suggestions?

Thanks,
Peter Pedalstire

Use _____ to
     bicycle grease/water

_____ friction.
increase/reduce

4

Dear Editors,
We have new shiny wooden floors in our house, but we keep slipping on them when we wear socks. What should we do?

Sincerely,
Rebecca Salks

Wear _____
      bigger socks/slippers with rubber soles

to _____ friction.
   increase/decrease

Science Fact

It is not because ice is really slippery that you can skate so fast. When you glide over the ice, the heat caused by the skate blade rubbing against the ice causes the ice to melt underneath it. You are actually gliding on water, and that is what reduces the friction and makes sliding so easy.

14

Magnets

- A magnet is a piece of iron that has a special force: magnetism.
- Magnetism is a force that can push or pull other objects that are magnetic.

A. Which objects are magnetic?   Draw lines from the magnetic objects to the horseshoe magnet.

ISBN: 978-1-77149-031-3

B. Read what the mouse says. Unscramble the letters to find out which materials are not magnetic.

1

2

lsasg

thloc

3

4

odow

sclipla

> Not all metals are magnetic. Iron, or metal that is mostly iron, is always magnetic.

C. Where are magnets used? Circle the magnets in each picture.

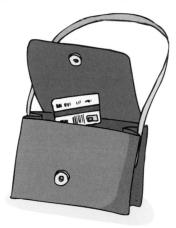

Experiment – Turn a needle into a magnet!

- Stroke the end of the magnet along the length of the needle about 30 times. Stroke in only one direction – do not rub back and forth.
- Test your "magnet". Try to pick up some pins with the needle.

Things needed:
- 1 magnet
- 1 needle
- pins

Science Fact

You can pick up dust from outer space with a magnet. Since tiny meteorite particles contain iron, a magnet will pick them up.

15

Magnetic Poles

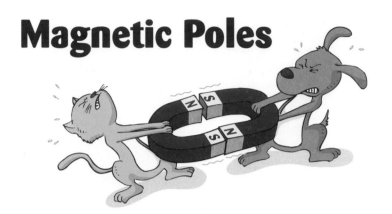

- Every magnet has a south pole and a north pole.
- The Earth behaves like a magnet, with both a south pole and a north pole. Because of this, a magnetic compass can show us which way is north.

A. Look at the pictures. Then fill in the blanks with the given words.

south   north   repels   attracts

1. A magnet has a _____ pole and a _____ pole.

2. The north pole of one magnet _____ the south pole of another magnet.

3. The north pole of one magnet _____ the north pole of another magnet.

B. Write "N" for north pole and "S" for south pole in the circles to complete the diagrams.

Magnets Attract

Magnets Repel

ISBN: 978-1-77149-031-3

C. Fill in the blanks to complete what Dr. Cowan says. Complete each diagram to show how a triangle is formed with three bar magnets.

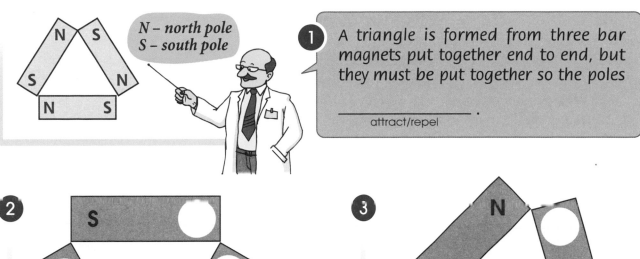

N – north pole
S – south pole

1. A triangle is formed from three bar magnets put together end to end, but they must be put together so the poles

_____.
attract/repel

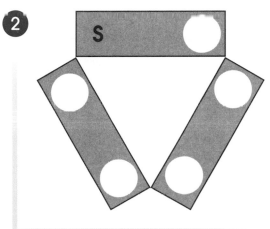 2.

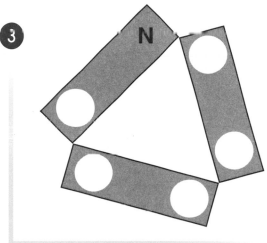 3.

D. For each compass, write "N" in the correct shaded part to show which direction is north.

1.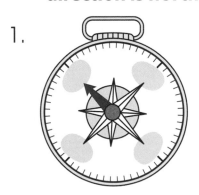

2.

3.

 **Science Fact**

Repelling magnets are used to give some roller coasters a boost at the start of the ride. Instead of starting slowly and gradually gaining speed, the fun starts right away!

16

Stability

- Stable structures are those that are not likely to fall down, overturn, or break when reasonable forces are applied to them.
- There are many ways to make a structure more stable.

A. Fix the unstable situations. Check ✔ the correct answers.

1

2

(A) Add one more leg to the table.

(B) Remove one leg from the table.

3

(A) Use training wheels.

(B) Use bigger wheels.

4

(A) Put a bigger book on top.

(B) Stack the books more neatly.

(A) Use a longer ladder.

(B) Pull the "feet" of the ladder farther away from the wall.

ISBN: 978-1-77149-031-3

B. **These fairy tale characters have problems with stability. Help them circle the correct words to fix the problems.**

1.

   > Every time I climb this skinny beanstalk, I think it's going to break and fall down, so I don't get to climb very high.

   Solution:

   Climb a   thicker / rough   beanstalk.

2.

   > I've lost two brothers. How can I build my house to keep the wolf out?

   Solution:

   Build the house out of a   thicker / stronger material.

3.

   > Those goats make such a racket on my bridge. I'm afraid they may be too heavy and will make it collapse right onto me!

   Solution:

   Use   beams / sticks   to support the bridge.

Try this!

> Use an ordinary deck of cards to make a house of cards.

Science Fact

Eggshells are not easily crushed when being squeezed because of their arch shape. The arch is a very strong structure that has been used to build bridges for many years.

17

Levers

- Levers are simple machines that can make movement and force either larger or smaller.
- The point on which the lever pivots, or turns around, is called the fulcrum.

A. Colour the tools that are levers.

1.

2.

3.

4.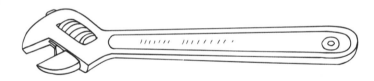

5.

6.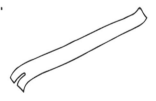

7.

B. Circle the fulcrum in each lever.

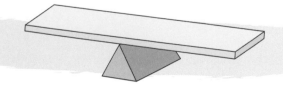

ISBN: 978-1-77149-031-3

C. **Read what Daniel says. Help him do the experiment. Then use the given words to complete the record.**

You need a broom and an open space to do this experiment. This experiment will tell you what happens when the fulcrum in a lever changes position.

easy   little   easier   harder   greater   lesser

Record

Part 1

Grab the handle of the broom with both hands. Sweep, being careful not to move the fulcrum.

fulcrum

- _____ to sweep
- broom's sweep length: _____

Part 2

Slide your lower hand higher up the handle so that it is closer to your other hand. Sweep, noting any change in the force required to move the broom.

- _____ to sweep
- broom's sweep length: _____

Part 3

Slide your lower hand as far down the broom handle as you can. Sweep, again noting any changes in force.

- _____ to sweep
- broom's sweep length: _____

Science Fact

The lever is the oldest of the simple machines. A shaduf was used by the ancient Egyptians around 3000 BCE. The counterweight made getting water from the river easier.

18

More about Levers

load

effort

fulcrum

- A lever has three parts: the fulcrum, or pivot point, an effort, or a force that is put into the lever, and the load, which is the force that comes out of the machine.
- Changing the order of the fulcrum, effort force, and load force results in different machines that do different things.

A. Label each lever with "fulcrum", "effort", and "load".

1

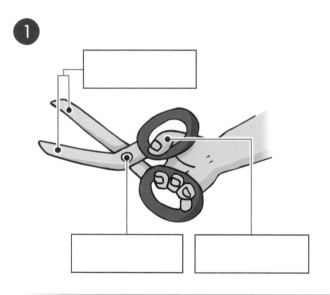

2

3

4

ISBN: 978-1-77149-031-3

B. **Look at the pictures. Fill in the blanks with the correct words to complete what Tom says.**

1.

A shovel is an example of a _____ (lever/screw).

2.

Levers are simple machines that make work _____ (harder/easier) for us.

3.

The farther the effort force is from the fulcrum, the _____ (harder/easier) it is to move the load.

4.

When we use scissors, the small movement our fingers make will result in a _____ (greater/smaller) movement made by the blades.

Science Fact

What do pianos, self-filling fountain pens, and old water pumps have in common?

They all make use of **LEVERS!**

19

Soil

Hi, Mr. Soil.

- Soil is the top layer of much of the Earth's land surface.
- Soil is a mixture of broken rock, humus (bits of dead plants and animal waste), air, and water.

A. Colour the soil in the picture brown.

B. See how rock is broken down by nature in each picture. Write the missing letters to find the natural sources for this process.

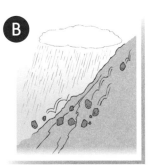

A __ a v e __

B r __ i __

C p __ a n __ s

D w __ __ d

E r __ v __ r

F g l __ c i e __

ISBN: 978-1-77149-031-3

C. **Humus is made from lots of things. Identify the things. Write the letters.**

A something that a rabbit has left behind

B a tree's fall offering

C living things

D something a bird has dropped

E fallen fruit

F what's left of a tree

Science Fact

Because rock erosion happens very slowly, it takes thousands of years to make one centimetre of soil.

20

More about Soil

- *We classify soil by the size of its rock particles.*
- *Each type of soil has different textures.*
- *The different types of soil can be found in different places.*

A. Fill in the missing letters to complete the names of the soil types.

Types of Soil

loam   clay   silt   sand

- __l__ __: has the smallest rock particles

- __ __l__: has rock particles between the size of clay and sand particles

- s__ __d: has the largest rock particles

- __o__ __: a mixture of clay, silt, and sandy soil

B. See what the children felt after touching the soil in the box. Write the names of the soil types given in part A on the lines.

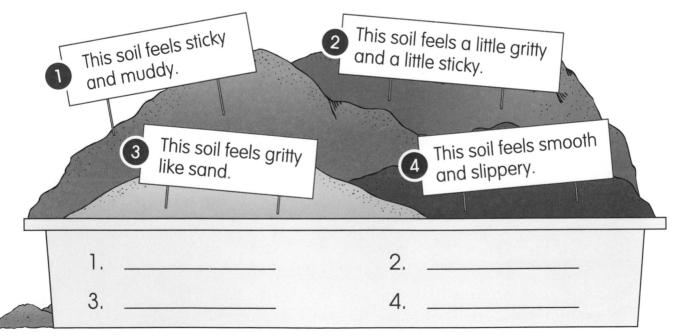

1 This soil feels sticky and muddy.

2 This soil feels a little gritty and a little sticky.

3 This soil feels gritty like sand.

4 This soil feels smooth and slippery.

1. _____   2. _____

3. _____   4. _____

ISBN: 978-1-77149-031-3

C. See what types of soil the children and the pig are describing. Write the names of the soil types on the lines.

clay   silt   sand   loam

1.

   The rock particles are so small in this soil, there is not a lot of room for air.

   _____

2.

   This soil holds just enough air and water to keep most plants happy.

   _____

3.

   With plenty of humus, this soil is used by plant nurseries.

   _____

4.
   a. Water drains easily from this soil.

   _____

   b. This soil absorbs water well.

   _____

   c. When this soil dries, it repels water.

   _____

   d. This soil is sometimes found near beaches.

   _____

Science Fact

We know air and water are ingredients of soil, but they are not just small ingredients. Air and water make up about half of most types of soil.

21

Soil Erosion

- Soil is lost when it is blown away by wind or carried away by rain or rivers. Mountain soil will gradually be lost due to gravity if the trees that hold it are cut down. This is soil erosion.
- Soil erosion can be prevented.

A. Fill in the blanks with the given words. Then draw lines to match the sentences with the correct pictures.

rain   waves   wind

Causes of Soil Erosion:

Soil can be washed away by heavy _____ .   ◉

Soil can be blown away by strong _____ .   ◉

Soil can be lost to the water by _____ .   ◉

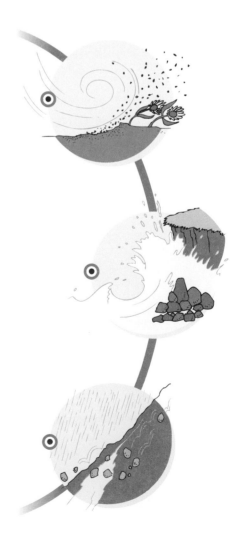

B. Match the methods of erosion prevention with the correct pictures. Write the letters.

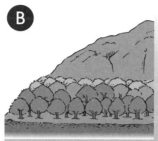
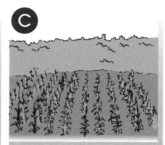

Methods of Erosion Prevention:

1. Planting in tiers prevents soil loss by gravity.   _____

2. Hedgerows prevent soil erosion by wind.   _____

3. Cover crops protect soil by holding it with the roots of plants.   _____

4. Replanting logged slopes prevents soil loss on mountainsides.   _____

Experiment

Things needed:

- a sample of soil
- an old cake pan
- water

1. Pile the soil on one end of the pan so it looks like a miniature beach.
2. Slowly pour water into the other side of the pan — just enough to touch the beach.
3. Gently rock the pan so the water hits the soil like waves.

What happens to the soil?

 Science Fact

When soil is repeatedly walked on, it compacts. Because little air is left in the soil and water cannot be absorbed, plants cannot grow. What will happen next? With no plants to hold the soil: soil erosion.

22

Earthworms

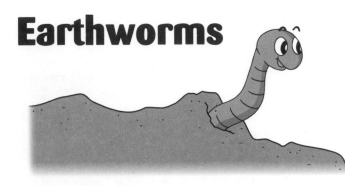

Importance of earthworms to soil:
- They mix up layers of soil and leave tunnels in the soil for air and water.
- They decompose dead leaves and animal waste, leaving nutrients for plants to grow well.

A. **Look at the picture that shows a worm's life underground. Fill in the boxes with the given words.**

habitat   predator   food   tunnel   castings

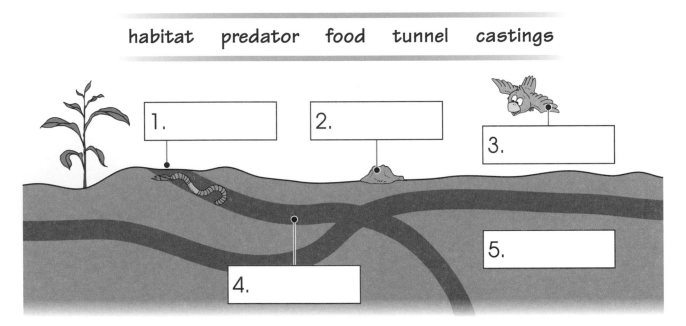

1. _____
2. _____
3. _____
4. _____
5. _____

B. **Match the words with their definitions.**

1. annelid _____

2. nocturnal _____

3. omnivorous _____

4. decomposer _____

5. castings _____

A eats both plants and animals or their waste

B helps break things down into smaller parts

C the waste products of worms

D active at night

E a kind of animal that is divided into rings

C. **Look at the picture. Fill in the blanks with the given words to complete the food chain.**

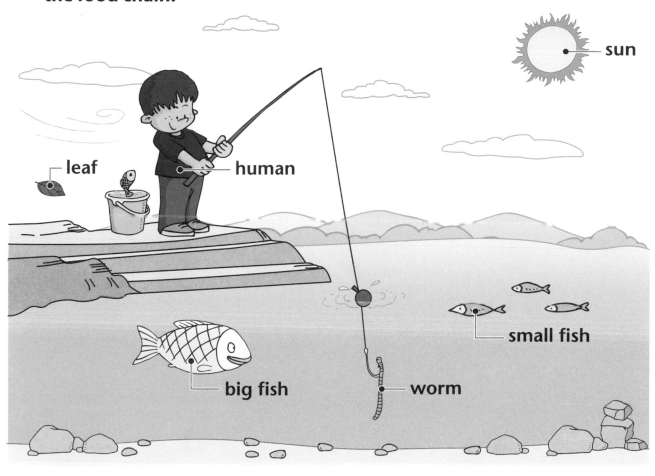

sun

leaf

human

big fish

worm

small fish

Food Chain

Science Fact

Ribbon worms are marine worms that can grow as long as 30 m.

23

Creatures that Use Soil

We love clay.

- People use soil for many different things.
- Soil is home to many animals.

A. People need soil for different things. Fill in the blanks with the given words to match the pictures.

soil field   china
skin mud mask
flowerpot with soil
clay brick   peat fuel

_____

_____

_____

_____

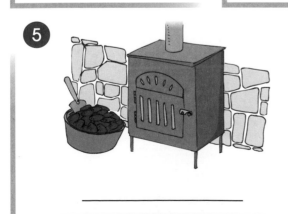

_____

_____

ISBN: 978-1-77149-031-3

B. What animals live in soil? Use the picture clues and the given words to complete the puzzle.

marmot   millipede   mite
nematode   pillbug   snail
ant   beetle   centipede
cicada   cricket   earwig

Science Fact

We can learn about the lives of ancient peoples through the discovery of buried pottery, such as clay pieces from thousands of years ago.

Compost

- Composting is a process of decomposing plant and animal materials. It happens naturally on the floor of every forest.
- We can make compost in our backyards with material from our gardens and kitchens.

A. Read the compost recipe. Then put a cross ✗ on the items that should not be put in the compost bin.

- **Items from the garden**

- **Items from the kitchen**

- **Items from other places**

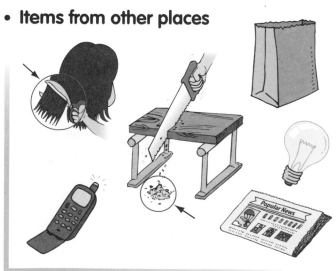

Compost Recipe

- **Organic matter** *
- **Air**
- **Water**
- **Micro-organisms** **

* Use organic matter that was once alive and will break down easily, such as leaves and apple cores.

** Micro-organisms will add themselves to the compost pile – you cannot keep them away.

ISBN: 978-1-77149-031-3

B. Write "true" or "false" for each statement.

1. Compost needs air to decompose. _____

2. A compost pile can get very hot in the middle. _____

3. A compost pile should be kept dry. _____

4. Micro-organisms, or very tiny creatures, are responsible for decomposition. _____

5.  Meat and dairy products should not be composted as they attract rodents. _____

C. Write the secret composting message on the line.

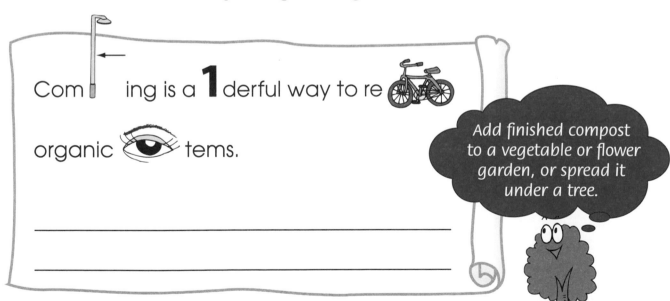

Com ⌐ ing is a **1** derful way to re 🚲

organic 👁 tems.

_____

_____

Add finished compost to a vegetable or flower garden, or spread it under a tree.

Science Fact

People who don't have backyards can still compost. Red wiggler worms kept in a bin are happy to receive kitchen wastes. This is called vermicomposting.

ISBN: 978-1-77149-031-3

ISBN: 978-1-77149-031-3

ANSWERS

ISBN: 978-1-77149-031-3

1   Numbers to 100

1. 37 ; 39 ; 40 ; 41 ; 43
2. 71 ; 72 ; 74 ; 75 ; 76
3. 89 ; 90 ; 91 ; 94 ; 95
4. 57 ; 59 ; 60 ; 61 ; 62
5. 49   6. 92   7. 70
8. 18, 39, 58, 63   9. 30, 44, 53, 81
10. 14, 16, 46, 64   11. forty-five
12. sixty-two   13. ninety-eight
14. 26   15. 45   16. 91
17. 80   18. 64   19. 38
20. 72   21. 53
22-25. (Suggested answers)
22. 66   23. 29   24. 10
25. 44
26.
75 70 65 60 55 50 45 40 35 30
27.
100 90 80 70 60 50 40 30 20 10
28.
88 86 84 82 80 78 76 74 72 70

29. 72 ; 66 ; 64 ; 60 ; 58
30. 80 ; 75 ; 65 ; 60 ; 55
31. 90 ; 80 ; 50 ; 40 ; 20
32. 34, 32, 30, 28 ; 2 ; 34
33. 60, 55, 50, 45 ; 5 ; 60
34. ;   35. ;
    50 ... 60   80 ... 90
    50   90
36. ;   37. ;
    60 ... 70   10 ... 20
    70   20
38. 84   39. 45 ; 54

2   Addition and Subtraction of 2-Digit Numbers

1. 53   2. 81   3. 81
4. 93   5. 87   6. 53
7. 80
8. 79 ;
$$\begin{array}{r} 50 \\ +\ 30 \\ \hline 80 \end{array}$$
9. 82 ;
$$\begin{array}{r} 20 \\ +\ 60 \\ \hline 80 \end{array}$$
10. 68 ;
$$\begin{array}{r} 10 \\ +\ 60 \\ \hline 70 \end{array}$$
11. 38 ;
$$\begin{array}{r} 10 \\ +\ 30 \\ \hline 40 \end{array}$$

12. A: 52   B: 23   C: 13
    D: 18   E: 35   F: 28
    G: 37   H: 6   I: 25
    J: 18
13. D and J   14. A
15. B
16. 35 ;
$$\begin{array}{r} 70 \\ -\ 40 \\ \hline 30 \end{array}$$
17. 27 ;
$$\begin{array}{r} 70 \\ -\ 40 \\ \hline 30 \end{array}$$
18. ✘ ; 49 ; 83
19. ✔ ;
$$\begin{array}{r} 45 \\ +\ 15 \\ \hline 60 \end{array}$$
20. 74 ;
$$\begin{array}{r} 16 \\ +\ 74 \\ \hline 90 \end{array}$$
21. 35 ;
$$\begin{array}{r} 24 \\ +\ 35 \\ \hline 59 \end{array}$$
22. 17 ;
$$\begin{array}{r} 16 \\ +\ 17 \\ \hline 33 \end{array}$$
23. 18 ;
$$\begin{array}{r} 66 \\ +\ 18 \\ \hline 84 \end{array}$$

24. a. 48 + 48 ; 96 ; 96
    b. 86 − 48 ; 38 ; 38
25. a. 42 − 36 ; 6 ; 6
    b. 36 + 42 ; 78 ; 78
26. a. 62 + 5 ; 67 ; 67
    b. 75 − 62 ; 13 ; 13

3   Numbers to 1000

1. 3 ; 5 ; 8 ; 358   2. 5 ; 4 ; 3 ; 543
3. 2 ; 9 ; 0 ; 290
4. A: 657   B: 524   C: 976
   D: 3 ; 7 ; 5   E: 5 hundreds 8 tens 1 one
5. 524, 581   6. 524, 581
7. 652, 625, 256   8. 887, 878, 788
9. 940, 904, 490   10. 423 ; 437 ; 449
11. 795 ; 821 ; 834
12. Mon: 645   Tue: 503   Wed: 296
13. Monday   14. 300
15. 500
16.
; 2
488 490 492 494 496 498 500 502
17.
; 100
200 300 400 500 600 700 800 900
18. 25 ; 550, 575, 600, 625, 650
19. 10 ; 750, 760, 770, 780, 790
20. 5 ; 715, 720, 725, 730, 735
21. 999 ; 100
22. 399, 400, 401, 402, 403
23. (Suggested answer)
    389, 390, 391, 392, 393
24. 6 ; 459, 495, 549, 594, 945, 954

ISBN: 978-1-77149-031-3

4 Addition and Subtraction of 3-Digit Numbers (1)

1. 339
2. 699
3. 495
4. 767
5. 568
6. 168
7. 836
8. 496
9. 398
10. 829
11. A: 448   B: 388
    C: 388   D: 497
    Answers greater than 450: D
    Answers smaller than 450: A, B, C

12.
$$\begin{array}{r} \overset{①}{} \\ 327 \\ +459 \\ \hline 786 \end{array}$$
13.
$$\begin{array}{r} \overset{①}{} \\ 436 \\ +127 \\ \hline 563 \end{array}$$
14.
$$\begin{array}{r} \overset{①①}{} \\ 85 \\ +516 \\ \hline 601 \end{array}$$

15.
$$\begin{array}{r} \overset{①①}{} \\ 652 \\ +149 \\ \hline 801 \end{array}$$
16.
$$\begin{array}{r} \overset{①①}{} \\ 584 \\ +266 \\ \hline 850 \end{array}$$
17.
$$\begin{array}{r} \overset{①①}{} \\ 298 \\ +298 \\ \hline 596 \end{array}$$

18. 446
19. 639
20. 822
21. 801
22. 494
23. 876
24. A: 537   B: 231   C: 490
    D: 555   E: 602   F: 251
    G: 318
    555 = D   251 = F
    231 = B   318 = G
25. 241
26. 421
27. 211
28. 309
29. 274
30. 338
31. 175
32. 221
33. 147
34. 249
35. A: 397   B: 236
    C: 142   D: 421
    D, A, B, C

36. a.
$$\begin{array}{r} 245 \\ +173 \\ \hline 418 \end{array}; 418$$
   b.
$$\begin{array}{r} 245 \\ -173 \\ \hline 72 \end{array}; 72$$

37. a.
$$\begin{array}{r} 318 \\ -57 \\ \hline 261 \end{array}; 261$$
   b.
$$\begin{array}{r} 318 \\ +261 \\ \hline 579 \end{array}; 579$$

38. a.
$$\begin{array}{r} 362 \\ -287 \\ \hline 75 \end{array}; 75$$
   b.
$$\begin{array}{r} 362 \\ +287 \\ \hline 649 \end{array}; 649$$

5 Addition and Subtraction of 3-Digit Numbers (2)

1. 507
2. 750
3. 229
4. 585
5. 253
6. 907
7. 773
8. 123
9. 362 ;
$$\begin{array}{r} 162 \\ +362 \\ \hline 524 \end{array}$$
10. 46 ;
$$\begin{array}{r} 154 \\ +46 \\ \hline 200 \end{array}$$

11. 232 ;
$$\begin{array}{r} 173 \\ +232 \\ \hline 405 \end{array}$$
12. 53 ;
$$\begin{array}{r} 318 \\ +53 \\ \hline 371 \end{array}$$

13. 613 ;
$$\begin{array}{r} 400 \\ +200 \\ \hline 600 \end{array}$$
14. 798 ;
$$\begin{array}{r} 700 \\ +100 \\ \hline 800 \end{array}$$

15. 644 ;
$$\begin{array}{r} 800 \\ -200 \\ \hline 600 \end{array}$$
16. 258 ;
$$\begin{array}{r} 600 \\ -300 \\ \hline 300 \end{array}$$

17.
$$\begin{array}{r} 319 \\ +254 \\ \hline 573 \end{array} ; \begin{array}{r} 319 \\ -254 \\ \hline 65 \end{array}$$
18.
$$\begin{array}{r} 608 \\ +73 \\ \hline 681 \end{array} ; \begin{array}{r} 608 \\ -73 \\ \hline 535 \end{array}$$

19.
$$\begin{array}{r} 462 \\ +353 \\ \hline 815 \end{array} ; \begin{array}{r} 462 \\ -353 \\ \hline 109 \end{array}$$
20.
$$\begin{array}{r} 224 \\ +537 \\ \hline 761 \end{array} ; \begin{array}{r} 537 \\ -224 \\ \hline 313 \end{array}$$

21.
$$\begin{array}{r} 176 \\ +413 \\ \hline 589 \end{array} ; \begin{array}{r} 413 \\ -176 \\ \hline 237 \end{array}$$
22.
$$\begin{array}{r} 821 \\ +117 \\ \hline 938 \end{array} ; \begin{array}{r} 821 \\ -117 \\ \hline 704 \end{array}$$

23. a. 321   b. 237
24. a. 503   b. 276
25. a. 413   b. 165
26. a. 735   b. 188
27. A: 240   B: 590   C: 181
    B
28. A: 307   B: 601   C: 237
    C
29. 218 + 174 ; 392 ; 392
30. 182 + 203 ; 385 ; 385
31. 182 – 79 ; 103 ; 103
32. 203 – 174 ; 29 ; 29
33. 154 – 68 ; 86 ; 86

6 Length and Distance

1. m
2. km
3. cm
4. m
5. km
6. cm
7. m
8. cm
9. km
10. m
11. cm
12. (Individual estimates)
    A: 11 cm
    B: a bit shorter than 10 cm
    C: a bit longer than 7 cm
    D: a bit longer than 9 cm
13. 5 cm ; Draw a pencil which is about 7 cm long.
14. A: 3 cm ; B: 5 cm ; Draw a tree which is a bit shorter than 5 cm.
15. A: 11 cm   B: 9 cm   C: 11 cm
16. a. 65   b. 65   c. 50

17 a. and 18 a.

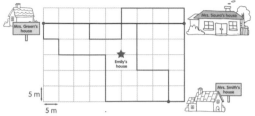

17. b. 45   18. b. 30
19. Mrs. Saura or Mrs. Smith

7 Perimeter and Area

1. 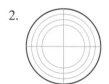   2.

3.

4. A: 12 cm   B: 14 cm   C: 10 cm
   D: 12 cm   E: 16 cm   F: 20 cm
5. (Individual estimates)
   Square: 16 cm   Hexagon : 22 cm
   Rectangle: 22 cm   Pentagon: 15 cm
   Triangle: 12 cm
6. (Suggested drawings)

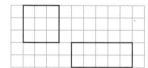

7.

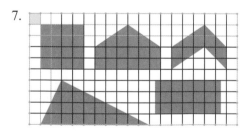

8. (Individual estimates)
   Square: 16   Pentagon: 18
   Hexagon: 10   Triangle: 20
   Rectangle: 18
9. the triangle
10. 8

11. (Suggested drawings)

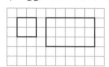

12. 48 ; 12   13. smaller
14.   ; 24

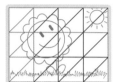

8 Time and Temperature

1. 05 ; 5   2. 6 ; 7   3. 20 ; 20
4. A: 10:25 ; 25 min past 10
   B: 5:55 ; 5 min to 6
   C: 2:35 ; 25 min to 3
   D: 12:10 ; 10 min past 12
   E: 11:50 ; 10 min to 12
5. B ; A ; F ; D ; C ; E
6.

Watch a movie
⑤ 5:54 (evening)
fifty-four minutes after
five o'clock

Visit Grandma
① 8:13 (morning)
thirteen minutes
after eight o' clock

Get a haircut
② 10:27 (morning)
twenty-seven minutes
after ten o' clock

Have lunch with Peter
③ 12:03 (afternoon)
three minutes after
twelve o'clock

Go to the library
④ 3:32 (afternoon)
thirty-two minutes after three o'clock

7. 39 ;
$$\begin{array}{r} 53 \\ -\ 14 \\ \hline 39 \end{array}$$

8. 13 ;
$$\begin{array}{r} 21 \\ -\ 8 \\ \hline 13 \end{array}$$

9. 12 ;
$$\begin{array}{r} 39 \\ -\ 27 \\ \hline 12 \end{array}$$

10. Sally

11. a.   12. a.

   b. B ; A   b. B ; A

13.   ; A

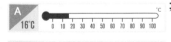

9 Money

1.

2.

3.

4.

5. (Individual estimates)
Jason: 9 ; 6
Elaine: 8 dollars 69 cents
Kevin: 7 dollars 50 cents
Sally: 5 dollars 50 cents
Bruce: 9 dollars

6. Jason   7. Sally

8. 4 ; 81 ; 4.81

9. 8 dollars 52 cents ; $8.52

10. 6 dollars 85 cents ; $6.85

11. 45 ; 2 ; 45 ; 2.45   12. 400 ; 4 ; 8 ; 4.08

13.

| $5 | | $2 |

(25¢)(25¢)(5¢)(1¢)(1¢)(1¢)

14.

| $5 | ($2)($2)
(25¢)(10¢)(1¢)(1¢)(1¢)

15.

| $5 | ($2)($1)(25¢)(25¢)
(10¢)(10¢)(1¢)(1¢)(1¢)(1¢)

16.

| $5 | ($2)($2)
(10¢)(5¢)(1¢)

17.

| $5 | ($1)
(25¢)(25¢)(25¢)(10¢)(5¢)(1¢)(1¢)(1¢)

10 Addition and Subtraction with Money

1.
```
   3  21
+  2  38
   5  59
```

2.
```
   2  38
+  3  27
   5  65
```

3.
```
   3  21
+  4  49
   7  70
```

4.
```
   3  27
+  4  49
   7  76
```

5.
```
   2  38
+  4  49
   6  87
```

6.
```
   3  21
+  3  27
   6  48
```

7. C and D

8. 3.25 ;
```
   3  25
-  3  21
      04
```
0.04

9. 4.30 ;
```
   4  30
-  3  27
   1  03
```
1.03

10. 3.45 ;
```
   3  45
-  2  38
   1  07
```
1.07

11. 6 ;
```
   5  100
-  4  49
   1  51
```
1.51

12.

R & A Superstore	
Puzzle	$ 4.89
Crackers	$ 3.19
Total	$ 8.08
CASH	$ 10.00
CHANGE	$ 1.92

13.

R & A Superstore	
Detergent	$ 1.88
Bread	$ 2.16
Total	$ 4.04
CASH	$ 4.25
CHANGE	$ 0.21

14.

R & A Superstore	
Crackers	$ 3.19
Bread	$ 2.16
Total	$ 5.35
CASH	$ 6.00
CHANGE	$ 0.65

15.

R & A Superstore	
Detergent	$ 1.88
Detergent	$ 1.88
Total	$ 3.76
CASH	$ 5.00
CHANGE	$ 1.24

16.

R & A Superstore

Bread	$ 2.16
Puzzle	$ 4.89
Total	$ 7.05
CASH	$ 7.25
CHANGE	$ 0.20

17.

R & A Superstore

Crackers	$ 3.19
Detergent	$ 1.88
Total	$ 5.07
CASH	$10.00
CHANGE	$ 4.93

18. 1.23 ;
$$\begin{array}{r} 4\ 100 \\ -\ 3\ \ 77 \\ \hline 1\ \ 23 \end{array}$$

19. 2.17 ;
$$\begin{array}{r} 6\ 42 \\ -\ 4\ 25 \\ \hline 2\ 17 \end{array}$$

20. 7.32 ;
$$\begin{array}{r} 3\ 66 \\ +\ 3\ 66 \\ \hline 7\ 32 \end{array}$$

21. 8.91 ;
$$\begin{array}{r} 5\ 27 \\ +\ 3\ 64 \\ \hline 8\ 91 \end{array}$$

22. 4.77 + 4.77 = 9.54 ;
No, he needs 4¢ more.

11 Capacity and Mass

1. about 1 L: C, F
   less than 1 L: B, D, E, G
   more than 1 L: A, H, I
2. I
3. E
4.
5. (measuring cup marked to 5 L)
6.
7. more than 200 L
8. about 100 L
9. less than 1 L
10. A: three quarters
    B: three quarters of a litre
    C: a quarter of a litre
    D: half a litre
11. a quarter ; 4
12. 50 L ; 25
13. Flour: 3 kg
    Pumpkin: 5 kg
    Rock: 8 kg
    Frog: 6 kg
    Watermelon: 5 kg
    Tin Soldier: 4 kg
14. pumpkin ; watermelon
15. 2
16.

17. A: three quarters
    B: a quarter of a kilogram
    C: half a kilogram
    D: three quarters of a kilogram
18. a. 4   b. 8   c. 2
19. a. 5   b. more   c. 8

12 Multiplication (1)

1. (illustration of fish in 7 groups)

   3 + 3 + 3 ; 7 ; 7 ; 21

2. (illustration of fish)

   4 + 4 + 4 + 4 + 4 ; 6 ; 4 ; 6 ; 4 ; 24

3. (illustration of turtles)

   5 + 5 + 5 + 5 + 5 ; 6 ; 5 ; 6 ; 5 ; 30

4. 4 ; 4 ; 4 ; 28
5. 5 ; 5 ; 5 ; 45
6. 5 ; 5 ; 5 ; 25
7. 8 ; 8 ; 8 ; 16
8. 4 ; 6 ; 24
9. 6 ; 3 ; 18
10. 5 ; 4 ; 20
11. 2 ; 8 ; 16
12. (number line) 3 6 9 12 15 18 21 24 27
13. (number line) 4 8 12 16 20 24 28 32 36
14. (number line) 7 14 21 28 35 42 49 56 63
15. 6 ; 12 ; 18 ; 24 ; 30 ; 36 ; 42 ; 48 ; 54
16. 2 ; 4 ; 6 ; 8 ; 10 ; 12 ; 14 ; 16 ; 18
17. 5 ; 10 ; 15 ; 20 ; 25 ; 30 ; 35 ; 40 ; 45
18.

X	1	2	3	4	5	6	7
1	1	2	3	4	5	6	7
2	2	4	6	8	10	12	14
3	3	6	9	12	15	18	21
4	4	8	12	16	20	24	28
5	5	10	15	20	25	30	35
6	6	12	18	24	30	36	42
7	7	14	21	28	35	42	49

ISBN: 978-1-77149-031-3

19. 24   20. 15   21. 14
22. 36   23. 20   24. 42
25. 24

13 Multiplication (2)

1. 27   2. 32   3. 30
4. 42   5. 14   6. 25
7. 24   8. 15   9. 24
10. 28   11. 45   12. 36
13. 48   14. 35   15. 8
16. 7   17. 3   18. 7

19. 24 ;

$$\begin{array}{r} 4 \\ \times\ 6 \\ \hline 24 \end{array}$$

20. 18 ;

$$\begin{array}{r} 6 \\ \times\ 3 \\ \hline 18 \end{array}$$

21. 28 ;

$$\begin{array}{r} 7 \\ \times\ 4 \\ \hline 28 \end{array}$$

22. 6 key chains ;

$$\begin{array}{r} 7 \\ \times\ 5 \\ \hline 35 \end{array}$$; $$\begin{array}{r} 6 \\ \times\ 6 \\ \hline 36 \end{array}$$

23. a. $$\begin{array}{r} 4 \\ \times\ 4 \\ \hline 16 \end{array}$$; 16

b. $$\begin{array}{r} 7 \\ \times\ 4 \\ \hline 28 \end{array}$$; 28

24. a. $$\begin{array}{r} 6 \\ \times\ 3 \\ \hline 18 \end{array}$$; 18

b. $$\begin{array}{r} 5 \\ \times\ 6 \\ \hline 30 \end{array}$$; 30

25. a. $$\begin{array}{r} 6 \\ \times\ 5 \\ \hline 30 \end{array}$$; 30

b. $$\begin{array}{r} 2 \\ \times\ 7 \\ \hline 14 \end{array}$$; 14

26. Tina: 28 ; 8 ; 36
    Eva: 10 ; 16 ; 26
    Susan: 35 ; 5 ; 40
27. Susan   28. Eva
29. No   30. 18

14 Division (1)

1.  ; 15 ; 5

2. ; 21 ; 3

3. ; 20 ; 4

4. ; 7

5. ; 2

6. ; 3

7. ; 6

8. 6 ;

9. 7 ;

10. 5 ;

11. 3 ;

12. a. 15   b. 3   c. 5
13. a. 24   b. 3   c. 6
14. A

15 Division (2)

1. 5 ; 5   2. 3 ; 3   3. 4 ; 4
4. 6 ;

$$3\overline{)18}\ \ \ \begin{array}{r} 6 \\ \hline 18 \end{array}$$

5. 4 ;

$$5\overline{)20}\ \ \ \begin{array}{r} 4 \\ \hline 20 \end{array}$$

ISBN: 978-1-77149-031-3

6.
$$5\overline{)30}$$
6
30

7.
$$8\overline{)24}$$
3
24

8.
$$2\overline{)16}$$
8
16

9.
$$7\overline{)42}$$
6
42

10. 5
11. 5
12. 4
13. 3
14. 3
15. 7
16. 5
17. 7
18. 5

19. 9 ;
$$3\overline{)27}$$
9
27

20. 8 ;
$$2\overline{)16}$$
8
16

21. 6 ;
$$5\overline{)30}$$
6
30

22.
$$4\overline{)15}$$ R 3
3
15
12
3

23.
$$3\overline{)20}$$ R 2
6
20
18
2

24.
$$7\overline{)18}$$ R 4
2
18
14
4

25. 2R1
26. 3R1
27. 4R2
28. 4R2
29. 25 ; 7 ; 3R4 ; 3 ; 4
30. 26 ; 3 ; 8R2 ; 8 ; 2

16 Multiplication and Division

1. 18
2. 36
3. 35
4. 16

5.
$$8\overline{)40}$$
5
40
40

6.
$$5\overline{)41}$$ R 1
8
41
40
1

7.
$$6\overline{)24}$$
4
24
24

8.
$$4\overline{)36}$$
9
36
36

9.
$$7\overline{)42}$$
6
42
42

10.
$$3\overline{)20}$$ R 2
6
20
18
2

11. 8
12. 36
13. 3R3
14. 4
15. 15
16. 48
17. 27
18. 8

19-22. (Suggested answers)
19. 3 ; 6 ; 18 ;
18 ; 3 ; 6
20. 2 ; 8 ; 16 ;
16 ; 2 ; 8

21. 4 ; 7 ; 28 ;
28 ; 4 ; 7
22. 5 ; 4 ; 20 ;
20 ; 5 ; 4

23-26. (Suggested answers)
23. 3 x 5 = 15
15 ÷ 3 = 5
24. 4 x 6 = 24
24 ÷ 4 = 6
25. 3 x 9 = 27
27 ÷ 3 = 9
26. 4 x 7 = 28
28 ÷ 4 = 7
27. B ; 28 ; 28
28. A ; 4 ; 4
29. C ; 48 ; 48
30. D ; 8 ; 8
31. 32 ;
$$\begin{array}{r} 4 \\ \times\ 8 \\ \hline 32 \end{array}$$
32. 4 ;
$$7\overline{)28}$$
4
28
28

33. 9 ;
$$3\overline{)27}$$
9
27
27

34. 7 x 5 ; 35 ; 35
35. 49 ÷ 5 ; 9R4 ; 10

17 Fractions

1. ;
eighths

2. ;
sixths

3.  ; tenths ; tenths

4. five
5. three sevenths
6. one fourth
7. five sixteenths
8. five tenths
9. four ninths
10. two fifths
11. three fourths
12. five sixths
13. four ninths
14.  ; eighths

15.  ; Two ; sixths

16.  ; Four ; fifths

ISBN: 978-1-77149-031-3

17. ★★★★★ ; Two ; thirds
★★★★★
☆☆☆☆☆

18. 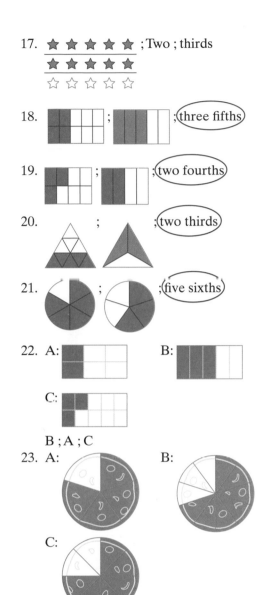 ; ;(three fifths)

19. ; ;(two fourths)

20. ; ;(two thirds)

21. ; ;(five sixths)

22. A: B:

C:

B ; A ; C

23. A: B:

C:

A ; C ; B

18 2-D Shapes (1)

1. Colour the shapes: A, C, D, E, F, G, H.
   A: triangle   C: pentagon   D: hexagon
   E: rectangle   F: heptagon   G: pentagon
   H: octagon
2. Irregular: A, C, E
   Regular: D, F, G, H
3. 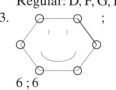 ;   6 ; 6
4. 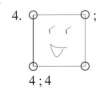 ;   4 ; 4

5. ;   6. ;
5 ; 5   8 ; 8
7. ;   8. ;
4 ; 4   4 ; 4
9. ✗ ; 5   10. ✗ ; square/rhombus
11. ✔   12. ✔
13. Check the pictures: B, E, F.
14.   15.
16.   17.
18.   19.

20. Square:
    side length longer than 2 cm: A, D
    side length shorter than 2 cm: I
    Pentagon:
    side length longer than 2 cm: F
    side length shorter than 2 cm: E
    Hexagon:
    side length longer than 2 cm: C
    side length shorter than 2 cm: B, G, H

19 2-D Shapes (2)

1.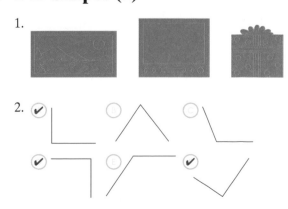

2. ✔ ○ ○
   ✔ ○ ✔

ISBN: 978-1-77149-031-3

3-6. (Suggested drawings)
3. greater than a right angle

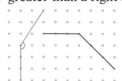

4. a right angle

5. smaller than a right angle

6. greater than a right angle

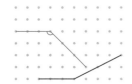

7. 8.

9. 10.

11.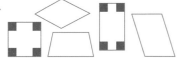

12. 4 ; 4 ; is   13. 2 ; 4 ; 2 ; is
14.   15.
16. ✔   17. ✔
18.

19.

20.

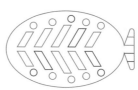

20 3-D Figures (1)

1. A: B: C:

D: E: F:

A: triangle ; triangular prism
B: rectangle ; rectangular prism
C: pentagon ; pentagonal prism
D: hexagon ; hexagonal prism
E: square ; square-based prism
F: pentagon ; pentagonal prism

2.   3.

rectangle ;   triangle ;
rectangular pyramid   triangular pyramid

4.   5.

hexagon ;   pentagon ;
hexagonal pyramid   pentagonal pyramid

6.   7.

square ;   hexagon ;
square-based pyramid   hexagonal pyramid

8. A: ; B: ;

6 ; 12 ; 8   4 ; 6 ; 4

C: ; D: ;

6 ; 10 ; 6   7 ; 12 ; 7

ISBN: 978-1-77149-031-3

E: 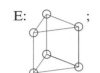 ;   F:  ;

5 ; 9 ; 6   8 ; 18 ; 12

9. B ; A, C, D, E, F   10. B, C, E ; A, D, F
11. B ; A, C, D, E, F
12. hexagonal prism   13. pentagonal pyramid
14. rectangular prism 15. triangular pyramid
16. D   17. C
18. A, C

21 3-D Figures (2)

1. Colour the nets: A, C, D, G.
2. 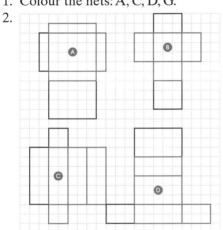 ;

C ; D ; B ; A

3. A:

B:

4. 6   5. rectangle
6. 3
7. rectangle ; triangle
8. hexagon ; rectangle
9. pentagon ; triangle
10. rectangle ; square
11.

rectangular pyramid ; 4 ; 1

12.

rectangular prism ; 6

13.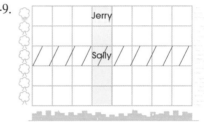

hexagonal prism ; 2 ; 6

14. A, C   15. A, B

22 Locations of Shapes and Objects

1. 5   2. 4   3. 5
4. 3   5. 4 ; 3   6. 2 ; 5

7-9.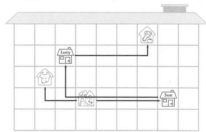

10. 1
11.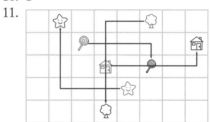

12-15. (Suggested drawings and answers)

12. 5 squares to the left and 2 squares up
13. 4 squares to the right and 1 square up
14. 2 squares to the left and 1 square up
15. 4 squares to the right

23 Transformations

1. A, D
2.   3.

4. 5.

6. 7.

8. 9.

10. 11.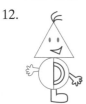

12. 13.

14. A, C   15. A, B   16. B, C

17.   18.   19.

20. slide   21. turn   22. flip
23. slide   24. turn   25. flip
26. flip

24 Patterns (1)

1.  ;   2. 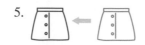 ;

3. ;   4. ;

5.  ;   6. 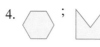 ;

2 ; 2 ; sizes   2 ; rectangle ; 2 ;
                       orientations

7.   ; 2 ; 2 ; hexagon ; pentagon

8. a. 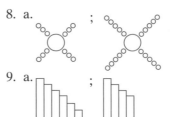   ;      b. growing

9. a.    ;   b. shrinking

10. a.   ;      b. growing

11. 30 ; 35 ; growing   12. 15 ; 12 ; shrinking
13. 50 ; 40 ; shrinking
14 and 17.

1	2	3	4	5	6	7	8	9	10
11	12	13	14	15	16	17	18	19	20
21	22	23	24	25	26	27	28	29	30
31	32	33	34	35	36	37	38	39	40
41	42	43	44	45	46	47	48	49	50
51	52	53	54	55	56	57	58	59	60
61	62	63	64	65	66	67	68	69	70
71	72	73	74	75	76	77	78	79	80
81	82	83	84	85	86	87	88	89	90
91	92	93	94	95	96	97	98	99	100

15. diagonally   16. in columns
18. Yes

25 Patterns (2)

1. 7 ; 14 ; 21 ; 28 ; 35 ; 42 ; 49 ; 56
2. 39 ; 36 ; 33 ; 30 ; 27 ; 24 ; 21 ; 18
3. 24 ; 28 ; 32 ; 36 ; 40 ; 44 ; 48 ; 52
4. 35 ; 30 ; 25 ; 20 ; 15 ; 10 ; 5 ; 0
5. 24 ; 30 ; 36 ; 42 ; 48 ; 54 ; 60
6. 80 ; 72 ; 64 ; 56 ; 48 ; 40 ; 32
7. a.
   b. 4 ; 7 ; 10 ; 13   c. 19
8. a.
   b. 3 ; 5 ; 7 ; 9   c. 13
9. a.
   b. 54 ; 40 ; 28 ; 18   c. 10

10. 7   11. 20   12. 8
13. 19   14. 9   15. 12
16. 7   17. 21   18. 16
19. 25   20. 3   21. 12
22. 18   23. 5   24. 6
25. 30   26. 17   27. 4

ISBN: 978-1-77149-031-3

28. $\heartsuit + 4 = 9$
$\heartsuit = 5$

29. $\stackrel{\wedge}{\sim} - 4 = 19$
$\stackrel{\wedge}{\sim} = 23$

30. $15 = 21 - \stackrel{\cdot}{\diamond}$
$\stackrel{\cdot}{\diamond} = 6$

31. $\stackrel{\frown}{\supset} - 6 = 23$
$\stackrel{\frown}{\supset} = 29$

32. $17 = 27 - \stackrel{\frown}{\circ}$
$\stackrel{\frown}{\circ} = 10$

33. $15 = 10 + \stackrel{\cdot\cdot}{\odot}$
$\stackrel{\cdot\cdot}{\odot} = 5$

34. $21 = 22 - \stackrel{\frown}{\cup}$
$\stackrel{\frown}{\cup} = 1$

26 Graphs (1)

1. 4
2. 105
3. 75
4. 10
5. 660
6. 40
7. 90
8. 120
9. 320

10. "The sports car" had the greatest sales because the number of sports cars left is the smallest.

11. (Suggested answer)
He should promote the "Octopus" because he has the most "Octopus" in stock.

12.

Flower buttons with 4 holes	Flower buttons with 2 holes	Square buttons with 4 holes	Square buttons with 2 holes
卌 卌 卌 卌 ‖‖	卌 卌	卌 卌 卌 卌 卌 卌	卌 卌 卌 卌 ‖‖

13.

Judy's Buttons

Flower buttons with 4 holes	Flower buttons with 2 holes	Square buttons with 4 holes	Square buttons with 2 holes

14. 34
15. 88
16. 51

27 Graphs (2)

1. 8
2. 5
3. ladybug
4. ant
5. 33
6.

7. Days Taken to Sell 10 Cartons of Juice
8. 5
9. A and B
10. E ; 1
11.

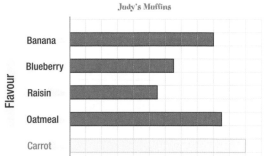

Judy's Muffins

12. 5
13. 42
14. 83
15. 83
16. 108 cm
17. 58 kg
18. 70 cm
19. $275

28 Probability

1. B
2. C
3. a. Apple, orange, or strawberry
   b. No
4. (Suggested answer)
   26 ; 12 ; 12
5. Happy face, flower, tree, or sun
6. Happy face : 10   Flower : 10
   Tree : 15   Sun : 5
7. B, D, E, F
8-9. (Individual colouring)
8.   9.

10. a. No
    b. No ; take out 1 heart marble.
11. a. Yes
    b. Cross out any 3 letter marbles and 1 shape marble.
12. (Suggested answer)

1 Groundhog Day

A. 1. B   2. A
 3. C   4. D
B. (Individual drawing and writing)
C. 1. c   2. h
 3. w   4. t
 5. l   6. k
 7. b   8. gh
D. 1. The knight was frightened by the lightning last night.
 2. Don't write the answers in the wrong column.
 3. He designed eight Christmas cards.
 4. The scientist stayed calm when he saw the ghost.
 5. The rhino is blowing a whistle beside the lamb.
E. (Individual answers)

2 The New Student

A. B
B. 1. No
 2. Yes
 3. No
 4. No
 5. Yes
 6. No
 7. Yes
C. Hard "C": A ; B ; C ; F ; H
 Soft "C": A ; C ; D ; E ; G
D.

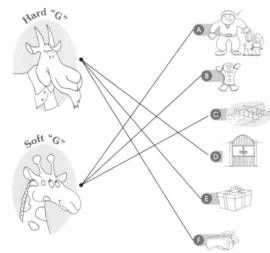

3 Acrostic Poems

A. (Individual drawing)
 1. Rainbow
 2. Mother
B. (Individual writing)
C.

D. (Colour the pictures of 1, 2, 5, 6, 7, and 9.)

4 What Are Things Made of?

A. 1. G   2. A
 3. H   4. E
 5. F   6. D
 7. B   8. C
B. 1. grow
 2. soil
 3. touch
 4. plants/places
 5. world
 6. things
C. 1. train
 2. day
 3. eight
 4. eat
 5. tree
 6. load
 7. know
 8. boot
 9. crew
 10. cause
 11. jaw

ISBN: 978-1-77149-031-3

D. 1.   2.
    3.   4. ✘
    5. ✘   6.
    7. ✘   8. ✘

5 A Special Gym Class

A.

B. (Individual writing)
C. (Cross out these words.)
    1. school
    2. player
    3. tail
    4. efforts
    5. fast
    6. peaches
D. (Individual new rhyming words)
    1. C   2. A
    3. G   4. B
    5. F   6. D
    7. E

6 The Frank Slide

A. 1.   2. ✔
    3.   4.
    5. ✔   6. ✔
B. 1. C   2. B
    3. F   4. A
    5. E   6. D

C. 1. <u>Aunt Rosaline</u> and her family moved to <u>Edmonton</u> last year
    2. Her daughter <u>Sherry</u> told me that <u>West Edmonton Mall</u> is the largest shopping centre in <u>North America</u>.
    3. You can find all types of shops in the mall
    4. Have you ever heard of <u>Turtle Mountain</u>?
    5. There was a town called <u>Frank</u> at the foot of the mountain
    6. <u>Alberta</u> is a province to the east of <u>British Columbia</u>.
    7. My family will take a trip to <u>Banff</u> next month.
    8. Our neighbour will take care of our dog <u>Mickey</u> for us.
D. (Individual answers)

7 A Gaggle of Geese?

A. 1. cattle
    2. fish
    3. penguins
    4. crows
    5. wolves
    6. lions
    7. sheep
    8. kittens
    9. geese
    10. seals
B. (Individual drawing and title)
C. 1. feet
    2. deer
    3. cities
    4. mice
    5. knives
    6. families
    7. teeth
    8. leaves
    9. offspring

D.
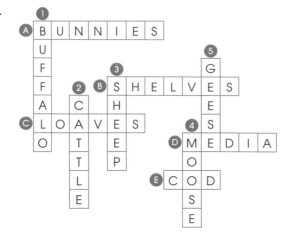

8 The Goat – Our Best Friend

A. 1. doe/nanny
2. kid
3. buck/billy
B. 1. wool ; clothing
2. meat
3. leather ; gloves ; boots
4. milk ; feta
C. 1. . ; T
2. ? ; A
3. . ; I
4. ! ; S
5. ? ; A
6. . ; T
7. ! ; S
8. . ; I
9. ? ; A
10. . ; T
D. (Individual writing)

9 The Narwhal – a Real-life Unicorn

A. 1. lucky
2. sure
3. tusk
4. amazing
5. real
6. whales
7. twists
8. blotches

B. 1. five metres
2. blue-grey
3. white blotches
4. brown
5. Canada
6. other northern countries
7. using sound waves
C. 1. My class|is doing a project on the narwhal.
2. Mrs. Reid|told us to look for information about the narwhal on the Internet.
3. The narwhal|is a whale.
4. The left tooth of the male narwhal|can grow up to three metres long.
5. The female|is slightly smaller than the male.
6. The skin of a baby narwhal|is brown in colour.
7. You|may see a narwhal in the Arctic seas.
8. Fish, squid, and shrimp|are what narwhals eat.
9. I|think a narwhal really looks like a unicorn.
D. 1. Our teacher
2. The main character
3. Bruce
4. The unicorn
5. The fairy tale
6. We
E. (Individual writing)

10 Skipping Rope

A.

a	J	e	s	p	b	a	n	a	n	a	s	J	p	a	c
p	a	C	F	e	b	r	u	a	r	y	b	a	l	p	p
p	n	e	M	a	c	u	m	p	l	M	a	n	u	F	l
e	o	a	n	c	s	a	s	p	e	a	n	u	S	e	u
k	c	y	h	e	r	p	l	u	m	s	a	e	o		
h	F	e	d	y	l	e	p	M	a	r	c	h			
a	s	f	t	u	s	e	a	e	v	s					

B. 1. exercise
2. friends
3. chant
4. skipper
5. caught
C. 1. There are four seasons in Canada. They are spring, summer, fall, and winter.
2. June, July, and August are the summer months in Ontario.
3. I like skipping, swimming, cycling, and rock climbing.
4. Sarah asked, "Would you like to skip with me?"

ISBN: 978-1-77149-031-3

5. "Let's ask Jerry to join us, " I said.
6. She reminded me, "Don't forget to take your skipping rope with you."
7. We sell all kinds of fruits: apples, oranges, bananas, peaches, cherries, mangoes – you name it.

D. 1. ✔
    2.
    3. ✔
    4.
    5. ✔
    6. ✔
    7.

11 I Love Haiku!

A. 1.
    2.
    3. ✔
B. 1. poems
    2. short
    3. three
    4. Japan
    5. frog
C. 1. 3
    2. 4
    3. 2
    4. 2
    5. 1
    6. 4
    7. 3
    8. 1
    9. 3
D. 1 Syllable: sound ; book ; bright
    2 Syllables: famous ; pizza ; author
    3 Syllables: acrostic ; Japanese ; lollipop
    4 Syllables: competition ; information ; stationery
E. 1. s y l / l a / b l e
    2. g a r / a g e
    3. a f / t e r / n o o n
    4. c o l / o u r / f u l
    5. c a r / r y
    6. e x / c i t / i n g
    7. i n / v i s / i / b l e
    8. n e / c e s / s a / r y

12 Why Do We Sneeze?

A.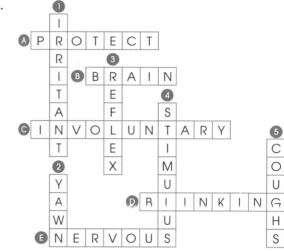

B. 1. They
    2. We
    3. It
    4. He
    5. You
    6. She
    7. I
C. 1. me
    2. them
    3. you
    4. ✔
    5. ✔
    6. him
    7. us

13 Girls' Festival in Japan

A.

B.

1. hina — a kind of Japanese clothing for girls and women
2. matsuri — festival
3. Hina Matsuri — Girls' Festival
4. peach blossom — a kind of pink flower
5. kimono — doll
6. sayonara — goodbye

C.
1. Girls'
2. Kiyoka's
3. grandma's
4. dolls'
5. sister's
6. friends'
7. Tanaka's
8. daughter's

D.
1. our
2. My
3. Her
4. his
5. its
6. their
7. your

14 A Visit to the Seniors' Centre

A. D ; B ; A ; C ; E

B.
1. She asked the writer to do a project about his favourite fish.
2. Some of the old people could not hear very well.
3. He thought that the people at the seniors' centre were very interesting and kind to him.

C.
1. this
2. That
3. those
4. This
5. that
6. These

D.
1. This book is mine.
2. These stickers are his.
3. Is this lunch box yours?
4. Those shoes are hers.
5. That puppy is ours.
6. These pictures are theirs.

15 A Letter to – and from – Ms. Naughton

A.
1. volunteering at the hospital twice a week
2. going for a long walk every day
3. working at the library
4. writing a book about being a principal for 30 years
5. learning to play golf

B. (Individual writing)

C.
1. helps
2. invites
3. wear
4. use ; read
5. asks
6. choose ; put
7. are

D.
1. ✔
2. goes
3. is
4. ✔
5. enjoy

E.
1. The kittens drink the milk happily.
2. The children are looking at the ladybug.
3. The pastries taste sweet and delicious.
4. The girls put away their books.

16 The Sugar Shack

A.

baked beans   bacon   sausages

ham   corned beef   fried eggs

waffles   pancakes   scrambled eggs

B.
1. little
2. right
3. perfect
4. done
5. collected
6. way
7. buckets

8. outdoors
9. delicious

C.

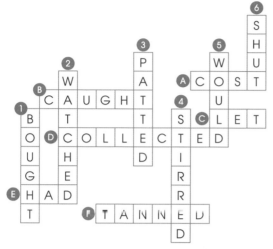

D.
1. promised
2. hurried
3. arrived
4. were
5. grabbed
6. bought
7. poured
8. did
9. spread
10. devoured
11. ate
12. choked
13. looked
14. saw
15. was
16. burst

17 The Amazing Coconut

A.

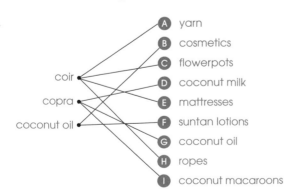

B.
1. Add boiling water to dried coconut.
2. Blend/Put it in the blender.
3. Strain out the bits.

C.
1. amazing
2. white ; large ; hard
3. young ; green ; tender
4. healthy ; refreshing
5. useful ; many
6. strong
7. brown ; tough
8. dried ; shredded ; delicious

D.
1. big ; tall
2. slimy ; wet
3. bright ; cold
4. Colourful ; early
5. stuffy ; crowded

E. (Individual writing)

18 Shooting Stars

A.

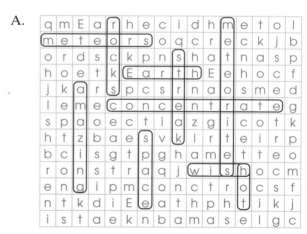

B.
1. ✔
2. ✔
3.
4. ✔
5. ✔
6.
7. ✔
8. ✔

C.
1. eagerly
2. patiently
3. high
4. late
5. gracefully

D. (Individual writing)

ISBN: 978-1-77149-031-3

19 The Circus School

A. 2. nutrition class
3. French class
4. music and rhythm class
5. balancing class
6. acrobatics class
7. aerials class
8. clowning arts class

B. (Individual writing)

C. (on) chairs
(in) the sky
(inside) the box
(at) sunset
(beside) the doll
(at) Christmas
(behind) the house
(at) two o'clock
(in) the morning
(on) weekends
(in) 2015
(above) Lydia

Where: on chairs ; in the sky ; inside the box ;
beside the doll ; behind the house ; above
Lydia

When: at sunset ; at Christmas ; at two o'clock ;
in the morning ; on weekends ; in 2015

D. 1. On   2. at
3. on   4. in
5. in   6. under
7. inside   8. in
9. at   10. on
11. in

20 My Brother Loves to Dance

A. 1. B
2. C
3. C
4. A
5. B

B. 1. Toller has won many awards.
2. The writer's father/Toller's father pretended
to be Morris in the role play.
3. Everyone cheered when Toller finished his
dance.

C. 1. didn't
2. I've
3. doesn't
4. there's
5. she's
6. we'll
7. shouldn't
8. he'd

D. 1. didn't
2. couldn't
3. hadn't
4. He'll
5. He'd

E. 1. Mr.
2. km
3. Blvd.
4. Nov.
5. no.
6. B.C.
7. Mt.

F. 1. Toller will join a dance competition on
Oct. 23.
2. It will take place in a school on Berry Dr.
3. He will go on a trip to P.E.I. afterwards.

21 Lacrosse

A. 4 ; 2 ; 3 ; 1

B. 1. F   2. F
3. F   4. T
5. T   6. T
7. F   8. T

C. (Cross out these words.)
re: result ; reach ; retrieve ; repeat
un: under ; unit ; unless ; uncle

D. 1. unpopular
2. redevelop
3. reset
4. replay
5. unwise

ISBN: 978-1-77149-031-3

E.

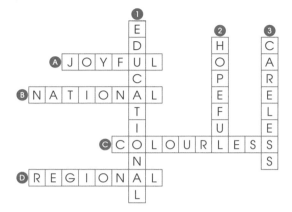

22 Rupinder the Reporter

A. Paragraph One: A
Paragraph Two: A
Paragraph Three: B
Paragraph Four: B
Paragraph Five: B

B.

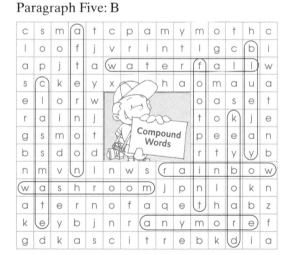

C.

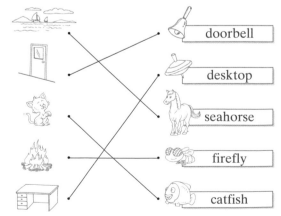

- doorbell
- desktop
- seahorse
- firefly
- catfish

D. (Individual drawing and word)

23 A Special Project

A. 1. wool and crochet hooks
2. 24
3. white wool
4. a large rainbow-coloured blanket
5. to an orphanage

B. (Individual writing and drawing)

C. 1. circle
2. very ; cloth
3. beside ; couch
4. dear ; loose
5. pass
6. It's
7. dessert

D. 1. quite
2. curb
3. pours
4. set
5. nine-storey
6. principal
7. bold
8. stripes

E. (Individual writing)

24 Durian

A. Fruit: cherries ; cranberries ; durians ; pears
Animal: wild pigs ; squirrels ; orangutans
Place: Malaysia ; Thailand ; Singapore ; Canada

B. 1. oval
2. 5
3. 40
4. 30
5. greenish-brown
6. yellowish

C. 1. large ; small ; huge
2. hate ; like ; dislike
3. speedy ; slow ; swift
4. yummy ; tasty ; flavourless
5. overcast ; sunny ; bright
6. pleasant ; warm ; stormy
7. boring ; absorbing ; amusing

D.   (Suggested answers)
   1. chilly
   2. vacation
   3. untidy
   4. hot
   5. permitted
   6. leaves
E.   (Suggested answers)
   1. I often try exotic fruits.
   2. This store closes on Sundays.
   3. The young lady is choosing a big durian.

25 The Story of Honey

A.   1. largest
   2. one
   3. laying all the eggs for the colony
   4. five years
   5. helping the queen make eggs
   6. up to eight weeks
   7. Worker Bee
   8. 60 000
   9. collecting nectar from flowers to make honey
   10. making the honeycomb from beeswax to store honey
   11. about five to six weeks
B.   1. ✔   2. ✔
   3. ✔   4.
   5.   6. ✔
   7.   8.
   9. ✔
C.   1. a ball
   2. snails
   3. coffee
   4. a stone
   5. a hotel
   6. birds
D.   (Individual writing)

26 Hello around the World

A.

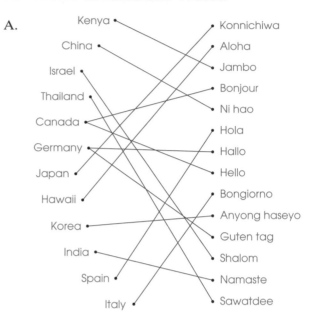

B.   1. but
   2. or
   3. but
   4. ✔
   5. but
   6. ✔
   7. and
C.   1. or
   2. but
   3. or
   4. and
   5. and
   6. but
D.   1. I tried to call Tracy but her line was busy.
   2. I will get some snacks and you can prepare the drinks.
   3. Put your shoes in the box or leave them on the rug.

ISBN: 978-1-77149-031-3

27 My Brother, the Babysitter

A. 1. B   2. B
    3. A   4. A
B. 1. He took special classes at a babysitter school
       last year.
    2. (Any one of these)
       Where are you going?
       When will you be back?
       What is your cellphone number?
       Where is the fire exit?
       What is the fire meeting point?
    3. (Individual answer)
C. 1. Does
    2. Do
    3. Is
    4. Were
    5. Are
    6. Did
    7. Was
D. (Individual writing)

28 Marsupials

A. 3 ; 1 ; 2 ; 4 ; 5
B. 1. Marsupial babies are born blind and hairless.
    2. The baby has to find its mother's pouch on its
       own.
    3. Most marsupials live in Australia.
    4. The opossum is about the size of a cat.
C. (Cross out these sentences.)
    Paragraph One:
    You cannot find other kinds of marsupials in
    Canada.
    Paragraph Two:
    Honeybees are hard-working insects.
    Paragraph Three:
    A spider is not an insect.
D. (Individual writing)

ISBN: 978-1-77149-031-3

1 Communities between 1780 and 1850

A.   1. First Nations
2. both groups were connected to nature
3. both wore animal skin clothing
4. longhouse
5. lived in one place all year round
6. grew corn, squash, and beans
7. wigwam
8. moved each season
9. hunted animals

B.

2 Roles: Then and Now

A.

Our Family Roles: (Individual answers)

B.   (Individual writing)

3 Early Canadian Travel

A.   A: horse and cart
B: snowshoes
C: canoe
1. C
2. B
3. A

B.   1. bark
2. large
3. lightweight
4. heavy
5. Fur Trade

C.   (Suggested answer)
Today, we usually use toboggans for fun. In winter, we use toboggans to slide down hills covered in snow.

4 Adapting to the Climate

A.

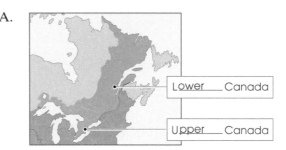

1. Lower
2. Upper
3. shelters
4. log
5. warm

B.   1. A
2. C
3. B

C.   • Everything liquid froze.
• The wood for the fire was green.
• The bread was frozen.
(Individual answer)

ISBN: 978-1-77149-031-3

5 Early Settlers' Challenges

A. A: ship
    B: log
    C: land
    D: grant
    A ; D ; C ; B
B. 1. B
    2. C
    3. D
    4. A
C. We get water from the faucet. ; We use electric light bulbs.

6 Canadian Identity

A. 1. French   2. English
    3. bilingual   4. two
    5. culture   6. multicultural
B. B ; A
    D ; C
    (Individual answer)

7 The Original Inhabitants

A. The Wendat
    Method: by farming
    Food: corn, squash, beans
    Tools: hoe, wooden spade

    The Anishnawbe
    Method: by fishing, hunting
    Food: fish, deer, buffalo, rabbits
    Tools: snare, fishing net
B. 1. hunting
    2. sleds
    3. women
    4. rivers
    5. baskets
    6. children
    7. (Individual answer)

8 Moving Out

A. (Suggested answers)
    1. Wenro ; Seneca ; Huron
    2. Bytown ; Kingston ; York
    3. Waterloo County: Neutral ; Mennonites
       Three Rivers: Algonquin ; French
B. 1. agreements
    2. land
    3. farming
    4. money
    5. reserves
    6. F
    7. T
    8. T
    9. F

9 Settling the Land

A. Check: A ; C ; D ; F
B. (Suggested answer)
    The settlers chose these areas because they were close to water sources.
C. D ; A ; C ; B ; E
D. 1. Women
    2. Children
    3. Men

10 Changing the Environment

A. Europeans: trading ; land ; farms
    Lifestyle: moved ; hunt
    Conflict: hunting ; fur
    Natural Environment: cleared ; animal
B.

ISBN: 978-1-77149-031-3

11 Hardships

A. 1. scurvy
2. vegetables
3. diseases
4. died

B. 1. metal
2. fur
3. overhunting
4. animals
5. The First Nations peoples did not have enough animal sources for food, clothing, and tools.
6. (Suggested answer)
It caused conflicts among First Nations tribes because different tribes would fight over these hunting grounds. Hunting for fur made the First Nations tribes very competitive.

12 Getting along Together

A. The Europeans to the First Nations:
B ; D ; E ; I ; J
The First Nations to the Europeans:
A ; C ; F ; G ; H

B. 1. land
2. poor
3. equal
4. last
5. lower
6. Sierra Leone
7. (Suggested answers)
The land they were promised was in poor condition. They were always the last to receive food and supplies.

13 Mapping Ontario

A. 1.

2. a. countries   b. oceans
c. provinces   d. capital cities
e. cities
3. (Individual answer)
4.

China	*Nova Scotia*	*Indian Ocean*
CHINA	NOVA SCOTIA	INDIAN OCEAN

Northwest Territories	*Barrie* (a city in Ontario)
NORTHWEST TERRITORIES	**Barrie**

B. 1. Ottawa ;

Toronto ; ●

(Suggested answer)
Timmins ; ●

2.

14 Ontario's Landforms

A.

1. three
2. a. Canadian Shield
   b. Great Lakes-St. Lawrence Lowlands
3. (Suggested answers)
   Hudson Bay Lowlands: Fort Severn
   Canadian Shield: Timmins
   Great Lakes-St. Lawrence Lowlands: Toronto

B. 1. marshes   2. polar bears
   3. fishing   4. Canadian Shield
   5. bedrock   6. minerals
   7. mining   8. plains
   9. fertile   10. agriculture

15 Where People Live

1. Toronto ; 2 615 060
   Ottawa ; 883 391
   Mississauga ; 713 443
2. Northern Ontario
   Land use: hunting ; forestry
   Features: wilderness ; natural
   Southern Ontario
   Land use: farming ; manufacturing
   Features: populated ; winter
3. (Suggested answer)
   The most populated cities are in Southern Ontario because it is warmer and it is closer to water access points like the St. Lawrence River.

4. (Suggested answer)
   Some reserves are located in Northern Ontario because the First Nations peoples value nature. Some reserves are located in Southern Ontario and are close to water sources which are important to their culture and lifestyle.

16 Enjoying Ontario Today

A. 1. Toronto
   2. variety
   3. recreational
   4. Thunder Bay
   5. hiking
   6. skiing

B. 1. Lake Ontario ; B
   2. North Ontario forests ; E
   3. Blue Mountain ; D
   4. Niagara vineyards ; C
   5. Thunder Bay Port ; A

17 Working in Ontario Today

A. 1. tour guide ; B
   2. factory worker ; A
   3. chef ; C

B. 1. a. 12
      b. 5
      c. 7
   2. snow removal and landscape gardening
   3. (Individual answers)

ISBN: 978-1-77149-031-3

18 Ontario's Valuable Land

A.

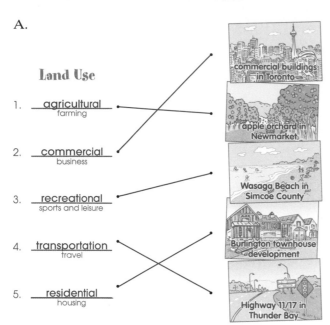

Land Use

1. __agricultural__
   farming

2. __commercial__
   business

3. __recreational__
   sports and leisure

4. __transportation__
   travel

5. __residential__
   housing

commercial buildings in Toronto

apple orchard in Newmarket

Wasaga Beach in Simcoe County

Burlington townhouse development

Highway 11/17 in Thunder Bay

B.

A. Conservation Area – The Oak Ridges Moraine

Lake Simcoe

Lake Ontario

1. green
2. water
3. protect
4. air
5. Ontarians

19 Using Our Land

A. 1. dominant
   2. west
   3. quarters
   4. habitat
   5. wood
   6. recreational

B. 1. Deforestation is needed for logging, building roads, growing crops, and raising cattle.
   2. animals: lose their habitats
      plants: lose their habitats
      people: lose natural environment
   3. (Individual answer)
   4. People are letting the deforested areas regenerate or planting seedlings if regeneration cannot occur.

20 Using Our Resources

1. People get precious resources, such as gold, copper, and nickel.
2. on land: the landscape is changed and polluted
   on plants and wildlife: lose their habitats
   on water and soil: polluted by toxic chemicals
3. Cover landfills with soil.
   Restore vegetation to the site.
4. C ; B ; D ; A

21 Developing the Land

A. 1. (Suggested answers)
      Mississauga ; Markham
   2. No, because Lake Ontario is south of Toronto.
   3. population: increased
      no. of households: increased
      area: stayed the same
      total length of bikeways: increased
   4. Toronto increased the length of bikeways so that cyclists can reach more places. Hence, more people are encouraged to ride bikes.

ISBN: 978-1-77149-031-3

B. 1.

2. (Suggested answer)
Fewer running cars means less impact on the environment and people spend less money on gas.

22 Local Governments

A. 1.

2. (Suggested answers)
Fort Severn, Kingfisher
3. (Individual answer)

B. Provincial Government:
province ; health ; premier
Municipal Government:
local ; police ; streets ; mayor
provincial ; municipal ; provincial

23 Municipal Lands

A. 1. Township of Pickle Lake
2. City of Toronto
3.

Land Use	Pickle Lake (a little / a lot / none)	Toronto
Residential	a little	a lot
Commercial	a little	a lot
Mining	a lot	none
Recreational	a lot	a lot
Transportation	a little	a lot

4. (Suggested answer)
When a community has a large population, there will be greater needs for certain types of land use, such as residential, commercial, and recreational land use.

B.

City of Toronto   Township of Pickle Lake

24 Municipal Jobs

A. Education: B
Mining Industry: D, F
Government: A, E
Recreational Industry: C

B. 1. C, D, F
2. Job B: Toronto ; large cities like Toronto have many schools
Job D: Pickle Lake ; there are mining activities around this area
3. (Individual answers)

ISBN: 978-1-77149-031-3

1 Plants

A. 1. flower
    2. leaves
    3. stem
    4. roots

B.

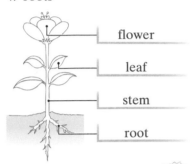

flower

leaf

stem

root

C.

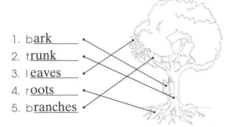

1. b<u>ark</u>
2. t<u>runk</u>
3. l<u>eaves</u>
4. r<u>oots</u>
5. b<u>ranches</u>

D. Broadleaf Tree: A, C, F
    Coniferous Tree: B, D, E

2 Leaves and Flowers

A.

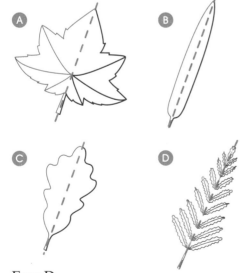

Ⓐ   Ⓑ

Ⓒ   Ⓓ

Fern: D
Maple: A
Grass: B
Oak: C

B. 1. grass
    2. fern
C. 1. pistil
       stamen
       petal
       ovary
       sepal
    2. ovary
    3. sepal

3 The Needs of Plants

A. 1. air
    2. water
    3. light
    Experiment (Individual observation)
    Light could not reach that part of the leaf.
B. 1. leaves ; thick
    2. float ; sunlight
    3. ground
    4. leaves
    alpine: C
    desert: A
    water: B
    woodland: D

4 Plants: Pollination

A. 1. moth
    2. butterfly
    3. bee
    4. wind
    5. hummingbird
B. Animal pollination: animals ; colours
    Examples: A, D
    Wind pollination: wind ; small
    Examples: B, C
C. 1. pollen
    2. stamen
    3. pistil
    4. seed
    5. scent
    6. nectar

ISBN: 978-1-77149-031-3

5 Seed Dispersal

A.

B.
1. 2 ; 1 ; 3 ; water
2. 2 ; 3 ; 1 ; wind
3. 1 ; 3 ; 2 ; animals

6 Plants: Life Cycles

A.

B. B ; C ; D ; A
C.
1. years ; months
2. leaves ; flowers
3. maple tree ; sunflower
D.

Annual plants	A pumpkin plant sprouts and dies within one year.
Biennial plants	Many plants, including trees, can live for many years.
Perennial plants	Parsley and foxgloves are examples of plants that live for two years.

7 Uses of Plants

A.
1. hard ; E
2. strong ; G
3. sweet ; C
4. soft ; light ; A
5. flexible ; strong ; B
6. soft ; fine ; D
7. flexible ; F
B.
1. needles
2. bark
3. trunk
4. sap
C. seed

8 Endangered Plants or Invasive Plants

A. A, C, D, E, H, I, J, K
B. Endangered ; Invasive
C.
1. habitat
2. extinct
3. endangered
4. protected
5. invasive
6. native

9 Rainforests

A.
1. A ; Emergent
2. D ; Floor
3. E ; Floor
4. B ; Canopy
5. C ; Understorey
B.
1. animals/plants
2. plants/animals
3. canopy
4. seeds/fruits
5. fruits/seeds
6. Birds
7. layer
8. dense
9. rainfall
10. understorey
11. forest floor
12. vines

10 Force as a Push or Pull

A. 1. Push
    2. Both Push and Pull
    3. Pull
    4. Push
    5. Pull
B. 1. gravity
    2. static electricity
    3. magnetism
C. 1. Direct Contact ; Push
    2. From a Distance ; Pull
    3. From a Distance ; Pull
    4. Direct Contact ; Push

11 Forces and Movement

A. 1.
    2.
    3.
    4.
    5.
    6.

B. 1. 3 ; 1 ; 2
    2. 1 ; 3 ; 2
    3. 2 ; 1 ; 3
    Colour picture number 2 for 1-3.

12 Gravity

A. 1-3 and 5. Draw an arrow pointing down.
    4. No Gravity
B. 1. Jupiter ; Earth ; Venus ; Mars
    2. Mars
    3. Jupiter

13 Friction

A. 1. friction
    2. friction
    3. FRICTION
    4. FRICTION
B. 1. rough ; increase
    2. harder
    3. bicycle grease ; reduce
    4. slippers with rubber soles ; increase

14 Magnets

A.
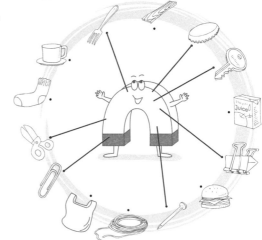

ISBN: 978-1-77149-031-3

B. 1. glass
   2. cloth
   3. wood
   4. plastic

C.

2.

3.

Experiment (Individual observation)

15 Magnetic Poles

A. 1. south, north
   2. attracts
   3. repels

B.

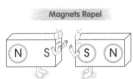

C. 1. attract
   2.

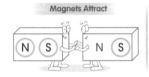

3.

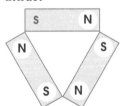

D. 1.

16 Stability

A. 1. B
   2. A
   3. A
   4. B

B. 1. thicker
   2. stronger
   3. beams

17 Levers

A. 1, 3, 4, 6, 7

B.

C. Part 1: easy ; little
   Part 2: harder ; greater
   Part 3: easier ; lesser

ISBN: 978-1-77149-031-3

18 More about Levers

A. 1.
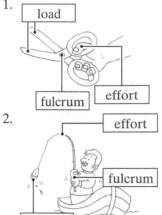

2.
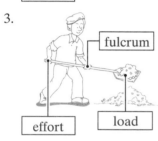

3.
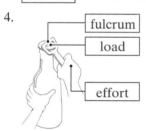

4.

B. 1. lever
2. easier
3. easier
4. greater

19 Soil

A.

B. A: waves
B: rain
C: plants
D: wind
E: river
F: glacier

C.
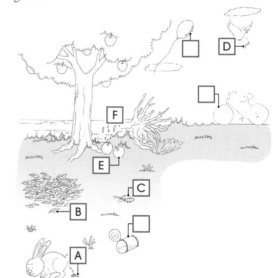

  ISBN: 978-1-77149-031-3

20 More about Soil

A. clay
   silt
   sand
   loam
B. 1. clay
   2. loam
   3. sand
   4. silt
C. 1. clay
   2. loam
   3. loam
   4. a. sand
      b. silt
      c. clay
      d. sand

21 Soil Erosion

A.

Soil can be washed away by heavy __rain__.

Soil can be blown away by strong __wind__.

Soil can be lost to the water by __waves__.

B. 1. B
   2. A
   3. C
   4. D
   Experiment (Individual observation)

22 Earthworms

A. 1. food
   2. castings
   3. predator
   4. tunnel
   5. habitat
B. 1. E
   2. D
   3. A
   4. B
   5. C
C.

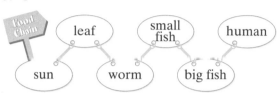

Food Chain — leaf — small fish — human — sun — worm — big fish

23 Creatures that Use Soil

A. 1. china
   2. skin mud mask
   3. soil field
   4. flowerpot with soil
   5. peat fuel
   6. clay brick

B.

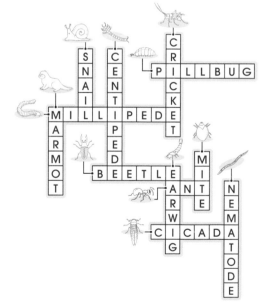

24 Compost

A. • Items from the garden

• Items from the kitchen

• Items from other places

B. 1. true
    2. true
    3. false
    4. true
    5. true

C. Composting is a wonderful way to recycle organic items.

ISBN: 978-1-77149-031-3